The Classroom Teacher's Guide to Special Education

SPECIAL EDUCATION LAW, POLICY, AND PRACTICE
Series Editors
Mitchell L. Yell, PhD, University of South Carolina;
David F. Bateman, PhD, American Institutes for Research

The Special Education Law, Policy, and Practice series highlights current trends and legal issues in the education of students with disabilities. The books in this series link legal requirements, evidence-based instruction, and practical applications for working with students with disabilities. The titles are designed to be textbooks for general education and special education preservice education programs and also for practicing teachers, administrators, principals, school counselors, school psychologists, parents, and others interested in improving the lives of students. The series is committed to research-based practices to provide appropriate and meaningful educational programming for students with disabilities and their families.

Titles In Series

Service Animals in Schools: Legal, Educational, Administrative, and Strategic Handling Aspects by A. O. Papalia, K. B. Ewoldt, and D. F. Bateman

Evidence-Based Practices for Supporting Individuals With Autism Spectrum Disorder, edited by L. C. Chezan, K. Wolfe, and E. Drasgow

Special Education Law Annual Review 2021 by D. F. Bateman, M. L. Yell, and K. P. Brady

Dispute Resolution Under the IDEA: Understanding, Avoiding, and Managing Special Education Disputes by D. F. Bateman, M. L. Yell, and J. S. Dorego

Advocating for the Common Good: People, Politics, Process, and Policy on Capitol Hill by J. E. West

Related Services in Special Education: Working Together as a Team by L. Goran and D. F. Bateman

The Essentials of Special Education Advocacy by A. M. Markelz, S. A. Nagro, K. Monnin, and D. F. Bateman

Disability and Motor Behavior: A Handbook of Research by A. S. Brian and P. S. Haibach-Beach

Supporting and Accommodating Students With Special Health Care Needs by A. D. S. Angelov and M. Rattermann

You're Hired! Practical Strategies for Guiding Individuals With Autism Spectrum Disorder to Competitive Employment by P. S. Arter, T. B. H. Brown, and J. Barna

Unraveling Dyslexia: A Guide for Teachers and Families by K. L. Sayeski

Disability, Intersectionality, and Belonging in Special Education: Socioculturally Sustaining Practices by E. A. Harkins Monaco, L. L. Stansberry Brusnahan, M. C. Fuller, and M. Odima Jr.

The Educator's Guide to Action Research: Practical Connections for Implementation of Data-Driven Decision-Making by M. E. Little, D. D. Slanda, and E. Cramer

The Essentials of Special Education Research by A. M. Markelz and B. Riden

The Classroom Teacher's Guide to Special Education: Essential Knowledge, Skills, and Mindsets by D. D. Slanda, L. Pike, and M. E. Little

For a full list of books in this series, visit https://rowman.com/Action/SERIES/_/RLSELPP/Special-Education-Law,-Policy,-and-Practice

The Classroom Teacher's Guide to Special Education

Essential Knowledge, Skills, and Mindsets

Dena D. Slanda, Lindsey Pike, and Mary E. Little

ROWMAN & LITTLEFIELD
Lanham • Boulder • New York • London

Rowman & Littlefield
Bloomsbury Publishing Inc, 1385 Broadway, New York, NY 10018, USA
Bloomsbury Publishing Plc, 50 Bedford Square, London, WC1B 3DP, UK
Bloomsbury Publishing Ireland, 29 Earlsfort Terrace, Dublin 2, D02 AY28, Ireland
www.rowman.com

Copyright © 2025 by The Rowman & Littlefield Publishing Group, Inc.

All rights reserved. No part of this publication may be: i) reproduced or transmitted in any form, electronic or mechanical, including photocopying, recording or by means of any information storage or retrieval system without prior permission in writing from the publishers; or ii) used or reproduced in any way for the training, development or operation of artificial intelligence (AI) technologies, including generative AI technologies. The rights holders expressly reserve this publication from the text and data mining exception as per Article 4(3) of the Digital Single Market Directive (EU) 2019/790.

British Library Cataloguing in Publication Information Available

Library of Congress Cataloging-in-Publication Data

Names: Slanda, Dena D., 1977- author. | Pike, Lindsey, 1986- author. | Little, Mary E. (Professor of education), author.
Title: The classroom teacher's guide to special education : essential knowledge, skills, and mindsets / Dena D. Slanda, Lindsey Pike, and Mary E. Little.
Description: Lanham : Rowman & Littlefield, [2025] | Series: Special education law, policy, and practice | Includes bibliographical references and index.
Identifiers: LCCN 2024058987 (print) | LCCN 2024058988 (ebook) | ISBN 9781538177464 (board) | ISBN 9781538177471 (paperback) | ISBN 9781538177488 (ebook)
Subjects: LCSH: Special education. | Special education teachers—Training of.
Classification: LCC LC3965 .S56 2025 (print) | LCC LC3965 (ebook) | DDC 371.9—dc23/eng/20250120
LC record available at https://lccn.loc.gov/2024058987
LC ebook record available at https://lccn.loc.gov/2024058988

For product safety related questions contact productsafety@bloomsbury.com.

∞™ The paper used in this publication meets the minimum requirements of American National Standard for Information Sciences—Permanence of Paper for Printed Library Materials, ANSI/NISO Z39.48-1992.

CONTENTS

Acknowledgments ix
Introduction xi

1   General Education Teachers Are Special Educators 1
   Chapter Objectives 1
   Key Terms 2
   Vignette 3
   Special Education Was Not Always Available 3
   Paving a Better Path Forward 4
   Changing Teacher Roles and Responsibilities 10
   Competencies for Classroom Teachers Who Teach Students With Disabilities 12
   Review and Reflect 14
   Guiding Questions 15
   Extend Your Learning 15

2   Special Education Is a Set of Services, Not a Place 19
   Chapter Objectives 20
   Key Terms 20
   Vignette 21
   What Is Inclusion? Understanding Models of Disability 22
   What Is Inclusion? Understanding Inclusive Education 25
   Inclusion as the Best Model for All Students 27
   The Classroom Teacher's Role in Advancing Inclusion 29
   Review and Reflect 34
   Guiding Questions 34
   Extend Your Learning 35

3 Valuing Student Identity 37
Chapter Objectives 38
Key Terms 38
Vignette 39
What Is Intersectionality? 40
Oppression, Privilege, and Systemic Inequity 41
Intersectionality and Students With Disabilities 44
Intersectionality for Inclusion and Equity in the Classroom 47
Review and Reflect 51
Guiding Questions 51
Extend Your Learning 52

4 Multitiered Approach to Inclusive Learning 55
Chapter Objectives 55
Key Terms 56
Vignette 57
Multitiered System of Supports 57
MTSS and Federal Legislation 58
Overview of a Multitiered System of Support Framework 59
Required Components of MTSS 64
Review and Reflect 70
Guiding Questions 71
Extend Your Learning 71

5 Using Data to Drive Student Success 77
Chapter Objectives 78
Key Terms 78
Vignette 79
Data-Driven Decision-Making: Using Data to Inform Instruction 80
Assessment 86
Equity in Data 91
Review and Reflect 94
Guiding Questions 94
Extend Your Learning 95

CONTENTS

6 Pathway to Student Services and Supports 99
Chapter Objectives 99
Key Terms 100
Vignette 100
Special Education: From Referral to Eligibility 101
Identifying Students Who Require Special Education and Related Services 101
The Path to Special Education 104
Eligibility for Specific Learning Disability 112
Challenges and Best Practices 113
Review and Reflect 116
Guiding Questions 117
Extend Your Learning 117

7 The IEP: A Blueprint for Individualizing Instruction 121
Chapter Objectives 121
Key Terms 122
Vignette 124
What Is an IEP? 125
Key Components of an IEP 128
Section 504: Protecting Students With Disabilities 146
Review and Reflect 148
Guiding Questions 148
Extend Your Learning 149

8 Access and Equity by Design 151
Chapter Objectives 151
Key Terms 152
Vignette 152
Promoting Access to the General Education Curriculum 153
Universal Design for Learning 154
Differentiated Instruction 155
High-Leverage Practices and Evidence-Based Practices 161

Foundational Framework: Culturally Inclusive Pedagogy and Practice (CIPP) 162
Review and Reflect 165
Guiding Questions 167
Extend Your Learning 168

9 A Shared Responsibility: Collaborating for Access, Inclusion, and Equity 171

Chapter Objectives 171
Key Terms 172
Vignette 173
Collaboration: Types, Purposes, and Collaborators 174
Essential Practices for Effective Collaboration 184
Effective and Culturally Informed Collaboration With Families 188
Collaboration for Professional Growth 191
Review and Reflect 193
Guiding Questions 193
Extend Your Learning 194

Index 197
About the Authors 207

ACKNOWLEDGMENTS

To all the exceptional educators we have had the privilege to learn from and collaborate with, this message is dedicated to you! Your dedication to equity and accessibility is genuinely motivating. You warrant boundless appreciation. Thank you for balancing lesson planning and managing the continuous paperwork—this book serves as a tribute to your daily efforts. You are making a significant impact on the world, one student at a time!

INTRODUCTION

Inclusion Includes You

Imagine a world where every student receives the education they need to thrive. We believe it's a vision that every educator—general education and special education alike—can share and contribute to. And, through this collaborative vision, the line between general and special education can continue to blur, transforming from a divide into a spectrum of opportunity.

In this book, we explore the transformative role the classroom teacher plays in the lives of their students, including the lives of students with disabilities. We lead you on a journey of discovery, introducing you to foundational practices that are not just beneficial but essential for every student. This text is not intended to be an exhaustive, comprehensive source on special education and disability, but rather to serve as a core resource for learning about and understanding key components of special education from the classroom teachers' role and perspective. We invite you to explore the resources provided in each chapter and go deeper in developing your knowledge on the topics and concepts discussed. Consider this book as more than a guide to special education in the general education setting—this book empowers you to embrace inclusive perspectives by building your knowledge, skills, and confidence to meet the diverse learning needs of all the students in your classroom. So let's turn the page and begin the transformation from classroom teacher into special education advocate, innovator, and champion.

Transformational Change

Embracing inclusive education involves rejecting the idea that students should conform to a "normal" (and arbitrary) standard. Rather, inclusive education focuses on establishing a safe and inviting classroom environment where all students feel affirmed, appreciated, and heard. Similarly, special education is not intended to mold students but instead acknowledges and values students by identifying their needs and developing an individualized instructional program that emphasizes access and equity.

Creating an inclusive environment begins with classroom teachers who are increasingly skilled and strategic in providing access to the general education curriculum through high-quality instruction. All students should have access to knowledgeable, skilled, and qualified educators. To feel confident in our ability to support students with disabilities, we must also feel assured that our practices are grounded in research and aligned with policy.

This book synthesizes research and policy to boost educators' confidence, strengthen their self-efficacy, and build their capacity. And we recognize that building confidence begins with building knowledge. This book is organized to answer some of the biggest questions teachers have around special education. We recognize that even though supporting students with disabilities can seem complex and even overwhelming at times, we know how rewarding it can be when we provide effective instruction.

As You Read

This book is organized to include predictable chapter features to support your journey. These features include:

- A list of *chapter objectives* that reflect the knowledge, skills, and mindsets you will develop through your engagement with the chapter content.
- A set of *key terms* that introduces terminology used throughout the chapter and commonly employed in the field. These key terms serve as a preview to chapter concepts.
- An opening *vignette* that introduces the central focus of the chapter. The vignette is not just a story but an opportunity to apply your learning to authentic examples.
- A compilation of *high-leverage practices* (HLPs) aligned with the chapter topic. The emphasis on HLPs is rooted in their intersection of general and special education.
- *Guiding questions* that not only check your understanding but also offer a chance to deepen your knowledge of concepts discussed in the chapter.
- Links to *supplementary resources* carefully curated to complement the chapter's focus. These resources are designed to expand your understanding.

Chapter Overviews

Chapter 1: General Education Teachers Are Special Educators

This chapter shares a brief history of special education and its blending with general education in practice and legislation. Chapter 1 highlights pivotal legislation to protect and educate students with disabilities. This chapter also considers how the legislation has influenced the roles and responsibilities of classroom teachers.

Chapter 2: Special Education Is a Set of Services, Not a Place

Chapter 2 emphasizes the significance of special education as a set of services and not as a place and discusses the role of the classroom teacher in ensuring the provision of a free appropriate public education (FAPE) in the least restrictive environment (LRE). In addition, this chapter examines the multiple models of disability, their influence on inclusion, and the impact of deficit perspectives and sociocultural factors on the education of students with disabilities.

Chapter 3: Valuing Student Identity

Serving the whole child in an inclusive setting begins with understanding their multiple, intersecting identities and how their identities shape their educational experience. Unpacking the concept of intersectionality, this chapter considers best practices for the integration of students' ability, race, culture, gender, language, sexual orientation, socioeconomic status, and other markers of identity into educational and instructional decision-making.

Chapter 4: Multitiered Approach to Inclusive Learning

This chapter provides a detailed understanding of the multitiered system of supports (MTSS) and emphasizes its role as a support system, not a road to special education placement. The major tenets of MTSS are shared and discussed. In addition, the chapter explores the classroom teacher's roles and responsibilities across the tiers.

Chapter 5: Using Data to Drive Student Success

This chapter shares the problem-solving approach to data-driven decision-making. This chapter emphasizes the comprehensive and iterative nature of using various types of assessment and progress monitoring to drive instruction and intervention.

Chapter 6: Pathway to Student Services and Supports

This chapter includes an overview of the process for identification and eligibility for special education services and supports, including prereferral, referral, identification, eligibility, and determination. In addition, this chapter discusses eligibility for protections under Section 504.

Chapter 7: The IEP: A Blueprint for Individualizing Instruction

The chapter details the required components of an individualized education program (IEP) and underscores the significance of the classroom teacher's participation in its development and implementation.

Chapter 8: Access and Equity by Design

This chapter details the theories and practices for providing access to the general education curriculum and planning and delivering equitable instruction. A focus is placed on universal design for learning, differentiated instruction, high-leverage practices, evidence-based practices, and culturally inclusive pedagogies and practices. An emphasis is placed on how these frameworks can be used simultaneously by the classroom teacher to provide access and equity.

Chapter 9: A Shared Responsibility: Collaborating for Access, Inclusion, and Equity

Providing accessible, inclusive, and equitable education to students with disabilities is the shared responsibility of educators and caregivers/families. This chapter describes the key elements of collaboration and the necessary practices and strategies to make collaboration effective. The roles of collaborative team members, including educators, administrators, specialized instructional service personnel, and caregivers, are described. This chapter covers best practices in collaboration, effective communication methods, and other team-based tasks related to inclusive education.

1

General Education Teachers Are Special Educators

The number of students with disabilities who receive special education services in the general education classroom continues to increase, highlighting the critical need for classroom teachers to gain the necessary knowledge, skills, and dispositions to effectively meet diverse learning needs. This includes acquiring foundational knowledge of the laws and regulations that safeguard the rights of students with disabilities, such as Public Law 94-142, the Individuals With Disabilities Education Act (IDEA), and the Every Student Succeeds Act (ESSA). Federal law includes key principles that mandate the education of students with disabilities, including free appropriate public education (FAPE), least restrictive environment (LRE), systematic identification procedures, individualized education programs (IEPs), family involvement, and related services. In addition, federal laws influence the role of the classroom teacher, who assumes a shared responsibility to educate students with disabilities.

Chapter Objectives

After reading this chapter, readers will be able to

- Identify and explain key legislation that governs the rights of students with disabilities
- Explain key principles of legislation and analyze their influence on the responsibilities of classroom teachers
- Evaluate the influence of legislation on the roles and responsibilities of classroom teachers
- Explain high-leverage practices (HLPs) and evidence-based practices, and describe how each can be used to improve student outcomes

Key Terms

evidence-based practices: Instructional techniques that meet a rigorous, prescribed set of research criteria and have been shown to have a statistically significant impact on student achievement when implemented with fidelity (Cook & Cook, 2013). Additionally, evidence-based practices are "supported by empirical research and professional wisdom so that research-based instructional methodologies could be implemented in the unique systems represented by each preK-12 public school" (Burns & Ysseldyke, 2009, p. 3).

free appropriate public education (FAPE): All students, regardless of the severity of their disability, are entitled to a free appropriate education under federal law. Schools have the responsibility to provide an appropriate education, which includes special education and related services, without any financial burden on the parent or guardian, to meet the unique needs of a student with a disability to support their preparation for further education, employment, and independent living.

high-leverage practices (HLPs): HLPs reflect a compilation of "frequently used" practices that "have been shown to improve student outcomes" (McLeskey & Brownell, 2015, p. 7). Further, they are "practices that can be used to leverage student learning across content areas, grade levels, and student abilities and disabilities" (McLeskey et al., 2017, p. 9). These HLPs can be used across grade levels, are important for student learning, and enhance and advance teaching (McLeskey et al., 2017; TeachingWorks, 2016).

individualized education program (IEP): A formal, legally binding document that delineates the specially designed instruction, supports, and services required by a child with a disability to ensure their academic growth and success within a school setting. IDEA further defines an IEP as a "written statement for each child with a disability that is developed, reviewed, and revised in accordance with section 614(d)" (Individuals With Disabilities Education Act, 2004).

least restrictive environment (LRE): LRE is a principle within the Individuals with Disabilities Education Act (2004) that ensures that students with disabilities (1) learn alongside their peers without disabilities to the greatest extent possible and (2) are not removed from the general education classroom unless their learning needs are not met even with supplementary aids and services.

specially designed instruction (SDI): SDI ensures students with disabilities can access the general education curriculum by adapting the content, methodology, or delivery of instruction to meet their unique needs.

Vignette

As you read this chapter, consider the interactions between Mrs. Trujillo and Ms. Rinehart. Connect the information you learn about Mrs. Trujillo and Ms. Rinehart to a shared responsibility. There will be prompts and examples related to this vignette throughout the chapter.

Ryan, a third grade student at Sunshine Elementary, receives special education services. The IEP Team identified the general education classroom as the least restrictive environment for Ryan. In accordance with his IEP, Ryan receives special education services in the general education classroom from Mrs. Trujillo, the special education teacher, three times a week for 30 minutes each session. Ryan's classroom teacher, Ms. Rinehart does not have a background in special education and does not feel confident providing specialized instruction or implementing accommodations. Instead, she relies on Mrs. Trujillo to fulfill these responsibilities during her designated times. While Ms. Rinehart believes this arrangement is sufficient, Mrs. Trujillo has continually emphasized that accommodations must be provided at all times so Ryan can access the curriculum, including during her absence. Ms. Rinehart, on the other hand, firmly believes that her role is separate from Mrs. Trujillo's and that she is not responsible for providing special education services. Additionally, Ms. Rinehart has expressed discomfort with some of the accommodations, as she believes they give Ryan an unfair advantage.

Special Education Was Not Always Available

Public education has not always been considered a right for students with disabilities. During the early to mid-1900s, students with disabilities faced exclusion or unequal treatment within the public school system (Yell et al., 1998). Opponents for providing public education to students with disabilities argued that educating these students would burden schools with extra costs for differentiated instruction, specialized curriculum, trained teachers, and facility modifications to meet students' needs (Stevens & Stevens, 1948). Prior to 1975, decisions to provide a public education to students with disabilities was left to the discretion of individual schools, districts, or states and came with little to no guidance, oversight, or continuity in approach and implementation. Even when an education was available, there was a lack of procedures to identify and classify students (Smith, 1957) as well as an absence of standardized special education terminology (Kirk & Kolstoe, 1953). Additionally, the unclear understanding of disability characteristics made it difficult for educators to provide effective instruction, intervention, and support.

Even though there was great opposition for students with disabilities to receive a public education, there was a growing movement led by advocates who argued public education was a fundamental right. Advocates championed research to expand educational opportunities for students with disabilities and contended that although costly, special education fulfilled basic human needs. The civil rights movement of the 1950s–1960s propelled the efforts of advocates to give students with disabilities access to public schools. Landmark cases like *Brown v. Board of Education* established legal precedent for students with disabilities. By striking down racial segregation in schools as discriminatory, the courts paved the way for advocates to successfully argue that excluding students with disabilities was equally discriminatory. While the impact of the *Brown v. Board of Education* ruling took time to be realized, it was instrumental in driving policy changes for the education of students with disabilities.

Paving a Better Path Forward

In 1975, the efforts of advocates proved successful, and federal legislation known as Public Law 94-142, also known as the Education for All Handicapped Children Act (EAHCA), was passed guaranteeing a public education to students with disabilities. Between 1975 and 2006, PL 94-142 underwent multiple reauthorizations to stay current with research, address persisting issues, and respond to critical matters in special education. Each revision clarified terms and definitions, outlined processes and procedures, and provided guidelines for identification, evaluation, and informed service provisions for students with disabilities. Moreover, parameters were added to tackle problems stemming from implementation or growing field trends (Slanda, 2017). As a result, the roles and responsibilities of educators evolved, leading to an increased need to reimagine educator preparation to ensure all educators are prepared to meet the needs of all students. All educators must be prepared with the necessary skills, knowledge, and dispositions to effectively educate students with disabilities.

PL 94-142

Public Law 94-142 (1975) established the educational rights of students with disabilities (Yell & Drasgow, 2007). Six key provisions in PL 94-142 continue to form the basis for the educational guarantees for students with disabilities today (Turnbull & Turnbull, 2000) including the rights to

1. A free appropriate public education (FAPE), including related services like occupational and speech therapy, regardless of disability category

2. Be educated in the least restrictive environment (LRE) based on individual needs
3. An appropriate education as described and guided by an individualized education program (IEP) addressing present levels of academic achievement and functional performance (PLAAFP), goals, services, and more
4. Procedural due process
5. Nondiscriminatory assessments
6. Meaningful parental/caregiver participation in decision-making

Although litigation, research, and policies have clarified and expanded these provisions over time, the original six tenets remain the foundation of special education. Federal law initially included 12 disability categories: deaf-blindness, deafness, emotional disturbance, hearing impairment, intellectual disability, multiple disabilities, orthopedic impairment, other health impairment, specific learning disability, speech or language impairment, traumatic brain injury, and visual impairment. These original 12 categories remain today, and in 1990 autism was added as the thirteenth and final disability category recognized by federal law.

Individuals with Disabilities Education Act

As the implementation of PL 94-142 progressed, the need to clarify and expand key principles, including FAPE and LRE, became evident (Gamson et al., 2015). Consequently, in 1990 the law was reauthorized and renamed the Individuals With Disabilities Education Act (IDEA). Four fundamental revisions were authorized and included

1. Adopting person-first language
2. Replacing "handicapped" with "student with a disability"
3. Adding autism as a separate disability category
4. Mandating transition plans in students' IEPs by age 16

In addition, IDEA was structured into five sections: Parts A, B, C, D, and E. Table 1.1 details the provisions.

In 1990, IDEA was reauthorized. This reauthorization (1) expanded the law and shifted the focus from providing access and services designed to improve outcomes to implementing accountability measures (Bradley & Danielson, 2004), (2) mandated changes to the IEP, and (3) addressed discipline. The implications of these updates are outlined in table 1.2.

IDEA placed a strong emphasis on transforming special education from a physical location to a service provided to students with disabilities.

TABLE 1.1. *Provisions of IDEA*

Part	Provision Description
Part A	Justified the need for the legislation
	Provided general provision of the act
	Defined terms specific to special education
Part B	Included provisions of special education for students aged 3–21
	Designed to improve access to an FAPE for students with disabilities
	Guided by six main principles (Turnbull & Turnbull, 2000): 1. States must provide all children, regardless of their disability, with an *FAPE*, and no student can be excluded from public education. 2. Identification and evaluation is to be conducted by a team of qualified personnel and must be unbiased and culturally responsive. 3. Eligible students must be provided with a *uniquely designed education* that addresses their specific needs and be outlined in an individualized education program (IEP). 4. Eligible students must be educated in the *least restrictive environment* (LRE) "to the maximum extent appropriate" and are "to be educated with children who are not disabled" (IDEA, 2004, PL 108-446, Section 300.114[a][2]). 5. Parents and families have the right to exercise their *due process* rights as promised under the 14th Amendment and have the right to attain an independent evaluation, request a hearing, appeal, and keep records confidential. 6. Requires *parental/caregiver participation*, a key part of the special education process from identification to evaluation and placement.
Part C	Stipulated provisions and funding for the identification and early intervention services for infants and toddlers from birth to age two
Part D	Included provisions for the programs and services aimed to improve the education of students with disabilities, including parent services, technical assistance, professional development, and technology
Part E	Created the National Center for Special Education Research (NCSER), a center dedicated to conducting research to advance the education of students with disabilities

Note: Reprinted with permission from Slanda and Little (2018).

TABLE 1.2. *Outcomes of the 1990 Reauthorization of IDEA*

Component Added	Outcome
Accountability	• Expanded access to the general education curriculum • Required participation in state and district high-stakes testing • Integrated disaggregation of performance in accountability ratings and measures
IEP	Required the addition of the following: • Measurable annual goals • Description of how progress toward annual goals is measured • Explanation of student's progress toward annual goals • Revision of the IEP if goals are not met
Discipline	• Detailed IEP requirements for intervention • Provided guidelines for serious behaviors

Note: Yell et al., 1998.

Although not mandated, IEP teams increasingly interpreted inclusion as the general education classroom. As a result, the percentage of students with disabilities spending over 80% of their day in general education classrooms increased from 33% in 1990–1991 to 66% by 2020 (U.S. Department of Education, 2023). In fact, 95% of students with disabilities were educated in the general education classroom for at least some portion of their day (U.S. Department of Education, 2023).

Beginning with the 1997 reauthorization, IDEA encouraged schools to implement prereferral interventions to prevent unnecessary labeling of students to meet their learning needs. This shift allowed educators to proactively address students' educational needs through problem-solving strategies before resorting to special education placement (Prasse, 2006). Research has consistently demonstrated the impact of early intervention on narrowing the achievement gap between students with academic difficulties and their peers (Schwartz et al., 2012).

To determine special education eligibility for a specific learning disability (SLD; the most common disability category [U.S. Department of Education, 2024]), educators commonly used the discrepancy model. The discrepancy model mandated the presence of a gap between intellectual ability and academic performance (Fuchs et al., 2008). Although federal legislation required the documentation of a discrepancy, specific eligibility criteria were not described (Bradley et al., 2005), leaving interpretation and determination to the discretion of states and districts. The lack of standardized definitions and eligibility criteria led to underidentification or misidentification of students for special education services (Bradley et al., 2005). As a result, the discrepancy model left students struggling academically without support until the gap became significant enough to warrant services, which often occurred in the later elementary school years (Bradley et al., 2005).

When IDEA was reauthorized in 2004 (becoming the Individuals With Disabilities Education Improvement Act, IDEIA), states were given the opportunity to replace the discrepancy model with the problem-solving approach, known as response to intervention (RtI), for identifying learning disabilities. The transition to a problem-solving model had the potential to decrease the prevalence of academic difficulties and improve the accuracy of identifying specific learning disabilities. The 2004 reauthorization also emphasized early intervention services, allowing special education funds to be allocated to address the needs of students who were at risk. School districts were authorized to utilize up to 15% of their IDEA Part B funds for prereferral and early intervention services (SEC 613[a][2][C] IDEIA).

RtI was developed based on research on early screening, progress monitoring, and the positive impact of small group interventions and tutoring. These elements are essential to the RtI process. RtI, now known as a multitiered system of supports (MTSS), is a prevention model that aims to provide intervention and support to students as soon as they show signs of struggling. Through ongoing progress monitoring, MTSS encourages teachers to provide personalized instruction and data-based intensive intervention as necessary. Within the MTSS framework, educators assess students' response to evidence-based instruction and intervention and deliver flexible support within the general education classroom and in line with eligibility processes.

By emphasizing a problem-solving approach, IDEA aimed to enhance fairness and accessibility to services by addressing ongoing challenges and acknowledging the need to be responsive to an increasingly diverse society. The problem-solving approach was also designed and implemented to address the persistent disproportionate placement of marginalized and minoritized students, including multilingual students, in special education. By including requirements for various supports such as assistive technology, increased practice opportunities, evidence-based practices, and regular progress monitoring, the problem-solving MTSS framework shifted the focus from perceived student deficiencies to improving instruction to enable all students to access the general education curriculum.

Every Student Succeeds Act

The Elementary and Secondary Education Act (ESEA) was passed in 1965 on the heels of the historic *Brown v. Board of Education* decision.

Designed to combat racial segregation in schools and ensure equitable access to education by low-income students, ESEA has been reauthorized (and renamed) multiple times. Most recently, ESEA was reauthorized in 2002 as the No Child Left Behind (NCLB) Act and again in 2015 as the Every Student Succeeds Act (ESSA). To ensure all students experienced academic success, had access to highly qualified teachers, and entered the workforce ready to compete globally, NCLB introduced accountability requirements measured by high-stakes testing. NCLB soon became a topic of debate, with critics arguing that its accountability measures results in an undue emphasis on test scores, leading to a situation where educators felt compelled to focus their teaching primarily on test preparation. To address these and other issues, ESSA was enacted in 2015. Garnering bipartisan and bicameral support, ESSA was welcomed as a more favorable approach for all students, especially students with disabilities. ESSA was responsive to local educational needs and returned control to states, districts, and schools by allowing for flexibility. Under ESSA, state education agencies were able to identify and adopt rigorous state standards, design and employ accountability assessments, and implement instruction and intervention using an MTSS framework.

Although states were responsible for establishing and implementing their own academic achievement standards, ESSA emphasized the importance of increasing the rigor of the curriculum by adopting academic standards that align with college and career objectives. Most importantly, ESSA requires that *all* students, including students with disabilities, access and master the same academic standards regardless of their individual needs. Alternate academic achievement standards and aligned alternate annual assessments could only be offered to students with the most severe cognitive disabilities as long as the total number of students did not exceed one percent of the total number of all students in the state who are assessed (Section 1111[b][2][D][i][I], ESSA).

Furthermore, ESSA required states to adopt accountability goals for *all* students that address proficiency on annual state assessments, English proficiency, and graduation rates. These goals must target achievement gaps between student groups to promote equity, especially for historically marginalized and minoritized students. States were required to implement strategies to close gaps through research- and evidence-based instruction and targeted goals outlined in school improvement plans for both students and educators. The flexibility provided by ESSA allowed states to innovate and tailor their education strategies to better meet the needs of their students by providing the freedom to develop education-responsive policies and accountability measures.

Most significantly, ESSA blurred the historical divisions between general education and special education in unprecedented ways by integrating provisions from both ESEA and IDEA. This integration promoted

TABLE 1.3. *Changes in Major Tenets of Federal Legislation Impacting Students With Disabilities*

PL 94-142	IDEA (1997)	IDEA (2004)	ESSA
Free appropriate public education	Person-first language	Response to intervention	Multitiered system of supports
Least restrictive environment	Replaced IQ-achievement discrepancy requirement	Accountability measures	Inclusion of 99% of all students in school assessment
Specially designed instruction		Early intervention and prereferral services	
Procedural due process	Guidelines for early identification, evaluation, and placement		Accountability structures
Nondiscriminatory assessment		Scientifically based instruction	State control
Parental/caregiver participation	Transition requirements	Measurable annual goals	
	Autism added as a separate category		

educational equity and access for all students, as President Obama affirmed: "Every child, regardless of race, income, background, [or] zip code . . . deserves the chance to make of their lives what they will." Table 1.3 presents the fundamental principles of the legislation governing the education of students with and without disabilities.

> Pause and Reflect:
>
> What changes in federal legislation may influence Mrs. Trujillo's responsibility to provide Ryan with access to the general education curriculum?

Changing Teacher Roles and Responsibilities

The adoption and implementation of federal legislation such as IDEA and ESSA have led to an expansion of teachers' roles and responsibilities

(Slanda, 2017). These mandates shaped the knowledge and skills required of educators as they take on the responsibility of providing evidence-based instruction in the least restrictive environment. Educating students with disabilities has increasingly become a joint effort between general and special educators, necessitating collaboration for the effective implementation of inclusive practices. Like the special educator, it is the duty of the classroom teacher to ensure students with disabilities have access to the general education curriculum, receive necessary accommodations, and are provided with specially designed instruction. This obligation extends beyond the responsibility of the special education teacher. To clarify, both the classroom teacher and special education teacher are responsible for providing access to the general education curriculum by providing adaptations, including accommodations and specially designed instruction. This shared responsibility requires all educators, including classroom teachers, to have a foundational understanding of special education services by enhancing their knowledge and skills in this area.

Fuchs and colleagues (2010) contended that there is a "blurring of special education in a new continuum of services" (p. 310) that necessitates the reorganization of the duties and obligations of educators operating in inclusive environments. Tremblay (2013) further suggested that to proficiently instruct students with and without disabilities to attain demanding academic standards and objectives, the roles and responsibilities of classroom teachers would undergo some restructuring. This restructuring expands the required competencies, knowledge, and skills of classroom teachers to include evidence-based instruction and high-leverage practices as well as data-driven decision-making, progress monitoring, tiered instruction and intervention support, and compliance to guide IEP implementation. Table 1.4 lists overarching competencies required as a result of legislation.

> **Pause and Reflect:**
>
> Consider Ms. Rinehart and Ryan in the vignette at the beginning of the chapter. How do the changes in legislation influence her role and responsibility to provide high-quality instruction for Ryan or other students with disabilities in her classroom? What are Ms. Rinehart's legal responsibilities for educating students with disabilities? How does Ms. Rinehart share the responsibility to provide specially designed instruction, including accommodations, for Ryan?

TABLE 1.4. *Impact of Legislation on Teacher Knowledge and Skills*

	IDEA	ESSA
Knowledge	Disability categories	Multitiered systems of support
	Compliance	Evidence-based instructional practices
	Response to intervention, eligibility requirements	
Skills	Implement adaptable and responsive assessments	Provide access to the curriculum
	Analyze data	Ensure 99% of all students are ready to participate in assessment measures
	Adjust and modify instruction and intervention in response to data	Implement instruction and intervention within a tiered framework
	Provide accommodations	
	Identify and implement evidence-based practices	Collaborate with specialized instructional support personnel (SISP)
	Monitor progress	
	Collaborate with multiple professionals	

Competencies for Classroom Teachers Who Teach Students With Disabilities

High-leverage practices (HLPs) are effective instructional practices that have demonstrated success for students with disabilities and are effective for all students and can be implemented across settings, content areas, and grade levels (Aceves & Kennedy, 2024). HLPs are practices identified from decades of research as effective and frequently utilized by educators (McLeskey & Brownell, 2015). These are "practices that can be used to leverage student learning across content areas, grade levels, and student abilities and disabilities" (McLeskey et al., 2017, p. 9). HLPs are important for student learning and enhance and advance teaching in inclusive classrooms (McLeskey et al., 2017; TeachingWorks, 2016). When used with

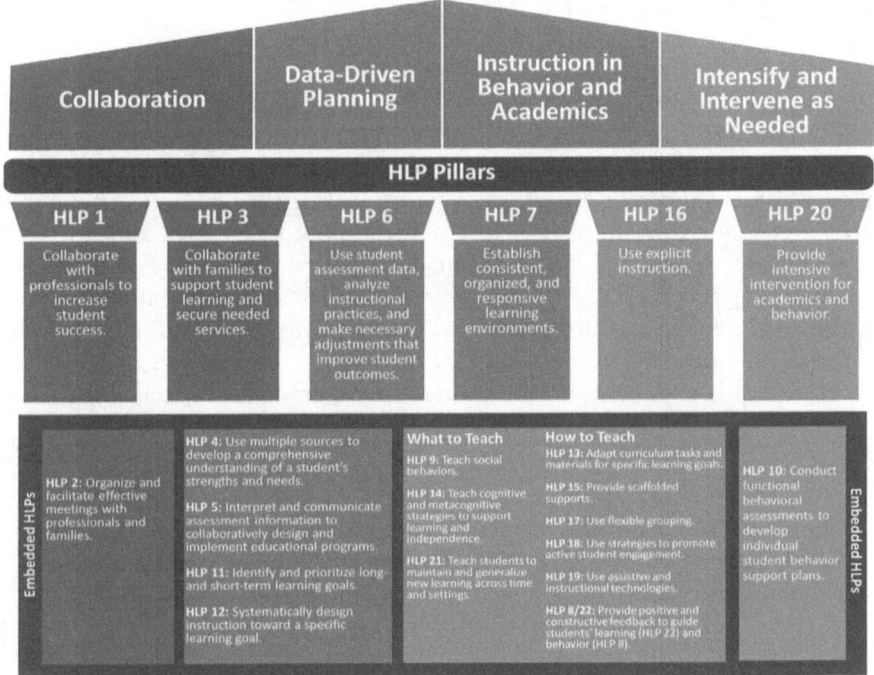

FIGURE 1.1. *High-Leverage Practices: A Continuum of Learning That Improves Teacher Efficacy and Student Learning.* Reprinted with permission from the Council for Exceptional Children.

evidence-based practices (EBPs), the impact of HLPs can be amplified to improve outcomes for all students.

In 2024, the Professional Standards and Practice Committee (PSPC) of the Council for Exceptional Children (CEC) and the CEEDAR Center refreshed and restructured the HLPs to better align with the latest research, changing education landscape, and growing diversity of the student population. The reorganized HLPs emphasize culturally inclusive pedagogies and practices and are designed to fit within an MTSS framework. The 22 HLPs are organized in four domains: (1) collaboration, (2) data-driven planning, (3) instruction in behavior and academics, and (4) intensify and intervene as needed. Seven of the HLPs are designated as pillar practices: (1) collaboration among professionals; (2) collaboration with families; (3) using data, analyzing instruction, and adjusting as necessary; (4) establishing a consistent, organized, and responsive learning environment; (5) using explicit instruction; (6) providing intensive instruction for academics and behavior; and (7) creating individualized function-based support plans. Figure 1.1 outlines how HLPs are organized.

Braiding HLPs and EBPs

When HLPs are used in conjunction with EBPs, teachers are well positioned to advance student learning. EBPs are research-validated instructional and behavioral strategies and are defined as "an activity or intervention that demonstrates a statistically significant effect on improving student outcomes" (Every Student Succeeds Act, 2015). Unlike HLPs, EBPs are bound by content area and grade level (must be developmentally appropriate) and are skill specific (McCray et al., 2017; Robinson & Brownell, n.d.). For example, summarizing text is an EBP that improves a student's reading comprehension and is best applied in third grade and beyond (McCray et al., 2017). And, *using data, analyzing instruction, and adjusting instruction as necessary* is an HLP that is applicable across content areas, grade levels, and skills.

> Pause and Reflect:
>
> How can Ms. Rinehart use HLPs to support Ryan? How can Ms. Rinehart braid HLPs with EBPs to support all students? HLPs emphasize collaboration. How can Ms. Rinehart collaborate with Mrs. Trujillo to support students with disabilities in her classroom?

Several resources exist to help educators identify EBPs to influence instructional and behavioral outcomes, including the National Center on Intensive Intervention (https://intensiveintervention.org/), the IRIS Center (https://iris.peabody.vanderbilt.edu/), the CEEDAR Center (https://ceedar.education.ufl.edu/), and the What Works Clearinghouse (WWC). Although locating resources that list and describe EBPs is relatively simple, difficulty arises when translating knowledge of EBPs into instructional practice and routine.

Review and Reflect

The increasing inclusion of students with disabilities in general education classrooms underscores the importance for educators to develop the necessary competencies to address diverse learning needs. This includes understanding foundational legislation such as PL 94-142, IDEA, and ESSA. Federal laws outline fundamental principles that mandate the education of students with disabilities, which includes FAPE, LRE, identification procedures, IEPs, family involvement, and related services. Moreover, these laws shape the role of classroom teachers, who share the responsibility of educating students with disabilities. Each chapter of this book will further describe guiding principles for students with disabilities and help define the role of classroom teachers.

Guiding Questions

1. What are the major tenets of the Individuals with Disabilities Education Act (IDEA)?
2. Explain how IDEA and ESSA impact general education teacher roles and responsibilities.
3. What are the differences between HLPs and EBPs? How can HLPs support the implementation of EBPs?
4. Consider your roles and responsibilities in your current or future classroom. How will you positively impact outcomes for students with disabilities?

Extend Your Learning

TABLE 1.5. *Resources*

Resource	Description	Link
CEEDAR Center	Technical assistance, webinars, reports, briefs, tool kits	https://ceedar.education.ufl.edu
Council for Exceptional Children	Modules, resources for evidence-based practices, journal articles, peer-to-peer support, high-leverage practice briefs and resources	https://exceptionalchildren.org/
IRIS Center	Modules, briefs, webinars, resources, activities, microcredentials, videos	https://iris.peabody.vanderbilt.edu
National Center on Intensive Intervention	Tools, charts, modules, sample lessons, strategies, resources, overviews, briefs	https://intensiveintervention.org

References

Aceves, T. C., & Kennedy, M. J. (Eds.). (2024). *High-leverage practices for students with disabilities* (2nd ed.). Council for Exceptional Children and CEEDAR Center. https://ceedar.education.ufl.edu/wp-content/uploads/2024/03/High-Leverage-Practices-for-Students-with-Disabilties-updated.pdf

Bradley, R., & Danielson, L. (2004). The Office of Special Education Program's LD initiative: A context for inquiry and consensus. *Learning Disability Quarterly, 27*(4), 186–88.

Bradley, R., Danielson, L., & Doolittle, J. (2005). Response to intervention. *Journal of Learning Disabilities, 38*(6), 485–86.

Brittain, I. (2004). Perceptions of disability and their impact upon involvement in sport for people with disabilities at all levels. *Journal of Sport and Social Issues, 28*(4), 429–52.

Brown v. Board of Education of Topeka. (1954). 347 U.S. 483.

Burns, M. K., & Ysseldyke, J. E. (2009). Reported prevalence of evidenced-based instructional practices in special education. *Journal of Special Education, 43*(1), 3–11.

Cook, B. G., & Cook, S. C. (2013). Unraveling evidence-based practices in special education. *Journal of Special Education, 47*(2), 71–82.

Council for Exceptional Children. (n.d.). *Specially designed instruction.* https://exceptionalchildren.org/topics/specially-designed-instruction

Council for Exceptional Children and CEEDAR Center. (2024). *High-leverage practices for students with disabilities* (2nd ed.). https://ceedar.education.ufl.edu/wp-content/uploads/2024/03/High-Leverage-Practices-for-Students-with-Disabilities.pdf

Every Student Succeeds Act. (2015). Public Law 114-95, 114th Cong., 1st sess. https://www.congress.gov/bill/114th-congress/senate-bill/1177

Fuchs, D., Fuchs, L. S., & Stecker, P. M. (2010). The "blurring" of special education in a new continuum of general education placements and services. *Council for Exceptional Children, 76*(3), 301–23.

Fuchs, L. S., Fuchs, D., & Zumeta, R. O. (2008). Response to intervention. In E. L. Grigorenko (Ed.), *Educating individuals with disabilities: IDEIA 2004 and beyond* (pp. 225–33). Springer.

Gamson, D. A., McDermott, K. A., & Reed, D. S. (2015). The Elementary and Secondary Education Act at fifty: Aspirations, effects, and limitations. *RSF: The Russell Sage Foundation Journal of the Social Sciences, 1*(3), 1–29.

Individuals With Disabilities Education Act. (1997). 20 U.S.C. §§ 1400 et seq.

Individuals With Disabilities Education Improvement Act. (2004). 20 U.S.C. § 1400 et seq.

Kirk, S. A., & Kolstoe, O. P. (1953). The mentally retarded. *Review of Educational Research, 5,* 400–416.

McCray, E. D., Kamman, M., Brownell, M. T., & Robinson, S. (2017). *High-leverage practices and evidence-based practices: A promising pair.* CEEDAR Center. https://highleveragepractices.org/high-leverage-practices-and-evidence-based-practices-promising-pair

McLeskey, J., & Brownell, M. (2015). *High-leverage practices and teacher preparation in special education* (Document No. PR-1). https://ceedar.education.ufl.edu/wp-content/uploads/2016/05/High-Leverage-Practices-and-Teacher-Preparation-in-Special-Education.pdf

McLeskey, J., Council for Exceptional Children & Collaboration for Effective Educator Development, Accountability and Reform. (2017). *High-leverage practices in special education.* Council for Exceptional Children.

No Child Left Behind Act of 2001. (2002). Pub. L. 107-110. https://files.eric.ed.gov/fulltext/ED556108.pdf

Obama, B. (2015, December 10). *Remarks by the president at Every Student Succeeds Act signing ceremony.* https://obamawhitehouse.archives.gov/the-press-office/2015/12/10/remarks-president-every-student-succeeds-act-signing-ceremony

Prasse, D. P. (2006). Legal supports for problem-solving systems. *Remedial and Special Education, 27*(1), 7–15.

Robinson, S., & Brownell, M. (n.d.). *Situating high-leverage practices and evidence-based practices in literacy.* https://mocase.wildapricot.org/resources/Documents/Fall%202016%20Handouts/Situating%20High-Leverage%20Practices%20and%20Evidence-Based%20Practices%20in%20Literacy%20-%20Mary%20Brownell.pdf

Schwartz, R. M., Schmitt, M. C., & Lose, M. K. (2012). Effects of teacher-student ratio in response to intervention approaches. *Elementary School Journal, 112*(4), 547–67.

Slanda, D. (2017). Role ambiguity: Defining the elusive role of the special education teacher who works in inclusive settings [Doctoral dissertation, University of Central Florida]. https://stars.library.ucf.edu/etd/5563/

Slanda, D. D., & Little, M. E. (2018). Exceptional education is special. In G. E. Hall, L. F. Quinn & D. M. Gollnick (Eds.), *The Wiley handbook of teaching and learning* (pp. 277–300). John Wiley & Sons.

Smith, D. W. (1957). Public schools and the mentally retarded. *Elementary School Journal, 57*(7), 375–78.

Stevens, G. D., & Stevens, H. A. (1948). Providing for the education of the mentally handicapped child in the rural school. *Elementary School Journal, 48*(8), 442–46.

TeachingWorks. (2016). *High-leverage practices.* https://www.teachingworks.org/high-leverage-practices/

Tremblay, P. (2013). Comparative outcomes of two instructional models for students with learning disabilities: Inclusion with co-teaching and solo-taught special education. *Journal of Research in Special Education Needs, 13*(4), 251–58. doi:10.1111/j.1471-3802.2012.01270

Turnbull, H. R., & Turnbull, A. P. (2000). *Free appropriate public education: The law and children with disabilities* (6th ed.). Love.

U.S. Department of Education. (2023). *44th annual report to Congress on the implementation of the Individuals with Disabilities Education Act.* https://sites.ed.gov/idea/2022-individuals-with-disabilities-education-act-annual-report-to-congress/

U.S. Department of Education. (2024). *45th annual report to Congress on the implementation of the Individuals with Disabilities Education Act.* https://www.govinfo.gov/content/pkg/CMR-ED1-00187514/pdf/CMR-ED1-00187514.pdf

Yell, M. L., & Drasgow, E. (2007). Assessment for eligibility under IDEIA and the 2006 regulations. *Assessment for Effective Intervention, 32*(4), 202–11.

Yell, M. L., Katsiyannis, A., & Bradley, M. R. (2011). The Individuals with Disabilities Education Act: The evolution of special education law. In J. M. Kauffman & D. P. Hallahan (Eds.), *Handbook of special education* (pp. 61–76). Routledge.

Yell, M. L., Rogers, D., & Rogers, E. L. (1998). The legal history of special education: What a long, strange trip it's been! *Remedial and Special Education, 19*(4), 219–28.

2

Special Education Is a Set of Services, Not a Place

As discussed in chapter 1, current data indicates 66% of students with disabilities spend the majority of their day in the general education classroom and 95% of students with disabilities are educated in the general education classroom for at least some portion of their day (U.S. Department of Education, 2023). This number continues to increase, and although this progress is positive, the mission of responsible inclusion calls for education to design a classroom environment that is responsive to *all* students. Responsible inclusion is about much more than proximity and location—it requires providing the support and services needed for each student to make meaningful academic, behavioral, and social progress. As part of the team for advancing and facilitating inclusion, classroom teachers are essential to this mission. Inclusion rates continue to grow, and classroom teachers will provide a growing and significant portion of instruction and support to students with disabilities. As classroom teachers embrace this role and deepen their knowledge and skills to serve all students, understanding the core concepts, motivations, and practices for inclusion is key. This chapter begins with a summary of the essential components and importance of inclusive education and a description of the multiple models of disability in society. Then, research that supports inclusion as the best model for students with and without disabilities is presented. The chapter closes with a discussion of the classroom teacher's role in inclusive education.

Chapter Objectives

After reading this chapter, readers will be able to

- Define the medical and social models of disability
- Describe how the social model of disability informs inclusion and inclusive education
- List the core principles of inclusive education
- Summarize research that supports inclusive education as the best model for all students
- Select inclusive practices to utilize in multiple ways within the classroom environment

Key Terms

disability: Within the social model, disability is described as a disadvantage or restriction of activity caused by social organization and structures that do not take into account people who have physical impairments (Goodley, 2001; Haegele & Hodge, 2016). This excludes them from mainstream social settings and activities.

free appropriate public education (FAPE): All students, regardless of the severity of their disability, are entitled to a free appropriate education under federal law. Schools have the responsibility to provide an appropriate education, which includes special education and related services, without any financial burden on the parent or guardian, to meet the unique needs of a student with a disability to support their preparation for further education, employment, and independent living.

impairment: Within the social model of disability, an impairment is an abnormality of the body, such as the absence, restriction, or malfunction of a limb or a malfunction of a bodily mechanism or process (Forhan, 2009; Goodley, 2001).

inclusive education/inclusion: An inclusive education system is one where all children, including those with disabilities and diverse needs, learn together within the same schools and classrooms with equitable access to a continuum of support and services that match their needs (UNESCO, 1994, 2015). Inclusion means providing individual learning goals, modifications, accommodations, and high expectations for students with disabilities to ensure they can access the general education curriculum in the general education classroom.

least restrictive environment (LRE): A principle within the Individuals With Disabilities Education Act (2004) intended to ensure students with disabilities are served in the general education environment with peers who are not disabled to the maximum extent appropriate. LRE refers to the extent to which students with disabilities are educated alongside their nondisabled peers in the general education classroom (IRIS Center, 2019).

medical model of disability: An approach to the concept of disability that sets disability as an abnormality or deficiency that lies within the individual and focuses on the disability and needs of the individual (Shakespeare, 2017; Goodley, 2014). Disability-related problems are addressed through a cure or normalization of the individual facilitated by professionals or "experts" (Olkin, 2022). The focus of this model is on "fixing" the individual in order for them to function in society.

social model of disability: A model of disability in society in which disability is seen as an aspect of a person's identity. From this perspective, disability is believed to be a result of a "mismatch between the disabled person and the environment (both physical and social)" (Olkin, 2022). It is not the disability that creates barriers but the environment and lack of support for individual variability (Goodley, 2014; Olkin, 2022). The way to address disability is to change the environment and society rather than "curing" or "normalizing" people with disabilities.

Vignette

As you read this chapter, consider Ms. Chastain's incoming class and her goals for inclusion described in the vignette below. Connect the information you learn about inclusive education to what will be important for Ms. Chastain to consider and implement in her new class. There will be prompts and examples related to this vignette throughout the chapter.

Ms. Chastain is heading into her fifth year teaching seventh grade at Green Pines Middle School. The new school year begins in about one month, and preplanning and professional development sessions start in two weeks. Ms. Chastain receives a "welcome back" email sent to all teachers by her school principal. The email details the plans for summer professional development and preplanning and also emphasizes the school will be moving to an inclusive education model beginning in the fall. Ms. Chastain knows some information about inclusive education but has not taught within this model before. In the past, students with disabilities were typically pulled out of the classroom to receive services. Although she is excited to welcome all students in the same classroom, Ms. Chastain is unsure about best practices to support students with disabilities.

When Ms. Chastain received her tentative class roster, she noticed that she has six students with IEPs, one of which has multiple disabilities and uses a power wheelchair. Ms. Chastain contacted one of the veteran special education teachers, Mrs. Flores, to ask for help. She hoped this collaborative approach to preparing her classroom would put her on the path to providing an equitable and inclusive education to all her students.

What Is Inclusion? Understanding Models of Disability

Education legislation, school policies, research, and a host of other educational resources include many discussions of inclusion and inclusive practices. But what exactly is inclusion? To answer this question, it is important to begin with an understanding of the multiple models of disability. Each model serves as a framework that indicates the perceived causes of disability, appropriate responses, and deeper meanings (Olkin, 2022). Although some may adhere to just one model, the beliefs and practices of most are influenced by multiple models and related historical, social, and cultural trends and values (Goodley, 2014; Shakespeare, 2017). Table 2.1 provides a brief summary of the two most common models of disability within society, the medical model and the social model, and lists both positive outcomes and critiques of each perspective.

Medical Model

The medical model of disability considers disability as an abnormality or deficiency that lies within the individual and focuses on the disability and needs of the individual (Shakespeare, 2017; Goodley, 2014). This perspective asserts that disability-related problems should be addressed through "cures" or "normalizations" of the individual, and these are facilitated by professionals or "experts" (Olkin, 2022). The focus of the medical model is on "fixing" the individual in order for them to function in society. In the United States and other western societies, the medical model has largely replaced the older moral or Judeo-Christian perspective on disability. The moral Judeo-Christian model historically attributed disabilities to the work of a higher power (Humpage, 2007). Within this model, "disability presented itself as an opportunity for miracles to occur" (Haegele & Hodge, 2016) or as a consequence of moral failings (Olkin, 2022).

TABLE 2.1. *The Medical and Social Models of Disability*

Perspective	Medical Model	Social Model
Disability is . . .	an abnormality or deficit within the individual	the result of a disconnect between the variability in individual abilities and needs and the established structures of society and the environment
It should be addressed by . . .	treatments, normalizations, and cures established by experts and professionals	changing social perspectives and environmental conditions to provide access and equity for all individuals
People with disabilities . . .	have an abnormality that needs to be fixed	are unique and represent human variability
The model impacts society by . . .	maintaining structures and norms based on people who do not identify as having a disability	eliciting change and evolution in society to be more inclusive and representative of variability
The benefits of this perspective include . . .	a drive for medical and scientific breakthroughs and advances in technology	empowerment of individuals with disabilities, advocacy for equity, and reduction of deficit perspectives
The drawbacks of this perspective include . . .	perpetuating deficit perspectives, seeing disability as a negative, and giving authority to professionals and experts	neglecting to acknowledge the reality of difficult, day-to-day lived experiences of people with disabilities

Note: Olkin (2022), Cartagena & Pike (2022), and Haegle & Hodge (2016).

As medical and scientific knowledge expanded over the last several generations, doctors and scientists replaced religious leaders as the authorities on societal values, norms, and how to address "abnormalities" (Humpage, 2007). Because the medical field was able to define body parts, biological processes, injuries, and illnesses and also provide treatments and cures, it was established as this authority (Brittain, 2004). As a result, the medical profession became the leader in the discourse around disability and other issues of the body and mind and established disability as a biological issue (Brittain, 2004; Haegele & Hodge, 2016). This rooting in the medical field has led to many breakthroughs and advances in medicine and technology. However, taken on its own, the medical model maintains a deficit perspective on disability and does not place much emphasis, if any, on the role of the environment and society in creating barriers for individuals with disabilities. In this way, the medical model contributes to a continued perspective of people with disabilities as deficient or in need of "fixing" and reinforces societal norms that do not represent or reflect physical, cognitive, and other aspects of human variability (Cartagena & Pike, 2022).

Social Model

There are several theories and models that are categorized as a "social model of disability" (Mitra, 2006). Each of these models has its own specific tenets and perspective, but all of the social models of disability have common underpinnings. In general, the social model of disability asserts disability is an aspect of a person's identity and that disability or impairment is a result of a "mismatch between the disabled person and the environment (both physical and social)" (Olkin, 2022). In contrast to the medical model, the social model of disability emphasizes that it is the lack of support for individual variability within societal structures and environments that creates barriers for people with disabilities, not the individual's disability itself (Goodley, 2014; Olkin, 2022). The social model asserts the way to address disability is to change the environment and society, rather than "curing" people with disabilities. The terms *impairment* and *disability* are also seen as separate, with different definitions within the social model. Within the social model of disability, impairment is described as an abnormality of the body, such as the absence, restriction, or malfunction of a limb or a malfunction of a bodily mechanism or process (Forhan, 2009; Goodley, 2001). In the model, disability is described as a disadvantage or restriction of activity caused by social organization and structures that do not take into account people who have physical impairments (Goodley, 2001; Haegele & Hodge, 2016). This excludes them from mainstream social settings and activities. This distinction is important because it acknowledges the role of society in creating disability and suggests that it is society that limits a person's ability, not their individual body function (Haegele & Hodge, 2016).

Inherent in the social model of disability is a commitment to advocacy for systemic and structural change in society. The model rests on the belief that disability can be addressed by rooting out bias and changing societal systems and structures. Because the model emphasizes how society creates the barriers that disable people, proponents of the social model of disability advocate for changes to laws, policies, structures, and systems to increase accessibility, equity, and value for people experiencing impairments and disabilities. These kinds of changes must occur in all aspects of society to remove existing barriers and advance supports and resources. In this way, people with impairments will experience less disability within society.

> Pause and Reflect:
>
> What are the key aspects of the social model of disability that Ms. Chastain should know to inform her approach to inclusion in her classroom? What questions might Ms. Chastain prepare ahead of time for her meeting with Mrs. Flores?

What Is Inclusion? Understanding Inclusive Education

The social model of disability forms the foundation for inclusive education and informs the key components of inclusion. Inclusive education, or inclusion, refers to an education system where all children, including those with disabilities and diverse needs, learn together within the same schools and classrooms, with equitable access to a continuum of support and services that match their needs (UNESCO, 1994, 2015). An inclusive education system provides individual learning goals, modifications, accommodations, and high expectations for all students, including those with disabilities, to ensure access to the general education curriculum in the general education classroom. As discussed in chapter 1 and in other chapters in this book, federal policy language holds many parallels with inclusive education (Individuals With Disabilities Education Improvement Act, 2004; Every Student Succeeds Act, 2015). Specifically, the Individuals With Disabilities Education Act (IDEA) (2004) requires the provision of FAPE (free appropriate public education) within the LRE (least restrictive environment). Therefore, special education is not a place but a set of services designed to meet the strengths and needs of students with disabilities and is provided through the collaboration of education professionals.

Inclusion is designed to provide an equitable education in the least restrictive environment where students with and without disabilities receive the appropriate services and supports to learn alongside one another. In an inclusive setting, classroom teachers play an essential role in reducing barriers and advancing equity for all students. The key elements of inclusive education are shown in figure 2.1 below. These elements will be discussed further in this chapter and throughout the rest of the book.

Inclusive education is a transformative approach that seeks to provide equitable and accessible learning opportunities for all students, irrespective of their abilities, backgrounds, or identities. At its core, inclusive education is guided by key principles aimed at fostering an environment where every learner can thrive. These principles encompass multiple dimensions of the educational environment and culture,

CHAPTER 2

Accessible Physical Environment:
School buildings, facilities, and classrooms should be designed to be physically accessible, accommodating students with mobility challenges. This includes ramps, elevators, and other facilities.

Universal Design for Learning:
UDL principles involve designing instructional methods, materials, and assessments to meet the needs of all students from the outset, minimizing the need for subsequent modifications. Curriculum and learning materials should be designed to accommodate diverse learning abilities and preferences. Assistive technology plays a key role.

Collaboration & Teamwork:
Collaboration among teachers, support staff, caregivers, and specialists is crucial. Working together ensures that all aspects of a student's development are addressed comprehensively.

Individualized Education Plans:
For students with disabilities, individualized plans should be developed to address their unique learning requirements. These plans outline specific goals, accommodations, and support services.

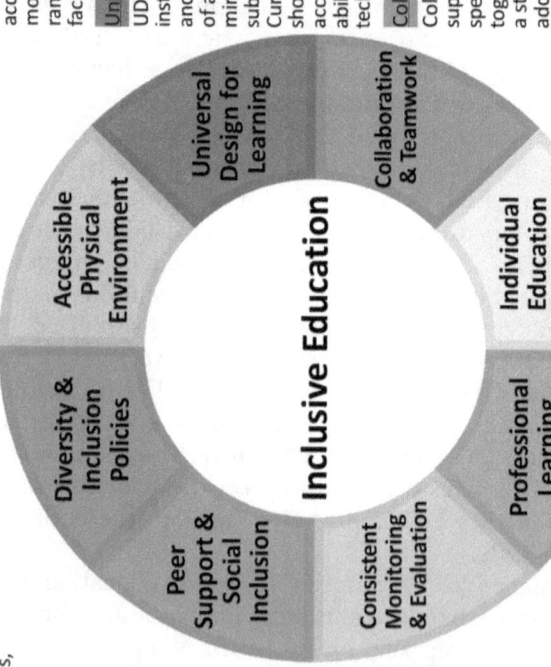

Diversity & Inclusion Policies:
Schools should have clear policies that promote diversity and inclusion, ensuring that students of all abilities, backgrounds, and identities are welcomed and supported.

Peer Support & Social Inclusion:
Encouraging friendships and social interactions among students of varying abilities helps create a sense of belonging and reduces social isolation.

Consistent Monitoring & Evaluation:
Schools and educators should regularly assess and evaluate their inclusive practices to identify areas for improvement and ensure that the needs of all students are being met.

Professional Learning:
Educators should receive training to effectively teach in inclusive classrooms. This includes understanding diverse needs, implementing inclusive teaching strategies, and fostering positive social interactions.

FIGURE 2.1. *Key Components of Inclusive Education.*

including the development and implementation of policies that promote inclusivity, the provision of accessible learning materials, and the creation of individualized education plans for students with special needs. Moreover, teacher training and ongoing professional development play a pivotal role in ensuring educators are equipped to employ inclusive teaching strategies. The concept extends to universal design for learning (UDL), collaborative teamwork among educators and support staff, and the cultivation of a positive and socially inclusive school culture. Through these interconnected elements, which are discussed in detail throughout this text, inclusive education strives to break down barriers, cultivate diversity, and create a learning environment that nurtures the potential of every student.

> Pause and Reflect:
> When they meet, what are some key considerations Ms. Chastain and Mrs. Flores should plan for to make the classroom and instruction inclusive for all students? What additional information might they need to support their planning?

Inclusion as the Best Model for All Students

While most understand how inclusion is beneficial to students who have identified disabilities, the significant benefits for all involved in inclusive education are not as widely known or accepted. Similarly, many believe students with more significant cognitive and intellectual disabilities have needs that are too complex to meet in an inclusive classroom. When discussing inclusion, it is important to understand how inclusive education benefits *all* students, not only those with an identified disability. Decades of research shows academic, social, behavioral, and functional outcomes improve for all students when they receive their education in an inclusive setting. Research also indicates educators, parents/caregivers, and community members also benefit from inclusive schools. Figure 2.2 synthesizes contemporary research findings demonstrating benefits of inclusion (e.g., Bui et al., 2022; Kart & Kart, 2021; IRIS Center; 2010).

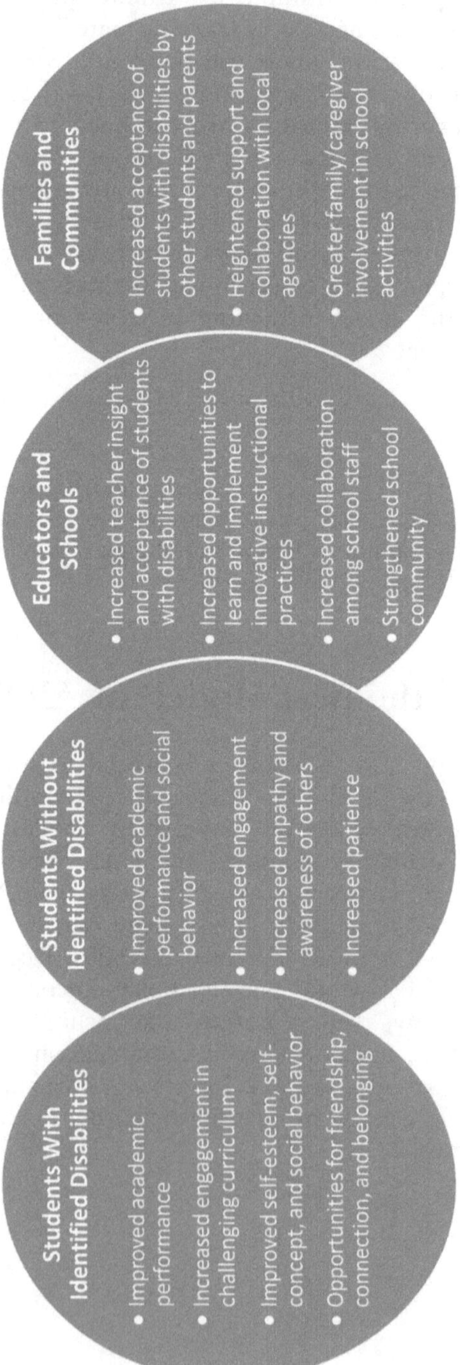

Students With Identified Disabilities
- Improved academic performance
- Increased engagement in challenging curriculum
- Improved self-esteem, self-concept, and social behavior
- Opportunities for friendship, connection, and belonging

Students Without Identified Disabilities
- Improved academic performance and social behavior
- Increased engagement
- Increased empathy and awareness of others
- Increased patience

Educators and Schools
- Increased teacher insight and acceptance of students with disabilities
- Increased opportunities to learn and implement innovative instructional practices
- Increased collaboration among school staff
- Strengthened school community

Families and Communities
- Increased acceptance of students with disabilities by other students and parents
- Heightened support and collaboration with local agencies
- Greater family/caregiver involvement in school activities

FIGURE 2.2. *The Benefits of Inclusive Education.*

The Classroom Teacher's Role in Advancing Inclusion

The classroom teacher plays an integral role in advancing inclusive education. Often, the classroom teacher is the primary source of prereferral intervention and initiates evaluation for special education services. They are also the primary provider of instruction and support for students with identified disabilities. Therefore, having a disposition toward inclusion is a critical quality as teachers fulfill their role in the identification and education of students with disabilities. It is important for classroom teachers to see all students as their own and to set high expectations for every learner. These are core beliefs and dispositions that underpin inclusive education. Classroom teachers are also part of a team and are collaborators in designing and delivering inclusive and equitable education. They have important insight into the curriculum and about their students and possess instructional and pedagogical skills. Additionally, classroom teachers can be strong advocates for inclusion. Within their classroom setting, their school, their district, and beyond, classroom teachers engage in multiple roles and practices that are essential to developing, implementing, and enhancing quality inclusive education for all students. The following section of this chapter discusses core inclusive practices for classroom education teachers. These and other related practices will also be discussed throughout the other chapters in this book.

Foundational Inclusive Practices

Within their classroom, teachers have the opportunity to create rich, inclusive spaces for learning that engage, support, and value the contributions of all learners. Building an inclusive classroom will look different depending on the school setting and students within the classroom, but all inclusive classrooms utilize similar core practices to meet the academic and behavioral/functional strengths and needs of all students. Table 2.2 shares five inclusive practices for academic achievement. These practices are discussed in detail throughout the rest of this book. For now, it is important to understand each of these practices in the context of viewing special education as a set of services and the provision of inclusive education—not as a program that is specific to a particular or separate place. This table does not represent an exhaustive list of inclusive practices but rather highlights essential instructional and classroom practices. By incorporating these instructional practices, educators can create an inclusive learning environment that promotes engagement,

TABLE 2.2. *Foundational Inclusive Academic Practices*

Practice	Description
Universal Design for Learning (UDL)	• Proactively design instruction • Accommodate learning preferences and abilities • Ensure content is accessible • Provide multiple means of engagement, representation, and action and expression
Differentiated Instruction	• Align teaching strategies to meet student's individual needs, strengths, and interests • Provide multiple pathways for learning • Allow students to progress at their own pace
Collaboration	• Encourage collaboration between educators • Implement co-teaching • Facilitate shared responsibility
Use of Assistive Technologies and Resources	• Integrate assistive technology and resources • Include a variety of technological programs, apps, and features to support reading, writing, and communication • Provide sensory accommodations
Assessment and Feedback	• Monitor student progress • Adjust instruction in response to student need • Provide immediate feedback

understanding, and success for all students, regardless of their abilities or backgrounds.

Inclusive education also provides for and supports the behavioral, functional, and social-emotional learning (SEL) strengths and needs of all students. Academics and behavior/social-emotional learning are inextricably connected and impact one another. Essential classroom practices for behavior and SEL in inclusive settings are crucial for fostering a positive and supportive environment. Table 2.3 describes four essential inclusive classroom practices for behavior and SEL. As with table 2.2, these are some of the core classroom practices for inclusion and are not intended as an exhaustive list. These practices contribute to a positive and inclusive classroom culture, supporting the social and emotional well-being of all students and creating an environment where everyone can thrive.

Inclusive education involves planning for and providing a high-quality education that is responsive to student ability and integrates students'

TABLE 2.3. *Inclusive Practices to Promote Positive Behavior and SEL Outcomes*

Inclusive Practice	Description
Clear Expectations and Procedures	• Establish behavioral expectations and classroom rules • Communicate expectations consistently and positively • Create a structured and predictable environment • Promote a sense of safety and belonging
Responsive Classroom Management	• Employ responsive and proactive strategies • Acknowledge and address root causes of behavior • Use restorative practices • Address individual needs • Reinforce positive behaviors
Positive Relationships	• Establish and nurture positive relationships • Create an atmosphere of trust, respect, and understanding • Build relationships with families and communities • Encourage positive social interactions between peers • Create a sense of community within the classroom
Explicit Instruction for Behavior and SEL	• Incorporate explicit behavior and SEL instruction • Teach skills including self-awareness, self-regulation, empathy, and effective communication

backgrounds, cultures, and other aspects of identity. Table 2.4 provides an overarching checklist of questions educators can consider when developing and evaluating an inclusive classroom setting. In reviewing and answering questions about their classroom and their school setting, educators can identify inclusive strengths to leverage and areas to improve in order to advance inclusion.

> Pause and Reflect:
>
> When Ms. Chastain and Mrs. Flores meet, what changes to the classroom environment might they consider making to create an inclusive space? What are some specific ways Ms. Chastain can build positive relationships with all of her students, including those with disabilities? What core inclusive practices should Ms. Chastain plan to implement daily to create an inclusive classroom culture?

TABLE 2.4. *Inclusive Classroom Checklist*

✓	Question	Classroom Evidence	Notes
	Is the classroom physically accessible, organized, and well equipped to support students' learning?		
	Is the physical layout of the classroom conducive to engaging, active learning as a whole class and in small groups?		
	Are classroom expectations and routines explicitly taught and consistently followed?		
	Are behavior expectations consistent and equitable for all students?		
	Are opportunities provided for all students to learn about, value, and respect individual differences?		
	Are the cultural backgrounds and experiences of all students integrated, valued, and celebrated?		
	Are a variety of learning experiences and activities provided for students?		
	Are students provided with ample opportunities to express themselves, their ideas, and their learning?		
	Is technology leveraged to engage students, assist them in accessing and understanding curriculum content, and support their participation and expression in the classroom?		
	Is there a system in place to address student individual needs and concerns?		
	Are students given feedback on their progress regularly?		

HIGH-IMPACT: THE CONNECTION WITH HIGH-LEVERAGE PRACTICES

HLP 1: Collaborate with professionals to increase student success

HLP 2: Organize and facilitate effective meetings with professionals and families

HLP 3: Collaborate with families to support student learning and secure services

HLP 4: Use multiple sources of information to develop a comprehensive understanding of a student's strengths and needs

HLP 5: Interpret and communicate assessment information to collaboratively design and implement educational programs

HLP 6: Use student assessment data, analyze instructional practices, and make necessary adjustments that improve student outcomes

HLP 7: Establish consistent, organized, and responsive learning environments

HLP 9: Teach social behaviors

HLP 10: Conduct functional behavior assessments to develop individual student behavior support plans

HLP 11: Identify and prioritize long- and short-term learning goals

HLP 12: Systematically design instruction toward a specific goal

HLP 13: Adapt curriculum tasks and materials for specific learning goals

HLP 14: Teach cognitive and metacognitive strategies to support learning and independence

HLP 15: Provide scaffolded supports

HLP 16: Use explicit instruction

HLP 17: Use flexible grouping

HLP 18: Use strategies to promote active student engagement

HLP 19: Use assistive and instructional technologies

HLP 20: Provide intensive intervention for academics and behavior

HLP 21: Teach students to maintain and generalize new learning across time and settings

HLP 8/22: Provide positive and constructive feedback to guide students' learning (HLP 22) and behavior (HLP 8)

Review and Reflect

Classroom teachers are at the center of building and delivering an inclusive education for all students, including those with disabilities. This role of the classroom teacher is critically important as it directly connects to equity in education. Promoting inclusive education through classroom culture and professional practices improves outcomes for all students, schools, and communities and reduces deficit perspectives around disability. Through collaboration with other professionals and essential foundational practices, classroom teachers help remove barriers for students and support the unique learning, progress, and development of every learner. Approaching the role of classroom teacher from the perspective of inclusion and equity creates a foundation of practice focused on promoting student strengths and removing barriers. In this inclusive classroom, all students are celebrated and get what they need, when and how they need it, in order to succeed.

Guiding Questions

1. Which model of disability do you see as the most common in education? What are some examples of this model? Why do you think it is the most common?
2. How can you use your understanding of multiple models of disability to support inclusion? Which aspects of each model do you think promote or hinder inclusion? Why?
3. How is inclusion connected to equity in education? Provide examples.
4. What are some of the challenges you perceive in developing and teaching within an inclusive classroom? What resources and supports do you think are essential for responsible and successful inclusion?

Extend Your Learning

TABLE 2.5 *Resources*

Resource	Description	Link
CEEDAR Center Course Enhancement Module on Inclusion	A comprehensive module reviewing the foundations of inclusive education and key practices for creating inclusive classrooms	https://ceedar.education.ufl.edu/cems/inclusive-education/
Maryland Coalition for Inclusive Education (MCIE) Resources	Library of resources to support the establishment and enhancement of inclusive education in schools, including research guides, conversation starters, and other applicable tools	https://mcie.org/resources/
TIES and IRIS Center Professional Development Module	"Inclusion of Students With Significant Cognitive Disabilities: Supports in the General Education Classroom"	https://iris.peabody.vanderbilt.edu/module/scd/
TIES Center Inclusive Practices Video Bank	Multiple videos discussing and demonstrating inclusive instructional practices	https://tiescenter.org/topics/inclusive-instruction/instructional-practices-videos

References

Brittain, I. (2004). Perceptions of disability and their impact upon involvement in sport for people with disabilities at all levels. *Journal of Sport and Social Issues, 28*(4), 429–52.

Bui, X., Quirk, C., Almazan, S., & Valenti, M. (2022). *Inclusive education research and practice.* Maryland Coalition for Inclusive Education. https://mcie.org/download/inclusion-works/

Cartagena, S., & Pike, L. (2022). Defying deficit thinking: Clearing the path to inclusion for students of all abilities. In R. Williams (Ed.), *Handbook of research on challenging deficit thinking for exceptional education improvement* (pp. 101–26). IGI Global.

Every Student Succeeds Act. (2015). Public Law 114-95, 114th Cong., 1st sess. https://www.congress.gov/bill/114th-congress/senate-bill/1177

Forhan, M. (2009). An analysis of disability models and the application of the ICF to obesity. *Disability and Rehabilitation, 31*(16), 1382–88.

Goodley, D. (2001). "Learning difficulties," the social model of disability and impairment: Challenging epistemologies. *Disability & Society, 16*(2), 207–31.

Goodley, D. (2014). *Dis/ability studies: Theorising disablism and ableism.* Routledge.

Haegele, J. A., & Hodge, S. (2016). Disability discourse: Overview and critiques of the medical and social models. *Quest, 68*(2), 193–206. https://doi.org/10.1080/00336297.2016.1143849

Humpage, L. (2007). Models of disability, work and welfare in Australia. *Social Policy & Administration, 41*(3), 215–31. https://doi.org/10.1111/j.1467-9515.2007.00549.x

Individuals With Disabilities Education Improvement Act. (2004). 20 U.S.C. § 1400 et seq.

IRIS Center. (2010). *Creating an inclusive school environment: A model for school leaders.* https://iris.peabody.vanderbilt.edu/inc/

IRIS Center. (2019). *Information brief: Least restrictive environment.* https://iris.peabody.vanderbilt.edu/information-brief/least-restrictive-environment-lre/

Kart, A., & Kart, M. (2021). Academic and social effects of inclusion on students without disabilities: A review of the literature. *Education Sciences, 11*(1), article 16.

McLeskey, J., & Brownell, M. (2015). *High-leverage practices and teacher preparation in special education* (Document No. PR-1). https://ceedar.education.ufl.edu/wp-content/uploads/2016/05/High-Leverage-Practices-and-Teacher-Preparation-in-Special-Education.pdf

McLeskey, J., Council for Exceptional Children & Collaboration for Effective Educator Development, Accountability and Reform. (2017). *High-leverage practices in special education.* Council for Exceptional Children.

Mitra, S. (2006). The capability approach and disability. *Journal of Disability Policy Studies, 16*(4), 236–47.

Olkin, R. (2022, March 29). *Conceptualizing disability: Three models of disability.* https://www.apa.org/ed/precollege/psychology-teacher-network/introductory-psychology/disability-models

Shakespeare, T. (2017). The social model of disability. In L. J. Davis (Ed.), *The disability studies reader* (5th ed., pp. 195–203). Routledge.

UNESCO. (1994). *The Salamanca statement and framework for action on special needs education.* World Conference on Special Needs Education. https://unesdoc.unesco.org/ark:/48223/pf0000098427

UNESCO. (2015). *Incheon declaration: Education 2030; Towards inclusive and equitable quality education and lifelong learning for all.* https://uis.unesco.org/en/document/education-2030-incheon-declaration-towards-inclusive-equitable-quality-education-and

U.S. Department of Education. (2023). *44th annual report to Congress on the implementation of the Individuals with Disabilities Education Act.* https://sites.ed.gov/idea/2022-individuals-with-disabilities-education-act-annual-report-to-congress/

3

Valuing Student Identity

Students with disabilities have multiple identities and experiences outside of their disability. Language, race/ethnicity, culture, religion, socioeconomic status, immigration status, gender and sexuality, and other aspects of a student's identity influence how students experience their education and their disability. The concept of intersectionality explains the interaction between identities and can be used as a framework to consider the sociocultural and sociopolitical factors that simultaneously privilege and oppress certain groups of people. As educators, it is important to understand the multiple identities and lived experiences of students that may put them at risk for oppression in order to actively work to ensure inclusive and equitable education for all students. Similarly, the multiple identities of students should be meaningfully included in all aspects of the classroom and instruction. Pedagogy and practices that are culturally relevant (Ladson-Billings, 1995), culturally responsive (Gay, 2002), and culturally sustaining (Paris, 2012) serve as strong guidelines for considering, valuing, and incorporating student identity throughout the educational environment and all learning opportunities (see chapter 8 for more on these pedagogies and practices).

The Council for Exceptional Children (CEC), the largest international professional organization for special education, and the CEEDAR Center coined the term *culturally inclusive pedagogies and practices* (CIPP) (CEC & CEEDAR Center, 2024). CIPP refers to practices that have centered multiple layers of sociocultural diversity (CEC & CEEDAR Center, 2024). CIPP is further defined by "the wholeness of context, content, and constructs (e.g., people, resources, environments, etc.) that intersect and interact in the education space and influence life-centered outcomes" (CEC & CEEDAR Center, 2024, p. 26). Given its significance, CIPP is built into the high-leverage practices (HLPs; see chapter 1 for more on HLPs). This book underscores the importance of these pedagogies and practices and emphasizes intersectionality throughout. This particular chapter provides an overview of intersectionality, how it applies to students with disabilities, and ways to implement an intersectional equity lens in planning and instruction.

Chapter Objectives

After reading this chapter, readers will be able to

- Identify the key elements of the concept of intersectionality
- Describe how people have historically and contemporarily experienced oppression related to disability
- Describe identities students have in addition to their disability and how they interact to influence their educational experiences
- Apply the concept of intersectionality to the classroom teacher and how they can leverage intersectionality to support an equitable and accessible education
- Evaluate and select HLPs that integrate intersectionality to support students with disabilities

Key Terms

discrimination: The unfair or prejudicial treatment of a person or group based on characteristics like race, gender, age, ability, age, or sexual orientation.

disproportionality: The over- or underrepresentation of a group in a particular category that differs substantially from their percentage of the total population or representation of other groups in that category.

equality: Providing everyone the same resources and opportunities.

equity: Allocating resources and opportunities based on a person's individual circumstances to reach fairness and justice.

explicit bias: The attitudes and beliefs an individual holds about a person or group on a conscious level and related behaviors conducted with intent.

implicit bias: Unconscious attitudes and stereotypes held by all individuals that impact how they think about and act toward certain people and groups.

inclusion: An education model where all students are educated in the same classrooms within the same schools, meaningful learning opportunities are provided to groups who have traditionally been excluded (including children with disabilities and speakers of minority languages), and the unique contributions from students of all backgrounds are valued as a benefit to all.

inclusive language: Language that promotes respect and acknowledges diversity by avoiding expressions that communicate or imply ableist, racist, sexist, or otherwise biased, exclusionary, or insulting ideas.

intersectionality: The interconnected nature of social categorizations such as race, class, ability, and gender that creates overlapping and interdependent systems of discrimination, disadvantage, and oppression.

marginalization: Placing a person or group of people in a position of lesser importance, influence, or power where they have less access to resources, services, and opportunities.

oppression: A situation in which a person or group is governed or controlled in an unfair and cruel way by a person or group in a position of power and prevented from having certain opportunities and freedoms.

privilege: A special advantage, benefit, right, authority, or immunity available to a particular person or group and not to others.

social identities: The part of an individual's identity that is defined by their group memberships (e.g., race/ethnicity, gender, disability, sexuality, socioeconomic status/class).

systemic inequity: A system that implements unjust practices based on known or unknown prejudice.

zero-tolerance approach to discrimination: An approach used in organizations, businesses, and social groups that establishes expectations and policies that do not allow for discriminatory behavior from employees/members. Such policies and expectations leverage legal protections against discrimination and support justifiable termination of employees or expulsion of group members who violate antibias policies, whether through racism, homophobia, ableism, or other "isms."

Vignette

As you read this chapter, consider the student Naomi in the vignette below. How can you connect the vignette to what you learn about intersectionality and related teaching approaches and practices? There will be prompts and examples related to Naomi throughout the chapter.

Naomi is a 10-year-old fifth grade student. She enjoys music, drawing, and science and regularly participates during instruction. Her family immigrated to the United States from Haiti when she was four years old. Both of Naomi's parents work multiple jobs. Naomi has two older siblings, and her family lives with her mother's cousin and their family. Naomi was recently evaluated using culturally appropriate assessments in both English and Haitian-Creole. As a result of these assessments, she was identified as having a specific learning disability that stems from a processing disorder. Naomi's reading fluency is not on grade level, and she continues to struggle with decoding multisyllabic words, often guessing at the word after reading the first few letters. To support Naomi, her teacher provides intensive reading instruction and intervention to build her decoding skills. However, the frequency and duration of interventions has not been consistent due to chronic absenteeism.

What Is Intersectionality?

Intersectionality refers to how social identities (e.g., race, gender, class, ability, and other elements of identity) interrelate in multiple ways and contribute to overlapping systems of privilege and oppression experienced by individuals (Crenshaw, 1989; Collins, 1990). The concept of intersectionality was developed within the Black feminist movement of the 1970s and 1980s. According to Kimberlé Crenshaw (1989) and Patricia Hill Collins (1990), critical race and feminist researchers during the movement, analyzing only one marker of identity as primary limits the understanding of identity, difference, or disadvantage. Crenshaw (1989) coined the term *intersectionality* to express the difficulty she and her fellow researchers found in separating "race from class from sex oppression because in our lives, they are most often experienced simultaneously" (Combahee River Collective, 1977/1995, p. 234). Crenshaw (1991) emphasized how Black women found it difficult to identify with the predominantly White mainstream feminist movement because of the simultaneous oppressions they faced due to their race. Although Black women experienced sexism within the civil rights movement, they were often excluded from leadership positions due to their race.

In education, scholars and researchers interested in advancing equity emphasized the significance of intersectionality, giving rise to frameworks including disability/critical race theory (DisCrit) (Annamma et al., 2013), which highlighted the historical and contemporary link between racism and ableism. It creates a framework through which to analyze and address inequities based on race and disability, especially within education, at both the individual and systemic level. By considering students' multiple identities and the layers of oppression they may experience due to systemic bias and barriers, educators and advocates can leverage intersectionality and take

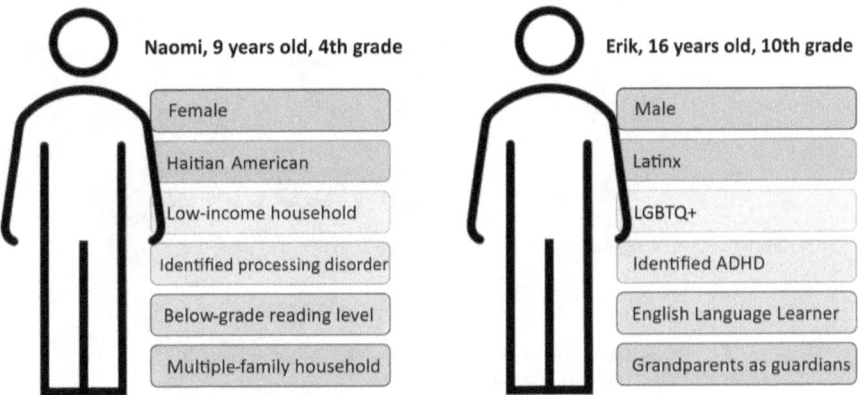

FIGURE 3.1. *Examples of Intersectional Identities.*

targeted action to remove systemic inequities in education (Annama et al., 2018; Boveda, 2016; Scott et al., 2022).

Today's students have multiple social identities that influence how they experience school. For some students, disability status represents one social identity. Just as their disability may influence their educational experience, their cultural background, socioeconomic status, gender, sexuality, and multiple other social identities may influence how they experience their disability. Similarly, disability may influence how they experience their other identities. Figure 3.1 illustrates examples of intersectional social identities.

Oppression, Privilege, and Systemic Inequity

Over the past 50 years, the concept and theory of intersectionality evolved to encompass all intersecting social identities (race, gender, sexuality, class, ability, age, language, etc.). Foundational to intersectionality theory is the acknowledgment of the multiple identities of every individual and the existence of biased and inequitable systems in society that inherently create privilege for some groups and oppression for others (Cochran-Smith, 2010). Privilege is any advantage, benefit, right, authority, or immunity available to a person or group from a particular social identity that is not afforded to other social identities. Oppression occurs when a person or group is prevented from accessing opportunities or freedoms by another person or group that is in a position of power.

Unfortunately, multiple social systems inherently oppress groups of people with particular social identities (Carbado et al., 2013). Examples of these systems are ableism, racism, heterosexism, and classism. These

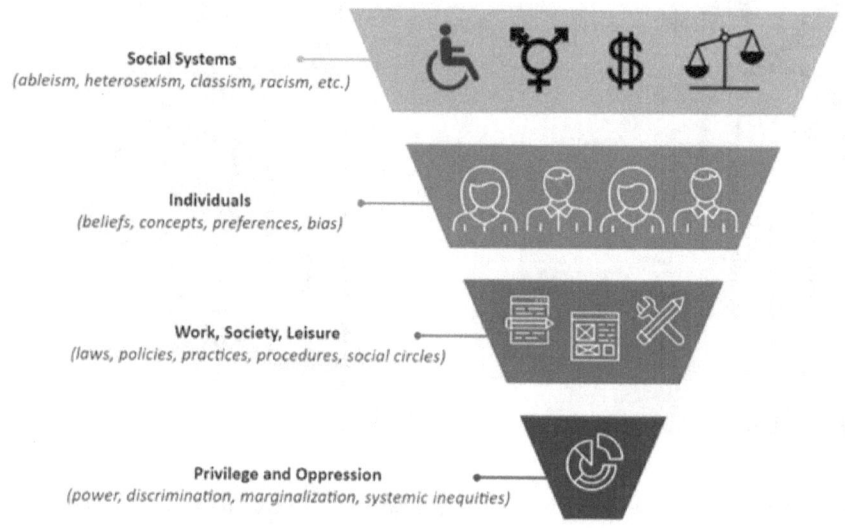

FIGURE 3.2. *The Funnel of Systemic Inequity, Bias, and Privilege and Oppression.*

social systems influence the structures, laws, policies, processes, and actions that guide everyday lives, creating systemic inequities that simultaneously privilege some individuals while oppressing others. For example, people from a lower socioeconomic status may experience more serious and more frequent health challenges, including a higher mortality rate, than individuals from a higher-income status (Daniel et al., 2018). The U.S. Department of Education (2020) reported that students attending schools that serve students of color are more likely to be taught by out-of-field and novice teachers than schools serving predominantly White students. Social systems also influence an individual's beliefs and actions, both conscious and subconscious. As individuals interact through work and leisure, they may create or maintain systemic inequities that oppress certain individuals or groups. Figure 3.2 illustrates how systems along with an individual's beliefs and bias result in social "norms" and practices that further lead to privilege or oppression.

Explicit and Implicit Bias

School systems, like businesses, are made up of individuals who are both aware and unaware of their bias and how they contribute to systemic inequity. Explicit bias refers to an individual's conscious beliefs and attitudes toward another individual or group that intentionally guides their actions and interactions (American Psychological Association, 2022a). Implicit bias, on the other hand, is the unconscious attitudes and stereotypes held by an individual that influence how they view or treat other individuals or groups (American Psychological Association, 2022b). Both explicit and implicit bias influence policies, programs, and practices. Figure 3.3 outlines details and examples of explicit and implicit bias.

Individuals or organizations can take various steps to combat bias and discrimination. For example, organizations can provide training and professional learning that encourages individuals to explore their biases and beliefs. Organizations can also adopt a zero-tolerance approach to explicit bias, which establishes expectations and policies that do not tolerate discriminatory behavior. Antidiscrimination practices and policies are enforced by various state and federal laws. Organizations can use these laws to protect against workforce discrimination.

Additionally, organizations can promote equitable and inclusive practices by ensuring diversity in its workforce. Diversifying the workforce leads to the development and adoption of inclusive and equitable policies, laws, procedures, and expectations and elevates diverse perspectives. For example, including the perspective of an individual with a mobility impairment ensures policies and practices address and reduce potential barriers. Similarly, including the perspective of a racially diverse workforce leads to inclusive policies and practices that are responsive to individuals' religious beliefs, dietary needs, or language. Including individuals from a broad range of backgrounds and experiences in decision-making can lead to an equitable and inclusive environment.

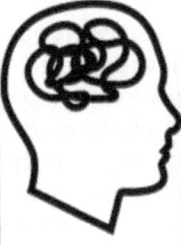

Implicit bias is unconscious and often ingrained in individuals beginning in childhood. It is based on what an individual observes and experiences within their environment as they develop.

Examples: When an employer, without realizing, assigns all technological tasks to younger employees instead of senior individuals. Automatically assuming a student with a learning disability will need significant help with every assignment.

Explicit bias is conscious, intentional, and may begin developing in childhood. It can be influenced by what an individual is taught and observes as a child and can become more pronounced as they age.

Examples: Bullying or harassing someone because of their race or ethnicity. Objecting to an employee who uses a wheelchair being promoted to a leadership role and questioning their ability to lead because they have a disability.

FIGURE 3.3. *Implicit and Explicit Bias.*

Intersectionality and Students With Disabilities

Because bias can influence systemic practices and policies, individuals with multiple intersecting social identities—including students—can experience oppression and marginalization. Marginalization is when an individual or group is forced to assume a position of lesser importance, influence, or power that reduces their access to resources, services, and opportunities. Students and their families may experience multiple forms of discrimination in response to their varied social identities. Table 3.1 describes various social systems rooted in bias that result in discriminatory practices. Although this table does not represent an exhaustive list of all social systems, it does provide examples of systemic discrimination in response to specific and multiple identities.

Bias and discrimination can be expressed by others both explicitly and implicitly. Within a school system, bias and discrimination can have dire consequences for students. Historically, identification for special education has been influenced by explicit and implicit bias that marginalizes students of color. Decades of research exposes that students from racially, culturally, and linguistically diverse backgrounds are identified for special education and placed in more restrictive learning environments at rates disproportionate to their percentage of the student population (Slanda et al., 2022; U.S. Department of Education, 2023). This occurrence is termed "disproportionality," which refers to the over- or underrepresentation of a group compared to their representation in the total population or the representation of other groups in that category.

Disproportionality in special education is an example of an intersectional or multiple marginalization. Racially, culturally, or linguistically diverse students experience increased oppression related to more than one social identity (e.g., disability and race). Disproportionality stems from various policies and practices and translates to overrepresentation in special education, placement in more restrictive environments, and harsher consequences for behavior and increased disciplinary action. For example, multilingual students whose primary language is not English are more likely to be identified for special education services than their White peers (Harry & Klingner, 2006; U.S. Department of Education, 2023). Disproportionality can also result in the underrepresentation of students of color. For example, students from racially diverse backgrounds face decreased access to gifted-and-talented programs.

These are just a few examples of how a student may experience multiple and simultaneous oppressions or challenges because of systemic inequities related to their identities. Given the impact of misidentification for special education, teachers should build their own cultural understanding to ensure they value students' multiple identities and lived experiences that

TABLE 3.1. *Social Systems That Are Inherently Biased*

Type of Bias	Description	Examples
Ableism	Bias based on the belief that typical abilities are superior and preferred and people with disabilities are less able.	A music event with no designated space for people with disabilities. Low expectations for what a person with a disability can achieve or participate in through work and socially.
Classism	Preference for or bias against people in a particular social or economic class.	Judging others to be lazy or unhygienic because they are from a low-income background. Assuming everyone has access to the same resources and technology at home.
Eurocentrism	A worldview or mindset that centers European, or White, and western ways of knowing as sole, central, or superior to all others.	Presenting lighter skin tones, straight hair, and other physical features as being more attractive. Portraying non-European cultures and peoples as exotic, primitive, or inferior and positioning European culture and history as the only "true" or "valid" culture and history.
Genderism/ Sexism	Preconception about attributes, characteristics, value, or expected roles of an individual based on their actual or perceived gender. This can include prejudice against women, stereotypical definitions of masculinity, and discrimination toward people who identify outside the gender binary of man and woman.	Assuming that all women are nurturing or that all men are aggressive. Asserting male and female as the only "real" or "valid" genders. Denying transgender and gender-nonbinary individuals access to places and resources. Misgendering someone intentionally.
Heterosexism	The belief that heterosexuality is the "normal" or "superior" sexual orientation. Prejudice toward anyone who is not heterosexual.	Lack of representation of nonheterosexual relationships in media. Assuming everyone is heterosexual. Asking invasive questions about someone's sexual orientation. Making jokes about nonheterosexuality.

(Continued)

TABLE 3.1. *(Continued)*

Type of Bias	Description	Examples
Linguicism	Bias or discrimination based on the language or dialect used by an individual or group.	Prioritizing English as the universal or superior language. Treating someone who does not speak English as less intelligent. Making fun of someone who has an accent or who makes grammatical or pronunciation mistakes.
Racism	Prejudice and discrimination against a person or group based on their race or ethnicity.	Refusing to rent or sell housing to someone, or providing different terms and conditions, based on their race or ethnicity. Assuming someone is less capable, reliable, or trustworthy because of their race or ethnicity.
Religious Bias/ Sectarianism	Preference toward a particular religion or sect over another. Discrimination against an individual or group based on their religious identity, beliefs, or practices.	Basing public school or work holidays on Christian holidays and traditions. Refusing to hire someone because they wear religious attire like a turban, hijab, or yarmulke.

are influenced by their culture, language, community, gender, sexuality, and other social markers. By learning about and understanding students, their experiences, and their backgrounds, educators can not only guard against the potential influence of biases in decision-making for serving students but also leverage social identities as strengths and points of engagement to serve equitably.

> Pause and Reflect:
>
> Consider what you know about Naomi from the vignette at the beginning of the chapter. Although it is important not to make assumptions, what possible types of bias, discrimination, and barriers might Naomi and her family experience? Think about experiences both within the education system and in other systems within society. How might experiences outside of the education system impact Naomi and her family's experiences within the education system?

Intersectionality for Inclusion and Equity in the Classroom

It is essential for educators to see students as their whole selves and consider and value the multiple identities and aspects of who they are. When working with students, educators should be conscious of the marginalization students may face because of their disability. However, they cannot stop there. It is important also to consider how the student's experience of disability is impacted by other identities they hold. Because various identities intersect, educators should consider the whole student by viewing identities collectively rather than individually (e.g., only seeing one identity) (Jones & Wijeyesinghe, 2011). When an educator is cognizant of students' multiple identities and the potential barriers they may face in their education because of bias and inequity, they can engage in targeted, intentional practices to reduce biases and eliminate obstacles to inclusion and equity.

Intersectional Practices

Examining Your Own Biases

Integrating an intersectional approach in the classroom requires educators to identify and examine their own bias. Individuals can have both explicit and implicit biases that influence their attitudes and actions. Teachers should explore their own biases, including those they may not be aware of, and take the time to reflect on how they might show up in their teaching practices (Starck et al., 2020). Reflective practices allow teachers to identify and mitigate their own biases (Starck et al., 2020). A variety of resources and tools have been developed to support educators in their own antibias journey (e.g., Broderick & Lalvani, 2017; Utt & Tochluk, 2020). Developing an antibias practice includes reflecting on and questioning the attitudes and actions taken each day as a teacher and actively engaging in activities that will address bias. This might mean increasing one's own knowledge and understanding about groups of people who are different from one's own or journaling about feelings of bias (positive or negative) toward an individual or group and what experiences or information might underpin these biases. When educators interrogate the biases they hold toward individuals and groups, they can begin to actively change their perceptions and their resultant actions. Educators who are critically conscious of their own biases enhance their ability to provide inclusive and equitable educational environments and experiences for all students.

Knowing Your Students

Taking time to connect with students on an individual level is an important practice for all educators. Activities like identity maps, journals, and one-on-one discussions allow students to explore their likes and dislikes and connect classroom teachers with their students by understanding and valuing their backgrounds, cultures, and experiences. Insight gained from identity-based activities can be used to enhance lesson-planning, engagement, and support strategies to ensure all students have access and feel included in the classroom. These activities also build educators' understanding that students who may share the same social markers may not experience their intersectionality the same way. Learning about the unique differences among students with similar social markers is essential to meeting their specific strengths and needs. By acknowledging students' disabilities as part of their greater, multifaceted identities, educators send a clear message: they view their students as more than their disabilities, recognize more than one aspect of their identity, and see them as a whole person.

Language Matters

Teaching from an intersectional perspective requires educators to be conscious of the language they use and how they talk about inclusion and equity in their own classroom. Inclusive language sets a foundation for communicating value for diversity and models this value as an expectation for students. Inclusive language promotes respect and acknowledges diversity by avoiding expressions that communicate or imply ableist, racist, sexist, or otherwise biased, exclusionary, or insulting ideas. When talking about disability or referring to a student with a disability, educators should use person-first language. This means referring to someone as a person first and then indicating their disability. For example, you could use the term *student with ADHD* instead of *ADHD student*. However, it is important to note that some people with disabilities prefer an identity-first reference as a matter of empowerment. For example, many people in the deaf community choose to refer to themselves as a deaf person, not a person with deafness. Similarly, many in the autistic community use identity-first language (e.g., autistic guy, autistic woman, autistic person). If able, educators should have conversations with students with disabilities about whether they prefer person-first or identity-first language. If this is not possible or the educator is speaking to or writing to a group audience, they should default to person-first language.

Another example of inclusive language for the classroom related to other identities or social markers would be greeting the class as "students," "scholars," or "everyone" instead of "boys and girls," "ladies and gentlemen," or "guys." This language acknowledges and demonstrates respect for a spectrum of gender identities. Similarly, educators can use the term *family members* or *caregivers* instead of *parents* to include students with various family structures. There are many examples of inclusive language, but the main message involves using language that includes and respects rather than excludes and devalues. Using inclusive language related to all identities, in addition to person-first language related to disability, communicates to students with disabilities that all of their identities are important and respected.

Differences as Assets: Elevating Voices and Experiences

As previously mentioned, it is also important that educators do not view or portray disability or other student identities as deficits or weaknesses. In fact, differences and diversities should be celebrated and valued, not only because they are the root of creativity, innovation, and progress but because they are what makes each individual unique and innately valuable as a human being. An intersectional approach to serving and supporting students with disabilities includes demonstrating appreciation for and elevating the voices and experiences of groups who have been historically marginalized or left out. For students with disabilities, this might include instruction around and exploration of disability history and ensuring students with disabilities are given opportunities to share their experience and serve as leaders and resources in the classroom. Inclusion and equity happen when a student is celebrated because of who they are.

Similar strategies can be used to include other aspects of students' identities in the classroom environment, instruction, and learning. For example, a teacher can ask a student how they might say something in their first language or what traditions or routines they engage in at home related to a class topic. Engaging students in activities that allow them to share their experiences, stories, and opinions related to disability, race, culture, and other identities communicates that these are important topics and their experiences matter. Celebrating students as sources of knowledge and experience that contribute to the classroom and to everyone's learning is empowering. Linking student stories and experiences to classroom topics and learning objectives supports deeper learning and belonging by connecting their education to their lives.

Activities and strategies that intentionally acknowledge, include, and value disability, culture, language, and other diverse identities are not as effective if they are implemented periodically. Instead of only celebrating racial and ethnic diversity during Black History Month or Hispanic Heritage Month, an intersectional approach to education ensures diversity is represented and integrated throughout all aspects of the classroom, every day, and all year. Encouraging students to share about their cultural, linguistic, and other background experiences within instruction and classroom materials supports their whole-person identity.

> Pause and Reflect:
>
> Review the vignette about Naomi at the beginning of the chapter. If you were Naomi's teacher, what are some examples of teaching practices and strategies you might use to include, teach, and support Naomi from an intersectional perspective?

Contributing to Systemic Change

In addition to transforming individual perspectives and practices in the classroom, professional educators are called to advocate for their students and contribute to advancing systemic equity. As discussed earlier in this chapter, inequity is often built into social and organizational policies and practices. Educators can play an essential role in the identification of inequity and transformation at the school/local, state/regional, and national/international level. One essential action educators can take is voting. Participating in local, state, and national elections and supporting candidates who develop and implement practices and policies to support equity within schools and communities is key to transforming systems. In addition to voting, there are many other ways educators can get involved with systemic change. Table 3.2 below provides a few examples and places to start.

TABLE 3.2. *Teacher Actions for Intersectional Systemic Change*

System/Level	Action	Organizations/Resources
School/Local	Start or join committees that address inequities	Mid-Atlantic Equity Consortium (MAEC) Equity Audit Toolkit: https://maec.org/equity-audit/
	Collaborate with families and community members to develop policies, practices, and programs	Great Schools Partnership Equitable Community Engagement Toolkit: https://www.greatschoolspartnership.org/resources/equitable-community-engagement/
State/Regional	Join a state or regional organization that improves education	Council for Exceptional Children (CEC) State Units: https://exceptionalchildren.org/engage/units
	Serve on an education advisory committee for your state government official (representative, senator)	Find Your Member of Congress: https://www.congress.gov/members/find-your-member
National/International	Join a national education organization that engages in equity work	Council for Exceptional Children (CEC): https://exceptionalchildren.org/

HIGH-IMPACT: THE CONNECTION WITH HIGH-LEVERAGE PRACTICES

HLP 4: Use multiple sources of information to develop a comprehensive understanding of a student's strengths and needs

HLP 7: Establish consistent, organized, and responsive learning environments

HLP 18: Use strategies to promote active student engagement

Review and Reflect

Understanding intersectionality and the importance of students' multiple identities, as well as taking an intersectional approach to teaching, provides inclusive and equitable education to *all* students. It is important for educators to recognize and integrate students' identities into daily instruction and classroom interactions. In addition to learning about and understanding how the student experiences their disability, it is important for educators also to consider how the student experiences other identities. Learning about a student's experiences related to race, culture, language, socioeconomic status, and other social identities exposes how students' identities influence how they experience disability. Educators can seek, acknowledge, and value the multiple and intersecting identities of their students to promote an inclusive and equitable education. Acknowledging intersectionality creates an inclusive and equitable environment for all students and communicates that inclusion and equity are key components of the classroom culture. In this way, inclusive and equitable education for students with disabilities is not only about their disability but rather about their whole, inclusive identity.

Guiding Questions

1. Define intersectionality in your own words.
2. Identify your personal social identities. Have any of these identities been a source of privilege or oppression? If so, how?
3. List three examples of social identities a student may have. How might a student experience marginalization or privilege in their education due to these identities?
4. How can you use the concept of intersectionality as a framework to approach working with students who have disabilities?
5. In what ways can an intersectional approach to education support inclusion and equity for all students?

Extend Your Learning

TABLE 3.3. *Resources*

Resource	Description	Link
Learning for Justice Toolkit	"Toolkit for 'Teaching at the Intersections'": Curated resources, activities, and tools for teachers to embed intersectionality within their practice and their classroom	https://www.learningforjustice.org/magazine/summer-2016/toolkit-for-teaching-at-the-intersections
PROGRESS Center Handout and Resource Tool	"Fostering Belonging" handout: Resource with information, professional practices, and checklists to review and enhance feelings of belonging for students with and without disabilities in inclusive classrooms and educational spaces	https://promotingprogress.org/sites/default/files/2022-02/Fostering_Belonging_Handout.pdf
Center for Excellence in Teaching and Learning Resource Bank	"Equity Minded Teaching": Resource bank containing articles and tools for educators to serve the multiple identities of their students through equitable practices (includes information and resources specific to intersectionality)	https://cetl.uconn.edu/resources/equity-minded-teaching/
CEEDAR Center Resource Bank	"Culturally Relevant Education PD Pack": Website bank of videos and related resources focused on culturally relevant practices, including a section titled "Intersectionality & Inclusion in the Classroom"	https://ceedar.education.ufl.edu/portfolio/culturally-relevant-education-pd-pack/
Diverse Educators Toolkit	"Intersectionality Toolkit": Information about intersectionality and resources for integrating intersectionality into teaching and classroom practices	https://www.diverseeducators.co.uk/intersectionality-toolkit/
United Nations Women/United Nations Partnership on the Rights of Persons with Disabilities Resource Guide	"Intersectionality Resource Guide and Toolkit": Information, tools, and resources for organizations and individual practitioners to address intersectionality in their practices, policies, and programs	https://www.unwomen.org/en/digital-library/publications/2022/01/intersectionality-resource-guide-and-toolkit

References

Annamma, S. A., Connor, D., & Ferri, B. (2013). Dis/ability critical race studies (DisCrit): Theorizing at the intersections of race and dis/ability. *Race Ethnicity and Education, 16*(1), 1–31. https://doi.org/10.1080/13613324.2012.730511

Annamma, S. A., Ferri, B. A., & Connor, D. J. (2018). Disability critical race theory: Exploring the intersectional lineage, emergence, and potential futures of DisCrit in education. *Review of Research in Education, 42*(1), 46–71. https://doi.org/10.3102%2F0091732X18759041

American Psychological Association. (2022a). Explicit prejudice. *APA dictionary of psychology.* https://dictionary.apa.org/explicit-prejudice

American Psychological Association. (2022b). Implicit bias. https://www.apa.org/topics/implicit-bias

Boveda, M. (2016). Beyond special and general education as identity markers: The development and validation of an instrument to measure preservice teachers' understanding of the effects of intersecting sociocultural identities (2998) [Doctoral dissertation]. FIU Electronic Theses and Dissertations. https://digitalcommons.fiu.edu/etd/2998

Broderick, A., & Lalvani, P. (2017). Dysconscious ableism: Toward a liberatory praxis in teacher education. *International Journal of Inclusive Education, 21*(9), 894–905. https://doi.org/10.1080/13603116.2017.1296034

Carbado, D. W., Crenshaw, K. W., Mays, V. M., & Tomlinson, B. (2013). Intersectionality: Mapping the movements of a theory. *Du Bois Review: Social Science Research on Race, 10*(2), 303–12. https://doi.org/10.1017/s1742058x13000349

CEC and CEEDAR Center. (2024). *High-leverage practices for students with disabilities* (2nd ed.). https://ceedar.education.ufl.edu/wp-content/uploads/2024/03/High-Leverage-Practices-for-Students-with-Disabilties-updated.pdf

Cochran-Smith, M. (2010). Toward a theory of teacher education for social justice. In A. Hargreaves, A. Lieberman, M. Fullan & D. Hopkins (Eds.), *Second international handbook of educational change* (pp. 445–67). Springer.

Combahee River Collective. (1977). *The Combahee River Collective statement.* https://americanstudies.yale.edu/sites/default/files/files/Keyword Coalition_Readings.pdf

Cooc, N. (2019). Disparities in the enrollment and timing of special education for Asian American and Pacific Islander students. *Journal of Special Education, 53*(3), 177–90. https://doi.org/10.1177/0022466919839029

Collins, P. H. (1990). *Black feminist thought: Knowledge, consciousness, and the politics of empowerment.* Unwin Hyman.

Crenshaw, K. (1989). Demarginalizing the intersection of race and sex: A Black feminist critique of antidiscrimination doctrine, feminist theory, and antiracist politics. *University of Chicago Legal Forum, 1989*(1), 139–67.

Crenshaw, K. (1991). Race, gender, and sexual harassment. *Southern California Law Review, 65,* 1467–76. https://scholarship.law.columbia.edu/faculty_scholarship/2867?utm_source=scholarship.law.columbia.edu%2Ffaculty_scholarship%2F2867&utm_medium=PDF&utm_campaign=PDFCoverPages

Daniel, H., Bornstein, S. S., Kane, G. C., & Health and Public Policy Committee of the American College of Physicians. (2018). Addressing social determinants to improve patient care and promote health equity: An American College of Physicians position paper. *Annals of Internal Medicine, 168*(8), 577–78. https://doi.org/10.7326/M17-2441

Gay, G. (2002). Preparing for culturally responsive teaching. *Journal of Teacher Education, 53*(2), 106–16. https://doi.org/10.1177/0022487102053002003

Harry, B., & Klingner, J. K. (2006). The special education referral and decision-making process for English language learners: Child study team meetings and staffings. *Teachers College Record, 108*, 2247–81. https://nepc.colorado.edu/publication/special-education-referral-and-decision-making-process-english-language-learners-child-s

Jones, S. R., & Wijeyesinghe, C. L. (2011). The promises and challenges of teaching from an intersectional perspective: Core components and applied strategies. *New Directions for Teaching and Learning, 2011*(125), 11–20. https://doi.org/10.1002/tl.429

Kozleski, E. B. (2020). Disrupting what passes as inclusive education: Predicating educational equity on schools designed for all. *Educational Forum, 84*(4), 340–55. https://doi.org/10.1080/00131725.2020.1801047

Ladson-Billings, G. (1995). Toward a theory of culturally relevant pedagogy. *American Educational Research Journal, 32*(3), 465–91. https://doi.org/10.3102/00028312032003465

Paris, D. (2012). Culturally sustaining pedagogy: A needed change in stance, terminology, and practice. *Educational Researcher, 41*(3), 93–97. https://doi.org/10.3102/0013189X12441244

Scott, L. A., Cormier, C. J., & Boveda, M. (2022). Critical issues for the preparation and workforce development of racialized special educators. *Teacher Education and Special Education, 45*(1), 5–7. https://doi.org/10.1177/08884064211070571

Slanda, D. D., Pike, L., Herbert, L. W., Wells, E. B., & Pelt, C. (2022). Dismantling disproportionality in special education through anti-racist practices. In T. M. Mealy & H. Bennett (Eds.), *Equity in the classroom: Essays on curricular and pedagogical approaches to empowering all students* (pp. 221–64). McFarland & Company.

Starck, J. G., Riddle, T., Sinclair, S., & Warikoo, N. (2020). Teachers are people too: Examining the racial bias of teachers compared to other American adults. *Educational Researcher, 49*(4), 273–84.

U.S. Department of Education. (2020). *Civil rights data collection (CRDC) for the 2017–18 school year.* https://civilrightsdata.ed.gov/estimations/2017-2018

U.S. Department of Education. (2023). *44th annual report to Congress on the implementation of the Individuals with Disabilities Education Act.* https://sites.ed.gov/idea/2022-individuals-with-disabilities-education-act-annual-report-to-congress/

Utt, J., & Tochluk, S. (2020). White teacher, know thyself: Improving anti-racist praxis through racial identity development. *Urban Education, 55*(1), 125–52. https://doi.org/10.1177/0042085916648741

4

Multitiered Approach to Inclusive Learning

Supporting students with diverse learning needs can be complex and nuanced. The supports students require to achieve grade level standards are wide-ranging given they begin school with varied experiences, backgrounds, and abilities. This chapter will (1) introduce legislation that recognizes the need for a framework to support students, (2) provide an overview of the main tenets of MTSS and how the framework supports students in academics and behavior, and (3) detail the major components of a flexible and fluid MTSS framework, including a problem-solving approach, data-based decision-making, and evidence-based practices. Additionally, this chapter will explore the roles and responsibilities of the classroom teacher and special educator, who collaborate within the framework to enhance outcomes for students.

Chapter Objectives

After reading this chapter, readers will be able to

- Identify legislation that led to the framework of supports now used in schools known as a multitiered systems of support (MTSS)
- Explain the role of MTSS in supporting all students to achieve rigorous standards
- Describe the essential elements of the MTSS process, including universal screening, continuous progress monitoring, evidence-based practices, and improved student outcomes

- Explain all three tiers of the MTSS framework and how the tiers are fluid, flexible, and responsive to the needs of students
- Describe the roles and responsibilities of classroom teachers within the MTSS framework

Key Terms

high-intensity needs: Students with high-intensity needs have significant and persistent needs that require intensive instruction and intervention beyond Tier 1 core instruction (Slanda & Little, 2020).

multitiered system of supports (MTSS): ESSA defined MTSS as "a comprehensive continuum of evidence-based, systemic practices to support a rapid response to students' needs, with regular observation to facilitate data-based instructional decision making" (Section 8002[10][33]).

positive behavioral intervention and supports (PBIS): According to the Center on Positive Behavioral Interventions and Supports (n.d.), PBIS is "an evidence-based three-tiered framework to improve and integrate all of the data, systems, and practices affecting student outcomes every day."

problem-solving approach: A problem-solving approach allows teachers to create an intervention plan responsive to the needs of an individual student. There are four stages to the problem-solving approach: (1) identification of the problem, (2) analysis of the problem, (3) implementation of the plan to address the problem, and (4) evaluation of the plan (IRIS Center, 2024).

professional learning community (PLC): A team of educators who meet regularly throughout the school year to collaborate and engage in collective inquiry and data-based decision-making to improve student outcomes.

progress monitoring: Professionals or teams of professionals monitor the progress of a student and quantify their rate of improvement after implementing instruction and intervention to inform further instructional needs (National Center on Intensive Intervention, 2024).

response to intervention (RtI): RtI was the initial phrase used in IDEA (1997, 2004) to describe a multitiered system of supports and is defined as a framework for prevention and intervention that maximizes student achievement (Center on Response to Intervention, 2012).

Vignette

As you read this chapter, consider Ms. Campbell and her second grade class described in the vignette below. Connect the information you learn about MTSS to what plans and actions Ms. Campbell will need to develop and implement to ensure all students are receiving the support they need. There will be prompts and examples related to this vignette throughout the chapter.

It's the beginning of the year, which is always a busy time for Ms. Campbell. As she provides instruction, she is also gathering formal and informal data, building relationships, and determining students' strengths and areas for support. Ms. Campbell administered the required screening assessment and is collecting diagnostic data to determine current levels of performance. She is interested in how her students' current levels measure in comparison to their peers and to the grade level expectations. The screening tools and diagnostic assessments she administered were in reading and mathematics and were standards based and outcome driven.

When she reviewed the data, Ms. Campbell realized her second grade classroom of 22 children had diverse learning needs. At the beginning of the year, Ms. Campbell administered a screening diagnostic in reading that assessed students in phonics, vocabulary, and comprehension. Ms. Campbell knows that fluency influences vocabulary and comprehension performance, and she wanted to know more about her students' needs. When reviewing the oral reading fluency (ORF) assessment, she identified six students working significantly below grade level. Ms. Campbell knows it's important to immediately start providing intervention and additional support to her six students.

Multitiered System of Supports

As states set increasingly rigorous state standards, they "must also provide equally high support to help [students] reach those standards" (Elish-Piper, 2016, p. 111). A framework originally known as response to intervention (RtI) was adopted to provide such supports. Over time, RtI evolved, and now students with high-intensity needs (HIN) are provided supports within a comprehensive problem-solving framework that addresses behavior, social-emotional learning, and academics known as a multitiered system of supports (MTSS). MTSS is an equity-focused framework designed to improve educational access and outcomes for all students, including students from marginalized and minoritized groups. MTSS is based on the premise that *all* students deserve educators dedicated to providing access to grade level curriculum. Such access, however, may require additional supports or specialized instruction.

A multitiered system of supports framework is required by federal legislation and supported by research (e.g., Fuchs & Vaughn, 2012; Lemons et al., 2018). MTSS was first mentioned in the Individuals With Disabilities Education Act (1997) as RtI and was most recently reemphasized in the Every Student Succeeds Act (2015). ESSA described MTSS as a comprehensive continuum of evidence-based, systemic practices to support an immediate response to student needs through data-driven instructional decision-making (Slanda & Little, 2020). In response to federal legislation, states across the nation have adopted an MTSS framework providing established models for districts and schools.

MTSS and Federal Legislation

Individuals With Disabilities Education Act

In 1997, the Individuals with Disabilities Education Act emphasized "that special education can become a service . . . rather than a place where such children are sent" (Section 601[C][5][C]). This emphasis allowed educators to address the educational needs of students through a problem-solving approach before receiving a referral to special education (Prasse, 2006). Schools were incentivized by IDEA beginning in 1997 to implement "pre-referral interventions" that were meant to "reduce the need to label children as disabled in order to address their learning needs" (Section 601[C][5][F]). This legislation was based on research that showed that early intervention would reduce the gap between students with academic difficulties and their grade-level peers. By providing intervention designed to meet the unique needs of individual students at the first sign of struggle, educators would be able to reduce the inappropriate identification of students for special education (Lose, 2007).

MTSS was designed to provide services and supports to students at the earliest sign of struggling. Through continued progress monitoring, MTSS is designed to encourage teachers to provide students with individualized instruction and intensive interventions. Within the MTSS framework, educators should evaluate and assess students' response to high-quality, evidence-based interventions in the general education classroom. In this way, IDEA (2004) extended the use of interventions within a tiered framework to support a wider population of students (e.g., gifted, multilingual students, early childhood) and extended support across settings (e.g., classroom, schoolwide) (Batsche, 2014).

IDEA (2004) recognized that the "federal government must be responsive to the growing needs of an increasingly diverse society" (Section 601[C][10][A]). IDEA (2004) cited studies that "have documented apparent discrepancies in the levels of referral and placement of limited English proficient children in special education" (Section 601[C][11][B]) and that "more minority children continue to be served in special education than would be expected from the percentage of minority children in the general school population" (Section 601[C][12][B]). Under IDEA, it was asserted that a problem-solving tiered framework (i.e., MTSS) would address these discrepancies by shifting the focus from perceived student deficiencies to the evidence-based practices, curriculum, environment, and instruction provided to students to enable them to access the curriculum.

Every Student Succeeds Act

Under the Every Students Succeeds Act (2015), states garnered greater flexibility and choice in the application and implementation of instruction and intervention using MTSS. ESSA renewed the emphasis on strengthening standards and rigor for all students, the use of evidence-based practices to support student learning, and the use of data-based instructional decision-making using an MTSS framework. ESSA (2015) defined MTSS as "a comprehensive continuum of evidence-based, systemic practices to support a rapid response to students' needs, with regular observation to facilitate data-based instructional decision making." Specifically, ESSA recognized that to "increase the ability of teachers to effectively teach children with disabilities, including children with significant cognitive disabilities, and English learners" the use of "multi-tier systems of support and positive behavioral intervention and supports" was necessary to help students "meet the challenging State academic standards" (Section 2103[b][3][F]).

> Pause and Reflect:
> Revisit the vignette about Ms. Campbell and her second grade class at the beginning of the chapter. Ms. Campbell considers how she will provide support to the diverse range of learners in her classroom but wonders about students with disabilities. How are students with disabilities served within MTSS? In what ways does MTSS support access, inclusion, and equity for students with disabilities?

Overview of a Multitiered System of Support Framework

The MTSS framework is a three-tiered, problem-solving model that includes both instruction and intervention using evidence-based practices (EBPs) to address academic, behavioral, and social-emotional learning. MTSS is a general education initiative (i.e., Elementary and Secondary Education Act) that emphasizes a problem-solving approach and evidence-based practices (Batsche et al., 2005; Stoiber, 2014) that some researchers propose could *prevent* problems with learning or behavior (Miciak et al., 2018). MTSS includes responsive to intervention (RTI), positive behavior intervention strategies (PBIS), and a framework to address social and emotional development.

Response to Intervention

Response to intervention (RtI) is part of an MTSS framework and is designed to (1) provide targeted, high-quality, and evidence-based instruction to improve students' academic performance and outcomes, and (2) identify students for special education. RtI provides intensifying interventions for students who require additional support to master increasingly rigorous grade level standards by placing a focus on supporting students before they experience failure. RtI supports students through four essential components of RTI (IRIS Center, 2024): (1) universal screening, (2) evidence-based practices and high-quality instruction, (3) progress monitoring, and (4) tiered intervention.

Positive Behavioral Intervention and Supports

To support behavior outcomes within an MTSS framework, schools have adopted a tiered approach known as positive behavior intervention and supports (PBIS). To date, over 25,000 schools have adopted PBIS to advance their efforts to create an equitable, proactive, and responsive school environment (Center on Positive Behavioral Interventions and Supports, n.d.). To address behaviors and support student development, preventative and universal supports are delivered schoolwide. For students who require targeted or intensive support beyond the universal level, PBIS provides a framework to deliver individualized intervention. According to the Center on Positive Behavioral Interventions and Supports, effective PBIS frameworks prioritize equity by centering students, delivering evidence-based behavior strategies, utilizing data to drive intervention, and ensuring fidelity of implementation (Center on Positive Behavioral Interventions and Supports, 2024). Research indicates a strong link between behavior and academic outcomes, underscoring the significance of supporting students within a PBIS framework (Freeman et al., 2016; Kittleman et al., 2019).

Social-Emotional Learning Supports

Research indicates that embedding social-emotional learning (SEL) within an MTSS framework can provide a foundation to support student well-being (Lane, 2007; McCart & Choi, 2020) and advance educational equity and achievement. Supporting social and emotional development within an MTSS framework begins with universal support to build educator capacity to identify, select, and deliver social-emotional instruction and intervention strategies (Kim et al., 2022; Steed & Shapland, 2020). The Collaborative for Academic, Social, and Emotional Learning (CASEL) has been a leader in SEL since the term was established nearly 30 years ago. Through rigorous research, CASEL identified five key areas of social-emotional learning and development that form a strong foundation for SEL in schools (Collaborative for Academic, Social, and Emotional Learning, n.d.):

- self-awareness
- self-management
- social awareness
- relationship skills
- responsible decision-making

Classroom teachers deliver SEL lessons, connect SEL components to content area learning, and provide intervention for students needing additional support in behavioral, personal, and social skills. For students who do require targeted or intensive support in social-emotional development—including students who may have experienced or are experiencing trauma or who show signs of aggression or anxiety—educators can provide individualized and sustained supports. The classroom teacher is involved in providing SEL across all three tiers of MTSS/PBIS and is essential to supporting SEL for all students, including those with disabilities.

The MTSS framework includes the same features across RtI, PBIS, and SEL. Table 4.1 lists these identifying features.

TABLE 4.1. *Features of an MTSS Framework*

MTSS Framework Essential Components
• Supports students in the classroom setting
• Employs universal screening, assessment, and continuous progress monitoring
• Utilizes data-based decision-making and problem-solving approach
• Provides increasingly more intensive intervention
• Includes a continuum of evidence-based interventions
• Designed to be flexible and fluid
• Responsive to students' academic, behavioral, and social-emotional learning

Note: Adapted from CEEDAR Center (n.d.).

Tiers of Support

Tier 1

Tier 1 includes *all* students in the classroom and is considered core instruction designed to meet the needs of the majority of students (85–90%). Tier 1 requires that teachers first consider whether or not they created an environment conducive to learning, whether the curriculum was robust enough to meet the demands of the students and the classroom, and whether or not the instructional strategies used to deliver content were responsive and aligned to the learning needs of the student (Slanda et al., 2022). Within Tier 1, all students receive a high-quality curriculum delivered by the classroom teacher (Murawski & Hughes, 2009). Typically, progress monitoring at this tier consists of benchmark testing at three pre-identified times during the school year (usually fall, winter, spring) to evaluate student progress toward grade level standards (Vaughn & Fuchs, 2003). Tier 1 is considered universal classroom instruction in which all students receive evidence-based instruction in the classroom. According to Balu and colleagues (2015), the intention of Tier 1 instruction is to *prevent* academic, behavioral, or social failure and to reduce inappropriate referrals to special education.

Tier 2

Students who show insufficient progress in Tier 1 instruction are provided with additional supports through intensified interventions. Tier 2 instruction, intervention, and support supplement Tier 1 instruction (Bradley et al., 2007). Tier 2 interventions are conducted using increased instructional time (e.g., additional 30 minutes), reduced group size (e.g., three to five students), and delivery by the classroom teacher in consultation with a specialist. Tier 2 supports are implemented in a coordinated and purposeful manner that provides students with additional opportunities to practice their learning with guidance, increased progress monitoring, and intentional reinforcement (Harn et al., 2014). Increased progress monitoring is essential in Tier 2. Progress monitoring is often completed using curriculum-based measurements at more frequent intervals to assess and evaluate student progress and adjust intervention and instruction accordingly (Fuchs & Fuchs, 2007).

Tier 2 is defined by three characteristics: (1) evidence-based instruction (rather than research based), (2) teacher-led small group instruction, and (3) clearly articulated, validated intervention delivered with fidelity (Shurley, 2022). Tier 2 should not be more of the same instruction provided at Tier 1 but in smaller groups (Kramer et al., 2021). Instead, Tier 2 should be differentiated to meet the needs of the student. Students may struggle with Tier 1 instruction and meeting the grade level standards—but for different reasons.

Tier 2 is an opportunity to use assessment to determine why Tier 1 was not addressing their needs and then provide an intervention aligned with their specific needs. Therefore, Tier 2 interventions should look different than Tier 1 instruction not just in group size but also in strategy as there is no single intervention that meets every student's need. Giving students more of what did not work is not the answer. Instead, educators should address the content standard in a different way that matches the student's needs (Buffum et al., 2012; Hattie, 2009). At Tier 2 (and Tier 3), educators should be focused on evidence-based processes, strategies, and practices not programs. This is because purchased intervention programs and products are not designed to meet the individual needs of students in ways teachers can.

Tier 3

Tier 3 is the most intense level of intervention and provides the students with one-on-one instruction designed to meet their needs (National Center on Intensive Intervention, 2016). Progress monitoring in Tier 3 increases, and educators use "multiple interventions systematically to determine which approach best matches individual student needs" (Deno, 2016, p. 23). In Tier 3, students may receive intervention and instruction by specialized personnel (e.g., special education teacher) (Bean & Lillenstein, 2012). The National Center on Response to Intervention (2010) characterizes the third tier of intervention as the most individualized and targeted, where the student is receiving interventions that are more frequent and longer in duration, with increased progress monitoring allowing for evaluation of student progress and fidelity of treatment. This level of intervention is specialized, explicit, and individualized. Similar to Tier 2, Tier 3 interventions should be even more targeted and individualized. Tier 3 is not Tier 1 or Tier 2 strategies delivered one-on-one but an opportunity for educators to reexamine how they are delivering their instruction and intervention and adjust to meet the individual needs of the student.

Figure 4.1 illustrates a stacked three-tiered model of MTSS that addresses behavior, academic, and social-emotional support.

> Pause and Reflect:
>
> Revisit the vignette about Ms. Campbell and her second grade class at the beginning of the chapter. Ms. Chapman identified six students who performed below grade level expectations on the screening assessments administered to all students. How can she use her school's MTSS to begin providing support to those students? What type of support would they receive at each tier, and how will she know which students may need Tier 2 or Tier 3 interventions?

The MTSS framework provides access to the curriculum and equitable opportunity for educational outcomes. To increase access and equity, MTSS increases attention to EBPs in the classroom, increases the range of powerful interventions for students who need them, and improves the quality of

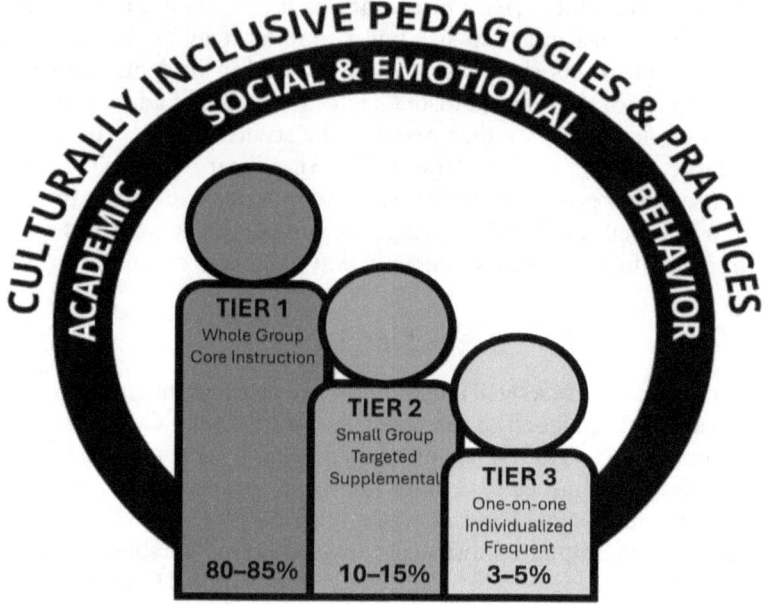

FIGURE 4.1. *An MTSS Framework.*

special education services provided to students with disabilities (Shinn et al., 2016). Research shows that students who receive intensive instruction (e.g., Tier 3) are able to make significant gains when interventions are aligned with their specific needs (Batsche, 2014; Shinn et al., 2016). MTSS serves as a framework for identifying students who struggle academically, socially, and behaviorally and provides immediate short-term intervention without having to experience the delays often associated with formal evaluation (O'Connor et al., 2013). Additionally, MTSS allows for special education eligibility determination if students are not responsive to the short-term interventions (O'Connor et al., 2013).

Required Components of MTSS

MTSS is a framework for providing supports in a flexible and fluid way that differentiates instruction and intervention that is unique to the individual. At the school level, MTSS is designed to prevent school failure by proactively addressing students' academic and behavioral needs through prevention, instruction, and intervention. At the classroom level, MTSS is designed to address the specific needs of students on an individual level. ESSA requires specific components (see tables 4.2 and 4.3) for MTSS to address academic and behavioral needs in a comprehensive way that is proactive and sustainable.

TABLE 4.2. *Essential Components of MTSS for Academics, Behavior, and Social Skills*

Assessment	Data-Based Decision-Making	Multilevel Prevention System	School Infrastructure and Support Mechanisms
Universal Screening	Decision-Making Process	**Tier 1** • Evidence Based • Differentiated Instruction • Standards Based • Whole Class	Support From School-Based Leadership
Progress Monitoring	Data System		Collaboration With Families
	Responsive to All Levels of Instruction and Intervention	**Tier 2** • Evidence Based • Complements Core • Supplemental to Tier 1 • Progress Monitoring • Small Group	Collaboration With SISP
	Allows for Fluidity and Flexibility Across the Tiers		Provides Professional Learning
			Responsive to School Master Schedule
		Tier 3 • Evidence Based • Frequent • Intensive Instruction • Progress Monitoring • Individualized	Includes Necessary Resources
			Cultural and Linguistic Responsiveness

Note: Adapted from "Multi-Tiered System of Supports Fidelity of Implementation Rubric," Center on Multi-Tiered System of Supports at the American Institutes for Research, 2023, https://mtss4success.org/resource/essential-components-mtss-rubric.

> Pause and Reflect:
>
> Think about Ms. Campbell and her students in the vignette at the beginning of the chapter. As she plans and prepares to provide instruction and support to all students through MTSS, who can she expect to collaborate with at each tier? How will her role change across each tier? Ms. Campbell has identified students in her class who may need additional academic support, but what about students with behavioral and social-emotional needs? How are those needs addressed through MTSS? How is addressing behavioral and social-emotional needs similar to or different from supporting academic needs within MTSS?

TABLE 4.3. *ESSA (2015) MTSS Requirements*

ESSA requires MTSS to include the following:	
Universal Screening	Screenings are universally administered assessments that are designed to gather student data schoolwide or grade-level-wide. The intent of the screenings is to identify challenges or areas of concern across the student population.
Progress Monitoring	The continuous process of monitoring student achievement in response to evidence-based instructional and behavioral strategies. Data are collected through multiple assessments and are utilized to make instructional changes that are classroom-wide or at the individual level. Progress monitoring provides students with multiple ways to show their learning.
Data-Based Decision-Making	Data-based instructional and behavioral decisions are made in response to identifying areas of strength and struggle. The dose of instruction and intervention is based on student need and provided in increasing intensity (i.e., tiers) based on student needs, which may change over time.
Team-Based Decision-Making	A comprehensive team of qualified professionals must be convened to make decisions about a comprehensive plan to address student needs. ESSA mentions the team in over 40 instances and refers to the team as "Specialized Instructional Support Personnel (SISP)."
Accountability Measures	ESSA requires states to establish an accountability system that measures progress toward "ambitious long-term goals." An annual measure for these long-term goals must be based on (1) state assessments, (2) at least one additional valid and reliable academic indicator that measures student growth, (3) at least one indicator of school quality (e.g., school climate and safety), and (4) for high schools, high school graduation rates.
Professional Development	Federal funds can be used to provide ongoing professional development for relevant school staff that is specific to building capacity within MTSS.

These components include having tiered levels of support that are fluid and flexible. At Tier 1, schools are obligated to ensure universal supports are available to all students. These supports can be provided schoolwide and can include strategies such as PBIS (e.g., CHAMPS, restorative justice, conscious discipline) or academic curriculums. At Tier 2, schools must establish targeted supports to students who are identified as needing additional services (e.g., small group). And at Tier 3 schools must provide intensive supports to individual students (e.g., individualized instruction, intensive therapy, wraparound services) who need specialized instruction.

The MTSS framework is designed to support students who have high-intensity needs and to sustain supports for students with disabilities. In the next section we will discuss how the framework is used to provide supports for both types of student groups.

A Collaborative Approach

Schools and districts have mobilized to implement a comprehensive framework of supports to ensure all students are college and career ready. Through a continuous problem-solving approach, teams of professionals utilize universal screeners and diagnostic assessments to identify students who need additional instruction and intervention. Although schools and districts may use a variety of teaming structures and labels (e.g., student study team), ESSA (2015) refers to teams of education professionals as specialized instructional support personnel (SISP). Depending on the school structure, the SISP may examine the sufficiency of Tier 1 instruction and determine the need for more intensive supports, provide consultative services and supports to the classroom teacher, or engage in data-based problem-solving processes. To effectively support students with high-intensity needs within the framework, the SISP shares responsibility for ensuring students meet rigorous grade level standards, have maximum access to the curriculum, and receive appropriate supports to enter a skilled workforce.

Educators who support students within the MTSS framework have a shared common belief that all students can learn and work to promote student achievement. They are dedicated to the delivery of high-quality, scientific, and research-validated instruction and intervention through evidence-based practices aligned with grade level standards. Their instruction and intervention is differentiated to meet individual student needs, as driven by data and assessment.

Providing Specialized Instruction to Students With Disabilities Within the Framework

If students receive Tier 3 instruction and intervention and it is determined by the SISP that evaluation for special education services is necessary, then formal evaluation procedures are initiated. However, the Tier 3 supports do not end. The student will continue to receive responsive and individualized tiered instruction and intervention. Additionally, if the student is eligible for special education services, their services and specially designed instruction will be delivered through the MTSS framework. This is so the student continues to receive the high-quality supports they need to be successful.

The Roles and Responsibilities of the Classroom Teacher in the MTSS Framework

Even though MTSS was generated from special education legislation (i.e., IDEA, ESSA), it is a general education initiative that begins in the classroom setting. Often there is a misconception that the staff member with a higher-level expertise in the student's target area of need should be the one providing intensive interventions or supports (Kramer et al., 2021). As Kramer and colleagues (2021) share, if we were to apply this line of reasoning, then the classroom teacher would be the perfect person to provide the interventions at Tiers 2 and 3 because they are the expert in the content area. The classroom teacher knows the grade level standards and content area best and how to effectively plan for students to meet those standards. They are the experts.

As classroom teachers meet within their professional learning community (PLC), they can engage in discussions about lesson planning and best practices and strategies to assist students in meeting rigorous state standards. These PLC discussions can focus on tiered instruction and intervention at all three tiers. The involvement of the classroom teacher across all three tiers allows for a shared responsibility for all students and maximum access to the classroom curriculum. Beginning in Tier 2, classroom teachers can reach out to specialized personnel to receive consultation on best practices to support struggling students. Specialized personnel (e.g., speech therapists, occupational therapists, school psychologists, social workers, special education teachers) allow the classroom teacher to match their expertise in their content area with the specialized personnel's knowledge of strategies and supports for struggling students (Scanlon et al., 2021). Through consultation, collaboration supports differentiated instruction that enables all students to access the classroom curriculum (Eisenman et al., 2011; Todd, 2012). Classroom teachers can share data with specialized personnel so they can engage in collaborative problem solving to implement instructional interventions. This collaboration can occur in Tiers 2 and 3. The team approach also includes parents/caregivers, instructional and behavior coaches, and site-based administrators. Table 4.4 shares the personnel that collaborate at each level and the ways for collaboration.

TABLE 4.4. *Tiers, Personnel Involved, and Focus of Instruction*

Tier	Personnel Involved	Focus
Tier 1	Student Parent/Caregiver Classroom Teacher(s) School Administrators Academic or Behavior Coach	• Universal screening • Core instruction using EBPs • Analyze and evaluate effectiveness of the curriculum • Monitor and document rate of academic growth • Adjust instructional strategies and grouping practices for all students • Identify students who struggle
Tier 2	Student Parent/Caregiver Classroom Teacher(s) School Administrators Academic or Behavior Coach Specialized Instructional Support Personnel Special Education Teacher	• Individual assessments/screening • Monitor progress on a more frequent basis • Identify and address strengths and weaknesses • Evaluate integrity of classroom instruction • Make decisions about effectiveness of instruction • Adjust instructional strategies based on student need • Design and deliver intervention in small groups • Increase academic engagement time • Narrow focus of instruction to maximize impact
Tier 3	Student who requires intensive supports and interventions Parent/Caregiver Classroom Teacher(s) School Administrators Instructional Coaches Specialized Instructional Support Personnel Special Education Teacher	• Individual assessment(s) • Assessment that can be analyzed for specific patterns • Pinpoint specific skills and missing foundational knowledge • Plan and implement targeted, specially designed intervention that is intense and individualized • Deliver multiple interventions simultaneously • Evaluate integrity of intervention • Make decisions about effectiveness of intervention • Adjust intervention strategies based on student need • Design and deliver intervention one-on-one • Increase academic engagement time • Monitor progress on a more frequent basis • Narrow focus of instruction to maximize impact • Monitor progress more frequently • Increase instructional time • Interventions may or may not include special education provisions

> ### HIGH-IMPACT: THE CONNECTION WITH HIGH-LEVERAGE PRACTICES
>
> **HLP 1:** Collaborate with professionals to increase student success
> **HLP 2:** Organize and facilitate effective meetings with professionals and families
> **HLP 3:** Collaborate with families to support student learning and secure services
> **HLP 4:** Use multiple sources of information to develop a comprehensive understanding of a student's strengths and needs
> **HLP 5:** Interpret and communicate assessment information to collaboratively design and implement educational programs
> **HLP 6:** Use student assessment data, analyze instructional practices, and make necessary adjustments that improve student outcomes
> **HLP 7:** Establish consistent, organized, and responsive learning environments
> **HLP 9:** Teach social behaviors
> **HLP 10:** Conduct functional behavior assessments to develop individual student behavior support plans
> **HLP 11:** Identify and prioritize long- and short-term learning goals
> **HLP 12:** Systematically design instruction toward a specific goal
> **HLP 13:** Adapt curriculum tasks and materials for specific learning goals
> **HLP 14:** Teach cognitive and metacognitive strategies to support learning and independence
> **HLP 15:** Provide scaffolded supports
> **HLP 16:** Use explicit instruction
> **HLP 17:** Use flexible grouping
> **HLP 18:** Use strategies to promote active student engagement
> **HLP 20:** Provide intensive intervention for academics and behavior
> **HLP 21:** Teach students to maintain and generalize new learning across time and settings
> **HLP 8/22:** Provide positive and constructive feedback to guide students' learning (HLP 22) and behavior (HLP 8)

Review and Reflect

Although legislation such as IDEA (1997, 2004) has historically guided educational equity within tiered intervention frameworks such as RtI and MTSS, legislation such as ESSA (2015) has also stressed its use and significance. ESSA has guided our use of a multitiered framework of supports that expanded to include social-emotional learning, behavior, and academic supports. Providing supports for the whole child requires an integrated approach that is grounded in collaboration and driven by data-based decision-making, assessment, and evidence-based practices to deliver individualized instruction and intervention. Additionally, there is an intentional fading of the line between general and special education, thereby impacting the role of the classroom teacher. Classroom teachers are responsible for providing instruction and intervention within the MTSS framework in the classroom. Providing prevention, intervention, and instruction requires increased knowledge, skills, and professional learning to support students with high-intensity needs.

Guiding Questions

1. Explain the essential components of the MTSS framework.
2. Describe how RtI, PBIS, and SEL fit within the MTSS framework.
3. Distinguish between the three tiers of instruction.
4. Explain how the MTSS framework is an equity-driven model created to support all students.
5. Describe the role of the classroom teacher in the MTSS framework.

Extend Your Learning

TABLE 4.5. *Resources*

Resource	Description	Link
CEEDAR Center	Technical assistance, webinars, reports, briefs, tool kits	https://ceedar.education.ufl.edu
Intervention Central	Accommodation finders, apps, checklists, videos, strategies, tools	https://www.interventioncentral.org
IRIS Center	Modules, briefs, webinars, resources, activities, microcredentials, videos	https://iris.peabody.vanderbilt.edu
National Center on Intensive Intervention	Tools, charts, modules, sample lessons, strategies, resources, overviews, briefs	https://intensiveintervention.org
Center on PBIS	Information, guides, videos, and other resources for developing and implementing classroom-level PBIS	https://www.pbis.org/classroom-pbis
CASEL	Research, information, tools, visuals, and implementation guides for building social-emotional learning capacity in the classroom	https://casel.org/systemic-implementation/sel-in-the-classroom/

References

Balu, R., Zhu, P., Doolittle, F., Schiller, E., Jenkins, J., Gersten, R., & Jacobson, J. (2015). *Evaluation of response to intervention practices for elementary school reading: Executive summary.* U.S. Department of Education, Institute of Education Sciences, National Center for Education Evaluation and Regional Assistance.

Batsche, G. (2014). Multi-tiered system of supports for inclusive schools. In J. McLeskey, N. L. Waldron, F. Spooner & B. Algozzine (Eds.), *Handbook of effective inclusive schools* (pp. 183–96). Routledge.

Batsche, G. M., Elliot, J. Graden, J. L., Grimes, J., Kovaleski, J. F., Prasse, D., Reschley, D., Schrag, J., & Tilly, W. D. (2005). *Response to intervention: Policy considerations and implementations.* National Association of State Directors of Special Education.

Bean, R., & Lillenstein, J. (2012). Response to intervention and the changing roles of schoolwide personnel. *Reading Teacher, 65*(7), 491–501.

Berkeley, S., Bender, W. N., Peaster, L. G., & Saunders, L. (2009). Implementation of response to intervention a snapshot of progress. *Journal of Learning Disabilities, 42*(1), 85–95.

Bradley, E. H., Curry, L. A., & Devers, K. J. (2007). Qualitative data analysis for health services research: Developing taxonomy, themes, and theory. *Health Services Research, 42*(4), 1758–72.

Bradley, R., Danielson, L., & Doolittle, J. (2005). Response to intervention. *Journal of Learning Disabilities, 38*(6), 485–86.

Buffum, A., Mattos, M., & Weber, C. (2012). *Simplifying response to intervention: Four essential guiding principles.* Solution Tree Press.

Burns, M. K., & Ysseldyke, J. E. (2009). Reported prevalence of evidenced-based instructional practices in special education. *Journal of Special Education, 43*(1), 3–11.

CEEDAR Center. (n.d.). *Multi-tiered system of support chapter.* https://ceedar.education.ufl.edu/mtssudldi-professional-development-module/mtss-chapter/

Center on Positive Behavioral Interventions and Supports. (n.d.). *About the center.* https://www.pbis.org/about/about

Center on Positive Behavioral Interventions and Supports. (2024). *What is PBIS?* https://www.pbis.org/pbis/what-is-pbis

Center on Response to Intervention. (2012). *What is RTI?* https://mtss4success.org/sites/default/files/2020-07/RTI_Placemat_2015.pdf

Collaborative for Academic and Social Emotional Learning. (n.d.). *What is the CASEL framework?* https://casel.org/fundamentals-of-sel/what-is-the-casel-framework/

Cook, B. G., & Cook, S. C. (2013). Unraveling evidence-based practices in special education. *Journal of Special Education, 47*(2), 71–82.

Deno, S. L. (2016). Data-based decision-making. In S. R. Jimerson, M. K. Burns & A. M. VanDerHeyden (Eds.), *Handbook of response to intervention: The science and practice of multi-tiered systems of support* (2nd ed., pp. 9–28). Springer.

Eisenman, L. T., Pleet, A. M., Wandry, D., & McGinley, V. (2011). Voices of special education teachers in an inclusive high school: Redefining responsibilities. *Remedial and Special Education, 32*(2), 91-104. doi:10.1177/0741932510361248

Elish-Piper, L. (2016). Elish-Piper: Response to "Beyond the common core: Examining 20 years of literacy priorities and their impact on struggling readers." *Literacy Research and Instruction, 55*(2), 111-13.

Every Student Succeeds Act. (2015). Public Law 114-95, 114th Cong., 1st sess.

Freeman, J., Simonsen, B., McCoach, D. B., Sugai, G., Lombardi, A., & Horner, R. (2016). Relationship between school-wide positive behavior interventions and supports and academic, attendance, and behavior outcomes in high schools. *Journal of Positive Behavior Interventions, 18*(1), 41-51. https://doi.org/10.1177/1098300715580992

Fuchs, L. S., & Fuchs, D. (2007). A model for implementing responsiveness to intervention. *Teaching Exceptional Children, 39*(5), 14-20.

Fuchs, L. S., Fuchs, D., & Zumeta, R. O. (2008). Response to intervention. In E. L. Grigorenko (Ed.), *Educating individuals with disabilities: IDEIA 2004 and beyond* (pp. 115-36). Springer.

Fuchs, L. S., & Vaughn, S. (2012). Responsiveness-to-intervention: A decade later. *Journal of Learning Disabilities, 45*(3), 195-203.

Harn, B. A., Fritz, R., & Berg, T. (2014). Effective literacy instruction in inclusive schools. In J. McLeskey, N. L. Waldron, F. Spooner & B. Algozzine (Eds.), *Handbook of effective inclusive schools: Research and practice* (pp. 229-46). Routledge.

Hattie, J. (2009). *Visible learning: A synthesis of over 800 meta-analyses relating to achievement.* Routledge.

Hoover, J. J., Baca, L. M., Wexler-Love, E., & Saenz, L. (2008). *National implementation of response to intervention (RtI): Research summary.* University of Colorado, Boulder-BUENO Center, National Association of State Directors of Special Education (NASDE).

Individuals With Disabilities Education Act. (1997). 20 U.S.C. §§ 1400 et seq.

Individuals With Disabilities Education Improvement Act. (2004). 20 U.S.C. § 1400 et seq. (Reauthorization of the Individuals With Disabilities Education Act of 1990.)

IRIS Center. (2024). *RTI (part 1): An overview.* https://iris.peabody.vanderbilt.edu/module/rti01/#content

Kim, E. K., Anthony, C. J., & Chafouleas, S. M. (2022). Social, emotional, and behavioral assessment within tiered decision-making frameworks: Advancing research through reflections on the past decade. *School Psychology Review, 51*(1), 1-5.

Kittelman, A., McIntosh, K., & Hoselton, R. (2019). Adoption of PBIS within school districts. *Journal of School Psychology, 76*, 159-67. https://doi.org/10.1016/j.jsp.2019.03.007

Kramer, S. V., Sonju, B., Mattos, M., & Buffum, A. (2021). *Best practices at tier 2: Supplemental interventions for additional student support.* Solution Tree Press.

Lane, K. L. (2007). Identifying and supporting students at risk for emotional and behavioral disorders within multi-level models: Data driven approaches to conducting secondary interventions with an academic emphasis. *Education and Treatment of Children, 30*(4), 135-64.

Lemons, C. J., Vaughn, S., Wexler, J., Kearns, D. M., & Sinclair, A. C. (2018). Envisioning an improved continuum of special education services for students with learning disabilities: Considering intervention intensity. *Learning Disabilities Research & Practice, 33*(3), 131–43.

Lose, M. K. (2007). A child's response to intervention requires a responsive teacher of reading. *Reading Teacher, 61*(3), 276–79.

McCart, A. B., & Choi, J. H. (2020). *State-wide social and emotional learning embedded within equity-based MTSS: Impact on student academic outcomes.* SWIFT Education Center.

Miciak, J., Roberts, G., Taylor, W. P., Solis, M., Ahmed, Y., Vaughn, S., & Fletcher, J. M. (2018). The effects of one versus two years of intensive reading intervention implemented with late elementary struggling readers. *Learning Disabilities Research & Practice, 33*(1), 24–36.

Murawski, W. W., & Hughes, C. E. (2009). Response to intervention, collaboration, and co-teaching: A logical combination for successful systemic change. *Preventing School Failure, 53*(4), 267–77.

National Center on Intensive Intervention. (2024). *Introduction to academic progress monitoring: Academic progress monitoring in intensive intervention part 1.* https://intensiveintervention.org/resource/introduction-academic-progress-monitoring-part1

O'Connor, R. E., Bocian, K. M., Beach, K. D., Sanchez, V., & Flynn, L. J. (2013). Special education in a 4-year response to intervention (RtI) environment: Characteristics of students with learning disability and grade of identification. *Learning Disabilities Research & Practice, 28*(3), 98–112.

Prasse, D. P. (2006). Legal supports for problem-solving systems. *Remedial and Special Education, 27*(1), 7–15.

Scanlon, D., Nannemann, A. C., & Baker, D. (2021). Lessons from research for implementing an instructional accommodations model in secondary inclusion. *Learning Disabilities: A Multidisciplinary Journal, 26*(1).

Scott, T. M., Gage, N. A., Hirn, R. G., Lingo, A. S., & Burt, J. (2019). An examination of the association between MTSS implementation fidelity measures and student outcomes. *Preventing School Failure, 63*(4), 308–16.

Shinn, M. R., Windram, H. S., & Bollman, K. A. (2016). Implementing response to intervention in secondary schools. In S. R. Jimerson, M. K. Burns & A. M. VanDerHeyden (Eds.), *Handbook of response to intervention: The science and practice of multi-tiered systems of support* (2nd ed., pp. 563–86). Springer.

Shurley, B. (2022). *What you need to know about utilizing tier 2 in MTSS.* Branching Minds. https://www.branchingminds.com/blog/mtss-tier-2-instruction-intervention

Siegel, L. S. (2019). Solving the problem of learning disabilities. *International Journal for Research in Learning Disabilities, 4*(1), 3–11.

Slanda, D. D. (2017). *Role ambiguity: Defining the elusive role of the special education teacher who works in inclusive settings.* [Doctoral dissertation]. University of Central Florida.

Slanda, D. D., & Little, M. E. (2020). Enhancing teacher preparation for inclusive programming. *SRATE Journal, 29*(2), 1–8.

Slanda, D. D., Pike, L. M., Herbert, L., Wells, E. B., & Pelt, C. (2022). Dismantling disproportionality in special education through antiracist practices. In T. M. Mealy & H. Bennet (Eds.), *Equity in the classroom: Essays on Curricular and pedagogical approaches to empowering all students* (pp. 218–64). McFarland.

Steed, E. A., & Shapland, D. (2020). Adapting social emotional multi-tiered systems of supports for kindergarten classrooms. *Early Childhood Education Journal, 48*, 135–46. https://doi.org/10.1007/s10643-019-00996-8

Stoiber, K. C. (2014). A comprehensive framework for multitiered systems of support in school psychology. In P. L. Harrison & A. Thomas (Eds.), *Best practices in school psychology: Data-based and collaborative decision making* (pp. 41–70). National Association of School Psychologists.

Todd, N. A. (2012). Assisting secondary support teachers to work in the recommended service delivery model: Introducing the concept of a subculture of learning support. *Support for Learning, 27*(4), 177–83.

Tomlinson, C. (2003). *Differentiating instruction.* Association for Supervision and Curriculum Development.

Vaughn, S., & Fuchs, L. S. (2003). Redefining learning disabilities as inadequate response to instruction: The promise and potential problems. *Learning Disabilities Research & Practice, 18*(3), 137–46.

Vaughn, S., Linan-Thompson, S., & Hickman, P. (2003). Response to instruction as a means of identifying students with reading/learning disabilities. *Exceptional Children, 69*(4), 391–409.

5

Using Data to Drive Student Success

When a nutritionist is presented with a client who would like to improve their health, they develop a nutrition plan. This plan begins with a comprehensive series of assessments including collecting information about the client's dietary practices, conducting laboratory assessments (e.g., bloodwork), reviewing their medical history, taking measurements, evaluating lifestyle habits, conducting a risk screening for malnutrition, and determining their food security level. Then assessment data are analyzed and synthesized to develop an understanding of their nutrition profile, and the nutritionist works with the client to identify and select an evidence-based intervention to optimize their health. The intervention is implemented for a set duration (e.g., length measured in hours, days, or weeks) and frequency (e.g., number of occurrences). As the intervention progresses, the nutritionist monitors the patient's response to the intervention by collecting data and adjusting the nutrition plan, if needed. Adjustments to the nutrition plan may result in increasing or decreasing frequency or duration of the intervention or identifying a different intervention altogether. This data-driven process ensures the client receives care that is responsive to their unique needs, underscoring the significance of individualizing care through a problem-solving approach.

Similarly, educators can design instruction that meets individual student needs by designing and delivering instruction through a data-driven approach. Data-driven decision-making (DDDM) provides an evidence-based approach to individualizing instruction and intervention within a multitiered system of supports (MTSS). This chapter will emphasize the comprehensive and iterative nature of DDDM to support all students and address academic, behavioral, and social learning.

Chapter Objectives

After reading this chapter, readers will be able to

- Explain the DDDM process, including its phases
- Evaluate the benefits of DDDM and how it can lead to improved student outcomes
- Describe and define the types of assessment educators use to make instructional decisions, including universal screening, diagnostic assessments, formative assessments, progress monitoring, and summative (outcome) assessments
- Explain best practices for ensuring equity in data collection, analysis, and interpretation

Key Terms

assessment: A critical aspect of the teaching and learning process that provides information and data on student performance, learning, and progress toward identified goals, objectives, and standards. Assessment comes in many forms, including universal screening, diagnostic measures, formative, and summative.

criterion-referenced assessment: A criterion-referenced assessment describes a student's performance against a predetermined standard, score, or criteria.

data-based individualization: A research-based process that is informed by assessment and is used to individualize and intensify instruction and intervention (National Center on Intensive Intervention, n.d.).

data-driven decision-making (DDDM): An interactive and structured process for informed decision-making that involves collecting and analyzing data for the design and evaluation of instruction and intervention.

diagnostic assessment: An assessment administered *prior* to instruction that measures a student's knowledge and skills in a specific area to identify strengths and weaknesses. By administering diagnostic assessments prior to teaching, educators can use the data to identify gaps in learning and plan instruction.

evidence-based practice: A teaching practice that is supported by rigorous research and is shown to have a positive effect on student outcomes.

fidelity of implementation: The degree to which educators follow the prescribed procedures to implement strategies, programs, and assessments.

formative assessment: A type of assessment that is used to monitor student learning, provide ongoing feedback, and reflect on teaching practices to improve student learning.

intensive intervention: Targeted and individualized instruction provided to students who are struggling academically or behaviorally and is often referred to as Tier 3 instruction.

norm-referenced assessment: A norm-referenced assessment describes a student's performance in comparison to a normed group.

progress monitoring: Assessment that is regularly administered and frequently analyzed to evaluate student performance, track student progress toward identified goals, and evaluate effectiveness of instruction.

qualitative data: Qualitative data are descriptive and provide details in a narrative form that can be gathered through interviews or observations.

quantitative data: Quantitative data are numerical and can be measured or counted.

standardized assessment: A type of assessment that follows strict guidelines when administered and is scored consistently.

summative assessment: An assessment administered to evaluate student learning and skill acquisition at the end of an instructional period to measure skill acquisition and mastery of benchmarks or curriculum standards.

universal screening: A series of assessments administered at multiple intervals during the academic year (e.g., fall, winter, spring) to identify students who may need additional support or intervention.

Vignette

As you read this chapter, consider Tomas, who is described in the vignette below. Connect the information you learn about Tomas to the special education referral and eligibility process. There will be prompts and examples related to this vignette throughout the chapter.

Tomas is a six-year-old first grader who enjoys reading picture books, especially when they are about animals found in the wild. Despite his interest in reading, Tomas is experiencing difficulty achieving grade level standards. Tomas is bilingual, and the primary language spoken in his home is Spanish.

His parents are bilingual and are proficient in English. However, his teacher, Ms. Locke ensures all written correspondence is provided in both English and Spanish.

After reviewing multiple sources of data, Ms. Locke recognizes that Tomas requires additional support and would benefit from targeted skill intervention. To ensure her interventions meet Tomas's specific needs, she collects and analyzes data to identify specific skills to target. Through this process, she learns that Tomas needs targeted instruction for decoding words, identifying high-frequency words, and making letter-sound associations. To address these needs, Ms. Locke identifies and selects evidence-based practices that are known to improve student outcomes in each of these areas.

Data-Driven Decision-Making: Using Data to Inform Instruction

Data-driven decision-making (DDDM), also known as data-*based* decision-making, is a powerful instructional practice influencing everything from planning to delivery. DDDM is the continuous use of assessment data to determine *when* and *how* to intensify instruction and intervention (Slanda & Little, 2021; Wilson, 2016). The heightened emphasis on DDDM stems from national trends and legislation (e.g., Individuals with Disabilities Education Act, Every Student Succeeds Act) resulting in changes to policy and practice.

As federal mandates underscored the significance of providing high-quality instruction to improve student outcomes, legislatures advanced policies requiring data collection and analysis. This emphasis on DDDM requires educators to bolster their knowledge and skills to analyze, interpret, and translate data into instruction (Datnow & Hubbard, 2016). Although the practice of data collection has long been an integral component of classroom practice—data use, not just data collection, serves as the cornerstone of DDDM (Schlidkamp, 2019). Data use makes instruction responsive, especially when implemented within an MTSS. Across the tiers within the MTSS framework, teachers use DDDM to identify students who are unresponsive to instruction, adjust instructional approaches, and provide intensified instruction (Mandinach & Schildkamp, 2021). DDDM enables educators to make informed decisions about the learning environment, curriculum materials and resources, and instruction strategies.

Defining DDDM

DDDM is described as the systematic collection and analysis of data to inform instruction, support learning, and adapt the learning environment (Marsh et al., 2006; Van der Kleij et al., 2015). In this way, DDDM allows educators to review, analyze, and synthesize data both to evaluate student learning and to address the conditions for learning. The Center on Multi-Tiered Systems of Support (n.d.) defines DDDM as "use of screening, progress monitoring, and other forms of data to make decisions about instruction, movement within the multi-level prevention system, intensification of instruction and supports, allocation of resources, and identification of students with disabilities."

The practice of using data to inform instruction is applicable across grade levels and content areas as well as important for driving behavior, functional, and social outcomes. Additionally, data can be used at the district, school, classroom, or student level to identify patterns and address pressure points as part of the cycle of continuous improvement and to make instructional decisions. Educators can use data to look for patterns and address pressure points across a district or school. For example, districts can review student performance data to make systems change in response. Similarly, if a school notices low performance of all sixth grade students on literacy benchmarks, then they may choose to explore the robustness of their Tier 1 literacy instruction, review their curriculum and resources, and review the need for continued professional learning to support staff. At the classroom level, teachers use data to identify patterns across students in their classroom and adjust instruction, environment, or pacing. At the student level, teachers can identify patterns in student thinking and adjust instructional approach, provide intervention, or track progress.

The DDDM Process

DDDM is a critical feature of an MTSS and occurs at all tiers. Teams utilize data from various assessments (universal screening, diagnostic, progress monitoring, classroom assessment) to make instructional decisions, including movement between the tiers, intensification of instruction and intervention, and determination for special education services. In addition, embedding DDDM within MTSS supports the evaluation of the extent to which instruction and intervention are sufficient to meet individual student needs. This evidence-based approach is cyclical and iterative, meaning it is a continuous process that permits revision and refinement in a flexible and responsive way.

Throughout the process, educators can follow steps and ask questions designed to identify and address an area of need. The DDDM steps across district, school, classroom, or student level include those in table 5.1. Figure 5.1 illustrates the cyclical and interactive process.

TABLE 5.1. DDDM Steps

Step	Description
Define	Aligned with state standards, define the objective students are expected to master.
Identify	Using data, identify the area of need.
Develop & Implement	In response to the data, develop a hypothesis as to why the problem is occurring and identify an intervention or approach to address the problem.
Evaluate	After implementing the intervention, collect and analyze data.
Reflect & Share	After collecting and analyzing data, reflect and share the results.

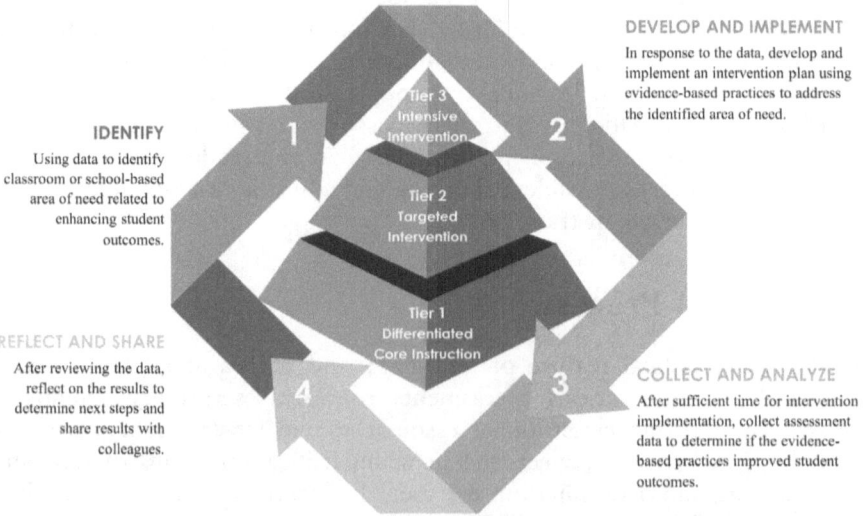

FIGURE 5.1. *Data-Driven Decision-Making Process.*

> Pause and Reflect:
> Review the vignette at the beginning of the chapter. How can Ms. Locke use the DDDM process to inform her instruction and intervention to meet the needs of Tomas?

DDDM requires "sensemaking" of the data (Mandinach, 2012) to align evidence-based instructional methods and resources and to make decisions about the intensity of instruction. To guide DDDM, Fuchs and colleagues (2017) developed a taxonomy of intervention intensity. The taxonomy provides a system of considerations across seven dimensions: strength, dosage, alignment, attention to transfer, comprehensiveness, support, and individualization. The taxonomy of intervention intensity is described in table 5.2.

TABLE 5.2. *Taxonomy of Intervention Intensity*

Dimension	Description	Implementation
Strength	Instruction and intervention are evidence-based	• Identify and select EBPs by visiting What Works Clearinghouse, the National Center on Intensive Intervention, or the PROGRESS Center
Dosage	Instruction and intervention provide the student with increased opportunities to respond and receive feedback	• Increase frequency of instruction (e.g., sessions) • Increase duration of instruction (e.g., additional time for each session) • Decrease group size (e.g., smaller groups, one-on-one)
Alignment	Instruction and intervention are aligned with student needs and grade level standards	• Align instruction with the targeted skill
Attention to Transfer	Instruction and intervention explicitly link skills across settings	• Connect skills in one setting to another (e.g., classroom to home)
Comprehensiveness	Instruction and intervention explicitly teach and scaffold preskills and principles	• Teach prerequisite skills • Scaffold the skill in steps
Support	Instruction and intervention consider and respond to behavior by providing engagement, motivation, and active participation	• Engage students in the learning process
Individualization	Instruction and intervention are guided by multiple sources of data and responsive to student need	• Monitor progress • Adjust instruction

Note: Adapted from Fuchs et al. (2017).

The Power of Data

Data serves as the foundation for all instructional decisions, providing valuable insights into student strengths and areas of need. Data is powerful for both educators and students and allows educators to

- Understand their students
- Adjust and refine instruction
- Provide the right amount of support
- Individualize instruction, support, or intervention
- Identify the need, duration, and frequency of intervention(s)
- Develop and monitor individualized education programs (IEPs)
- Identify, select, and allocate resources
- Organize small groups or pair students
- Reflect on their teaching practices

Types of Data

Although current practice heavily weights student instructional data, data from all sources should be considered (Mandinach & Schildkamp, 2021) since they can strongly influence student outcomes. When evaluating learning outcomes, Mandinach and Schlidkamp (2021) highlight the importance of considering data related to learning conditions (e.g., classroom environment, instructional approaches, fidelity of implementation) and student characteristics (e.g., health, attendance, motivation, home circumstances). Examining all available data provides a holistic understanding of the student, the classroom, and instruction. And although data for learning conditions and student characteristics can provide a holistic understanding of the student, these supplemental data points should be carefully collected and examined for the purpose of adjusting instruction, not for substantiating or discounting student outcome data.

There are several types of data that can be used to develop a comprehensive and holistic view of students. Data evidences student progress and describes a variety of skills, including academic, behavior, and functional or social skills. Used to inform instruction, data can be gathered from a variety of sources, including students themselves, teachers, and parents/caregivers. Typically, data falls into one of two categories, quantitative or qualitative. Quantitative data can be counted or measured, are nominal or numerical, and are often reported using a numerical value. Nominal data are variables such as gender, race, political affiliation, or other types of categorical variables. Numerical data are represented in numbers and can be measured or counted. Examples of numerical data include age, weight, height, or test scores. Numerical data can also describe frequency (how often something occurs, e.g., twice a week) or duration (how long something lasts, e.g., 15 minutes). Qualitative data describes characteristics or qualities, can be examined for patterns or meaning, and are often reported in a narrative format. The types of data that schools and teachers have access to are outlined in table 5.3.

TABLE 5.3. *Types of Data*

Demographic	Demographic data describes a student or population of students. Demographic data can include data related to
	• Age • Race/ethnicity • Gender • Economic status • Language • Disability status • Location
Academic Performance	Academic performance measures student achievement across domains and content areas. Academic performance data can include data related to
	• Academic achievement • Grades • Test scores • Course completion • Graduation rates
Behavior Performance	Behavior performance provides insights into patterns of student behavior inside and outside of the classroom. Behavior performance data can include data related to
	• Attention • Participation and engagement • Attendance • Discipline, including suspensions and expulsions
Functional and Social Performance	Functional and social performance refers to the skills that students need to function, live independently, and participate in everyday life. Functional and social performance can include data related to
	• Social skills • Communication skills • Organization and time management • Personal care • Activities of daily living

> Pause and Reflect:
> What types of data should Ms. Locke gather to support Tomas? How would multiple sources of data be helpful to Ms. Locke?

Assessment

Assessments are a tool to evaluate student performance and educator effectiveness and ensure accountability. Schools use data to determine adequacy of the curriculum and tiered supports, measure effectiveness of instruction and teacher quality, and provide targeted professional learning. Similarly, teachers can use data to (1) optimize the learning environment, (2) monitor student progress toward objectives and standards, (3) select instructional approaches and strategies, (4) guide instruction or intervention, and (5) uncover gaps in professional learning. Students can use data to reflect on their learning, identify their strengths, and engage in error analysis.

Types of Assessment

Various types of assessment can be used together to evidence student learning. The most common types of assessment used to drive instruction include (1) universal screening, (2) diagnostic, (3) formative, (4) summative, and (5) progress monitoring. Each of these assessments may vary in their purpose or use and have unique characteristics.

> **Universal screening:** A universal screener is a standardized assessment that measures a student's academic, behavior, or functional skill level to identify if the student needs additional support to meet grade level goals. By using universal screening, classroom teachers can quickly determine if (1) a student is performing on grade level for a specific skill (e.g., reading fluency, multiplication facts) and (2) if their core (Tier 1) instruction is sufficient for 80–85% of their students. Universal screenings are norm-referenced assessments. Norm-referenced assessments compare a student's current level of performance to grade level expectations individually or class-wide. For example, a classroom teacher can administer an oral reading fluency (ORF) assessment, which measures a student's ability to quickly and accurately read aloud a passage, to determine if a student's reading fluency meets grade level expectations. Protocols for the assessment are standardized, meaning all students have one minute to read the same passage at the same time of year, and guidelines for scoring are

implemented with fidelity. Typically administered three times a year in the fall, winter, and spring, these data points indicate the extent to which a student is making progress. These types of assessments are appealing because they provide critical information in a quick, easy-to-score, and inexpensive way that yields little discomfort to the student.

Diagnostic: Diagnostic assessments drive instruction by providing a baseline to plan and begin lessons that meet the students where they are. These baseline data are then used to leverage student's strengths, build background knowledge, address misconceptions, and fill gaps. Diagnostic assessments are also useful for conducting error analysis when they include a component that assesses a student's approach, strategy, or other metacognitive reasoning for a response. When administered at the start and end of a lesson, unit, or semester, diagnostic assessments can also be used to measure growth serving as a pretest and posttest. Although diagnostic assessments are informative, they are not typically included in classroom grades.

Formative: Formative assessments can be used to identify students' strengths and weaknesses to target instruction or intervention. Formative assessments are designed to provide ongoing feedback throughout a lesson or unit by measuring what a student has or has not yet learned. According to Heritage (2007), formative assessments are fluid and can include (1) gathering "on the fly" data during the course of a lesson, (2) asking planned questions or checking for understanding, or (3) using curriculum-embedded questions. In addition, formative assessments are focused on the learning process and learning progress (Mass & Brookhart, 2019). These assessments come in a variety of formats, from check-ins to quizzes and exit slips.

Summative: A summative assessment is a criterion-referenced assessment administered at the end of a lesson, unit, program, or course. A criterion-referenced assessment is an assessment that measures a student's learning by comparing it to a standard or a predetermined criteria. These types of assessments are usually high stakes, meaning they have a high point value or count for a high percentage of the student's grade. Because these assessments are high stakes, they are standardized, increasing the reliability and validity of the assessment. Assessments are reliable when they accurately measure what they are intended to measure and valid when they do so accurately. In addition, these assessments hold educators accountable for student learning. If a majority of students did not meet the learning objectives of the lesson, course, or program, then the teaching strategies, environment, or curriculum can be examined to determine areas for improvement. Examples of summative assessments include midterm exams, final exams, final projects, end-of-course exams, or standardized assessments.

Progress monitoring: Progress monitoring is a type of formative assessment that measures student performance and quantifies their progress over time (Center on Multi-Tiered Systems of Support, n.d.). An essential component of MTSS, progress monitoring identifies which students are not responding to instruction or intervention at each tier and increases in frequency at each tier. Progress monitoring provides data that helps educators examine student thinking, analyze data, and adjust instruction accordingly. A student's rate of progress, also known as their rate of growth, is demonstrated by showing their performance over time as they work toward an identified goal. Often represented by the slope of a line, the rate of progress is graphed by plotting data points that include the *baseline* (where a student starts), *mastery line* (point where mastery is achieved), *target line* (the individual goal for a student), and the *trend line* (current trend of progress). Figure 5.2 provides a graph to illustrate a student's rate of progress.

Although some assessment characteristics may overlap, each serves a different purpose. Assessments are meant to be used together to depict a holistic view of a student's abilities and should not be substituted for one another. Table 5.4 details types of assessment, their purpose, and their defining characteristics.

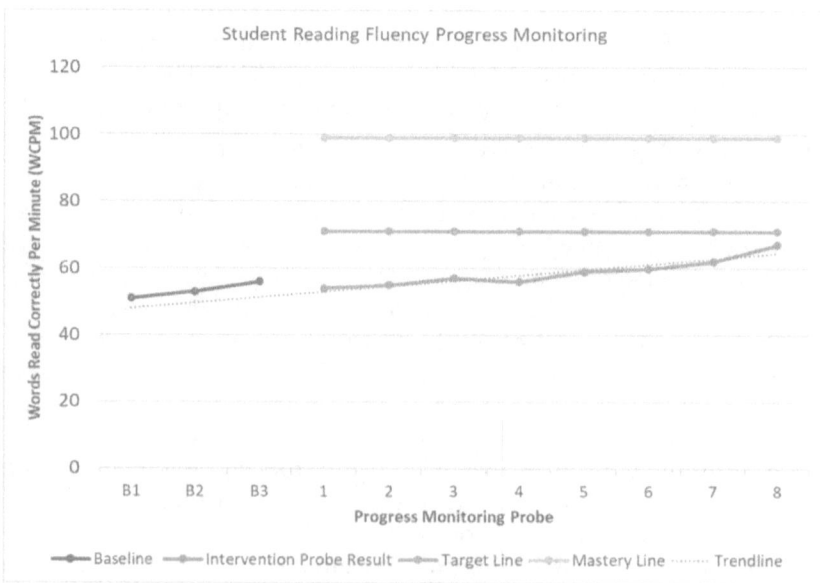

FIGURE 5.2. *Student Rate of Progress.*

TABLE 5.4. *Types of Assessment*

Type of Assessment	Purpose	Characteristics	Examples
Universal Screening	Measures how students are responding to instruction Identifies gaps in skill acquisition Determines which students may need additional support to achieve learning goals across academic, behavior, or functional skills	• **Brief:** Short in length and duration • **Targeted:** Content and grade-level specific; measures discrete skills • **Standardized:** Administered to every student in the same way • **Normed:** Scored consistently • **Inexpensive:** Little to no cost • **Routine:** Administered three times a year (fall, winter, spring)	• Oral reading fluency assessments • Dynamic Indicators of Basic Early Literacy Skills (DIBELS) • Phonological Awareness Literacy Screening (PALS) • AIMSweb • Social Skills Improvement System–Social Emotional Learning (SSIS-SEL)
Diagnostic	Identifies existing background knowledge Identifies strengths and weaknesses	• **Baseline:** Identifies where the student starts to measure growth • **Specificity:** Pinpoints learning gaps • **Error Analysis:** Identifies patterns and exposes the types of errors and why • **Informative:** Monitors progress, drives instruction	• Pretests • Surveys • Quizzes • Entry ticket • KWL charts • Observation

(Continued)

TABLE 5.4. (*Continued*)

Type of Assessment	Purpose	Characteristics	Examples
Formative	Identifies misconceptions, learning gaps Evaluates student learning	• **Student Centered:** Students own their learning • **Useful:** Informs instruction • **Immediate:** Allows for on-the-spot instructional adaptations • **Intentional:** Planned • **Informs:** Provides actionable feedback • **Ongoing:** Monitors progress	• Quizzes • Graphic organizers • Homework • Checklists • Comprehension checks
Summative	Measures students' knowledge or ability at a given point in time, usually the end of a unit or lesson Provides a summary of students' learning	• **Evaluative:** Demonstrates student learning • **Culminating:** Measures understanding at the end of a phase/unit/lesson • **Goal oriented:** Assesses if a student met the goals/objectives • **Valid/Reliable:** Measures what it is intended to measure • **High Stakes:** Awards a high point value or results in consequences	• Midterm exam • Final exams • Final projects • Standardized test
Progress Monitoring	Monitors students' progress towards a goal or objective Determines the extent to which a student is responding to instruction Used to make decisions about frequency and duration of instruction or intervention	• **Ongoing:** Frequently measures progress toward a goal • **Goal Driven:** Aligned with goals/objectives • **Individualized:** Uses data to drive decision-making • **Sensitive:** Identifies even small evidence of progress • **Rate of Growth:** Quantifies progress • **Quick:** Short in length and duration	• Curriculum-based measures • Computer-adaptive assessment • Observation • Rubrics

> Pause and Reflect:
>
> What type of assessment can Ms. Locke use to evaluate Tomas's performance and inform her instructional approach? Why is it important for Ms. Locke to use data from multiple assessments to inform instruction and provide targeted intervention?

Equity in Data

In the United States, data has long been used to promote inequitable access and limit educational outcomes (Bocala & Parker Boudett, 2022). This can be evidenced in accountability-driven reforms (e.g., No Child Left Behind) that promoted classification of students by their levels of proficiency. Although lawmakers intended to ensure all students were taught by highly qualified educators who used evidence-based practices, research indicated that accountability reforms restricted performance data to a single measure (e.g., standardized assessment), which was often unresponsive to student diversity (Bocala & Parker Boudett, 2022). Opponents to these high-stakes assessments cautioned that overreliance on a single data point would narrow teaching and learning and limit opportunity and reduce equitable access—especially for marginalized and minoritized students and students with disabilities (Villani, 2018).

The era of high-stakes accountability underscores the significance of equitable data collection and analysis procedures (Ward Biddle, 2022). The purpose of data is to identify what a student knows and is able to do (strengths), what a student does not yet know (needs), and which high-quality instructional practices can help them achieve their potential. In this way, data collection, analysis, and interpretation should be driven by creating the conditions every student needs to achieve to their full potential (Ward Biddle, 2022).

Equity in Data Collection, Analysis, and Interpretation

Analyzing and interpreting data is as important as collecting it. Data can be powerful when used to understand where students are performing, identify strengths and needs, and tailor instruction. But data can also be used to perpetuate beliefs about individual students or groups of students. Not all students have access to equitable learning opportunities, which impacts average reading and mathematics scores for some of our students (National Association of Secondary School Principals, 2021). These inequitable opportunities begin before students enter school and continue throughout their educational career.

Since 1968, the Office of Civil Rights of the U.S. Department of Education has collected state-level data that indicates the persistent disproportionate access students of color and students from low-income homes have to advanced coursework. In states that have intentionally designed policies to ensure equitable access, students are enrolling in advanced courses at higher rates (Leung et al., 2021). These policies promote access by addressing bias that has historically limited access. For example, in Washington State students who qualify are automatically enrolled in advanced courses rather than opted in by students, teachers, or parents/caregivers (Leung et al., 2021). Addressing achievement gaps requires addressing opportunity gaps—and this begins in the classroom with data analysis and interpretation. To ensure an equitable approach to data interpretation, consider the guiding principles in table 5.5.

> Pause and Reflect:
>
> What steps can Ms. Locke take to ensure equity in data collection, analysis, and interpretation? What can Ms. Locke consider while engaging with data to support Tomas?

Creating routine opportunities to collect and collectively analyze data supports equitable outcomes. When implemented through a collaborative approach, DDDM encourages educators to work together to use their diverse expertise to plan and deliver high-quality instruction to all students. Collaborative approaches enable educators to check each other for bias and ensure they are all working toward the goal of supporting all students. Additionally, a culture of collaborative inquiry can shift mindsets to see data as formative rather than evaluative (Ritchie & Gutmann, 2014). A formative approach to data promotes the continuous cycle of instructional improvement. When data is viewed as evaluative, the focus is on outcomes, stunting the commitment to driving change.

TABLE 5.5. *Ensuring an Equitable Approach to Data Interpretation*

Recognize Bias	Data can tell the story we want and choose to tell. As educators, we make judgments about students every day. And we can use data to reinforce (or debunk) our beliefs about individual students or groups of students (Knips, 2019). Data can also be used to create (or deny) opportunity.
	Ensure grading practices are driven by standards and are fair and equitable. This can be done by reducing the opportunity for subjectivity.
Understand Identity (e.g., culture, context, language, poverty)	There is a strong relationship between a student's cultural identity and achievement because cultural disconnection can influence their learning (Altugan, 2015). In addition, Aceves & Kennedy (2024) suggest analyzing data through an intersectional lens to uncover both hidden and observable layers of oppression and discrimination.
	Integrating students' cultural identity in their learning can positively influence learning, which can impact achievement data.
Set the Why	Addressing implicit and explicit bias in data analysis and interpretation begins with framing intention (Levinson, 2007). Essentially, why is the data being collected and what will the outcome of the data analysis lead to?
	Data is collected to provide and individualize instruction, intervention, and support. In this way, data is collected to ensure access rather than deny access.
Select Data	The data we select and interpret is critically important because educators may draw attention to something innocuous, which then could limit access or opportunity.
	We can select data that supports our preconceived notions of students, or we can select and interpret data that paints a holistic understanding of the student.
Identify Strengths	An asset-based approach to data analysis and interpretation begins by celebrating student strengths. Culturally inclusive pedagogies and practices (CIPP) challenge deficit thinking and presume students are capable (Aceves & Kennedy, 2024).
	Bocala and Parker Boudett (2022) emphasize, "While educators should use data to identify students who need targeted supports, they must ensure that those labels are not used to deprive students of opportunities" (n.p.).

> **HIGH-IMPACT: THE CONNECTION WITH HIGH-LEVERAGE PRACTICES**
>
> **HLP 1:** Collaborate with professionals to increase student success
> **HLP 2:** Organize and facilitate effective meetings with professionals and families
> **HLP 3:** Collaborate with families to support student learning and secure services
> **HLP 4:** Use multiple sources of information to develop a comprehensive understanding of a student's strengths and needs
> **HLP 5:** Interpret and communicate assessment information to collaboratively design and implement educational programs
> **HLP 6:** Use student assessment data, analyze instructional practices, and make necessary adjustments that improve student outcomes
> **HLP 10:** Conduct functional behavior assessments to develop individual student behavior support plans
> **HLP 11:** Identify and prioritize long- and short-term learning goals
> **HLP 12:** Systematically design instruction toward a specific goal
> **HLP 20:** Provide intensive intervention for academics and behavior
> **HLP 21:** Teach students to maintain and generalize new learning across time and settings
> **HLP 8/22:** Provide positive and constructive feedback to guide students' learning (HLP 22) and behavior (HLP 8)

Review and Reflect

DDDM empowers educators to evaluate classroom practices (e.g., environment, curriculum, teaching strategies), adjust and align instruction and intervention to meet student need, and improve student outcomes through informed decisions. By leveraging various types of assessment, educators gather meaningful data from a variety of sources to guide instruction and monitor student progress. As educators make sense of the data, they can apply an equity lens to examine why the data is being collected and ensure its intended purpose is to provide access and remove barriers to learning so all children can achieve their greatest potential.

Guiding Questions

1. Define data-driven decision making (DDDM) and explain how its cyclical nature helps to continually improve instruction and student outcomes.

2. What are the domains of the taxonomy of intervention intensity? Give an example of how you can use this in your current or future classroom.
3. What types of assessment can educators use to make instructional decisions? What are the similarities and differences between universal screening, diagnostic assessments, formative assessments, progress monitoring, and summative assessments?
4. What are best practices that can be implemented to ensure equity in data collection, analysis, and interpretation?

Extend Your Learning

TABLE 5.6 *Resources*

Resource	Description	Link
National Center on Intensive Intervention	Tools and resources to support DDDM and the taxonomy of intervention intensity	https://intensiveintervention.org/
IRIS Modules	Asynchronous modules to support DDDM in academics and behavior	https://iris.peabody.vanderbilt.edu/
PROGRESS Center	"Instructional Practice Brief: Reviewing and Intensifying Instruction"	https://promotingprogress.org/
Center on PBIS	Tools and resources for DDDM in behavior	https://www.pbis.org/

References

Aceves, T. C., & Kennedy, M. J. (Eds.). (2024). *High-leverage practices for students with disabilities.* 2nd edition. Council for Exceptional Children and CEEDAR Center.

Altugan, A. S. (2015). The relationship between cultural identity and learning. *Procedia-Social and Behavioral Sciences, 186,* 1159–62. https://doi.org/10.1016/j.sbspro.2015.04.161

Balu, R., Zhu, P., Doolittle, F., Schiller, E., Jenkins, J., Gersten, R., & Jacobson, J. (2015). *Evaluation of response to intervention practices for elementary school reading: Executive summary.* U.S. Department of Education, Institute of Education Sciences, National Center for Education Evaluation and Regional Assistance.

Bocala, C., & Parker Boudett, K. (2022). Looking at data through an equity lens. *Educational Leadership, 79*(5), 32–37. https://ascd.org/el/articles/looking-at-data-through-an-equity-lens

Brownell, M. T., Benedict, A. E., Leko, M. M., Peyton, D., Pua, D., & Richards-Tutor, C. (2019). A continuum of pedagogies for preparing teachers to use high-leverage practices. *Remedial and Special Education, 40*(6), 338–55.

Bruhn, A. L., Wehby, J. H., & Hasselbring, T. S. (2020). Data-based decision making for social behavior: Setting a research agenda. *Journal of Positive Behavior Interventions, 22*(2), 116–26. https://doi.org/10.1177/1098300719876098

Center on Multi-Tiered Systems of Support. (n.d.). *Essential components of MTSS: Progress monitoring.* American Institutes for Research. https://mtss4success.org/essential-components/progress-monitoring

Collaboration for Effective Educator Development, Accountability, and Reform (CEEDAR). (n.d.). *Multi-tiered system of support chapter.* https://ceedar.education.ufl.edu/mtssudldi-professional-development-module/mtss-chapter/#MTSS%20Components

Datnow, A., & Hubbard, L. (2016). Teacher capacity for and beliefs about data-driven decision making: A literature review of international research. *Journal of Educational Change, 17*(1), 7–28.

Every Student Succeeds Act. (2015). Public Law 114-95, 114th Cong., 1st sess.

Fuchs, L. S., Fuchs, D., & Malone, A. S. (2017). The taxonomy of intervention intensity. *Teaching Exceptional Children, 50*(1), 35–43.

Heritage, M. (2007). Formative assessment: What do teachers need to know and do? *Phi Delta Kappan, 89*(2), 140–45. https://doi.org/10.1177/003172170708900210

Hoover, J. J., Baca, L. M., Wexler-Love, E., & Saenz, L. (2008). *National implementation of response to intervention (RtI): Research summary.* National Association of State Directors of Special Education (NASDE).

Knips, A. (2019, June 13). 6 steps to equitable data analysis. *Edutopia.* https://www.edutopia.org/article/6-steps-equitable-data-analysis

Lemons, C. J., Sinclair, A. C., Gesel, S., Gruner Gandhi, A., & Danielson, L. (2017). *Supporting implementation of data-based individualization: Lessons learned from NCII's first five years.* National Center on Intensive Intervention.

Leonard, K. M., Coyne, M. D., Oldham, A. C., Burns, D., & Gillis, M. B. (2019). Implementing MTSS in beginning reading: tools and systems to support schools and teachers. *Learning Disabilities Research & Practice, 34*(2), 110–17.

Leung, M., Cardichon, J., Scott, C., & Darling-Hammond, L. (2021). *Inequitable opportunity to learn: Access to advanced mathematics and science courses.* Learning Policy Institute. https://files.eric.ed.gov/fulltext/ED626612.pdf

Levinson, J. D. (2007). Forgotten racial equality: Implicit bias, decision making, and misremembering. *Duke Law Journal, 57,* 345.

Mandinach, E. B. (2012). A perfect time for data use: Using data-driven decision making to inform practice. *Educational Psychologist, 42*(2), 71–85.

Mandinach, E. B., & Schildkamp, K. (2021). Misconceptions about data-based decision making in education: An exploration of the literature. *Studies in Educational Evaluation, 69,* article 100842.

Marsh, J. A., Bertrand, M., & Huguet, A. (2015). Using data to alter instructional practice: The mediating role of coaches and professional learning communities. *Teachers College Record, 117*(4), 1–40.

Marsh, J. A., Pane, J. F., & Hamilton, L. S. (2006). *Making sense of data driven decision making in education.* RAND Corporation. https://www.rand.org/pubs/occasional_papers/OP170.html

Mass, C., & Brookhart, S. (2019). The lay of the land: Essential elements of the formative assessment process. In *Advancing formative assessment in every classroom: A guide for instructional leaders* (2nd ed., pp. 5–23). ASCD.

National Association of Secondary School Principals. (2021, January). *Position statement: Racial justice and educational equity.* https://www.nassp.org/wp-content/uploads/2021/11/NASSP21ADV-0060_WS_Postion_Statements_Racial_Justice_P2b.pdf

National Center for Intensive Interventions. (n.d.). https://intensiveintervention.org/

Powell, S. R., Lembke, E. S., Ketterlin-Geller, L. R., Petscher, Y., Hwang, J., Bos, S. E., Cox, T., Mason, E. N., Pruitt-Britton, T., Thomas, E., & Hopkins, S. (2020). Data-based individualization in mathematics to support middle school teachers and their students with mathematics learning difficulty. *Studies in Educational Evaluation, 67*, article 100897. https://doi.org/10.1016/j.stueduc.2020.100897

Ritchie, S., & Gutmann, L. (Eds.). (2014). *FirstSchool: Transforming preK–3rd grade for African American, Latino, and Low-Income children.* Teachers College Press.

Schildkamp, K. (2019). Data-based decision-making for school improvement: Research insights and gaps. *Journal of Educational Research, 61*(3), 257–73.

Slanda, D. D., & Little, M. E. (2021). Data-driven decision-making to intensify literacy instruction and intervention. *Florida Literacy Journal, 2*(2), 69–84.

Van der Kleij, F. M., Vermeulen, J. A., Schildkamp, K., & Eggen, T. J. (2015). Integrating data-based decision making, assessment for learning and diagnostic testing in formative assessment. *Assessment in Education: Principles, Policy & Practice, 22*(3), 324–43. https://doi.org/10.1080/0969594X.2014.999024

Villani, S. (2018). *Exploring equity issues: Educators use data and find solutions to improve equity.* Center for Education Equity, Mid-Atlantic Equity Consortium. https://maec.org/wp-content/uploads/2018/09/Exploring-Equity-Educators-Use-Data-and-Find-Solutions-to-Improve-Equity-1.pdf

Ward Biddle, C. (2022, March 25). *Using student data for equity.* Relay Graduate School of Education. https://www.relay.edu/article/using-student-data-for-equity

Wilson, M. (2016). Becoming data and information rich in education. *BU Journal of Graduate Studies in Education, 8*(1), 5–9.

6

Pathway to Student Services and Supports

The special education referral and eligibility process is complex, nuanced, and steeped in legal compliance and guidelines. Special education determination involves several key steps, including identification and prereferral, parental notification and consent, and comprehensive evaluation. Providing students with disabilities the supports and services they need to improve their academic and functional performance begins by ensuring proper identification and evaluation. This process must be thorough and is designed to be collaborative by involving educators, specialists, and parents/caregivers who are committed to making informed decisions in the best interest of the student. In addition, the process requires compliance with federal and state legal guidelines. The importance of the process is underscored by the impact it has on a student's progress in the general curriculum and ultimately postsecondary outcomes.

Chapter Objectives

After reading this chapter, readers will be able to

- Describe the special education identification process, including the Child Find mandate, parent/caregiver-initiated referral, and public-school-initiated referral
- Identify and explain the steps of the referral and eligibility process
- Describe the defining characteristics of each of the 13 federal disability categories

- Understand the additional requirements for eligibility for specific learning disability (SLD)
- Identify challenges in the referral and eligibility process

Key Terms

Child Find: Child Find is a legal mandate that requires public schools to identify, locate, and evaluate all children ages birth to 21 who are known to or suspected to have a disability and may need special education and related services.

discrepancy model: To determine eligibility for special education services, Public Law 94-142 established a need to illustrate a discrepancy between intellectual ability and academic performance of students (Fuchs et al., 2008).

eligibility: Eligibility for special education is determined by evaluating if the child has a disability as defined in IDEA and if the disability affects their learning to the extent they require special education and related services.

evaluation: An evaluation refers to assessment tools that determine if a child has a disability and if the disability requires special education and related services to access the general curriculum.

prereferral: The prereferral stage is the stage before a formal referral is initiated and begins when a child experiences difficulty academically or functionally and receives targeted and intensive interventions to improve performance.

specific learning disability (SLD): According to IDEA, SLD refers to a disability in which a student's ability to listen, think, speak, read, write, spell, or do mathematical calculations is negatively affected. In addition, SLD includes conditions such as perceptual disabilities, dyslexia, and developmental aphasia.

Vignette

As you read this chapter, consider Elijah, who is described in the vignette below. Connect the information you learn about Elijah to the special education referral and eligibility process. There will be prompts and examples related to this vignette throughout the chapter.

Elijah is a second grade student who excels in math and loves science and social studies. He is often referred to as the class mayor due to his ability to get along with everyone in his class and school. To support his reading development, Elijah has been receiving Tier 3 intensive intervention in addition to core instruction. Despite the intensive support provided, including individualized one-on-one intervention and aligned instructional strategies, his progress has remained stagnant. Mr. Emmett is concerned and is not able to identify why Elijah is not responding to high-quality instruction. Given his concerns, Mr. Emmett schedules a meeting with the special education teacher, the academic coach, and Elijah's parents. During this meeting, they collectively review the intervention data, work samples, and other performance data to identify strengths and areas for continued support. The team highlights the need to determine if there is an underlying learning disability that may be impacting Elijah's ability to make progress. Elijah's parents agree that an evaluation would assist everyone to better understand his academic needs and if necessary develop a plan for specially designed instruction to meet his needs. The team decides to proceed with a referral for special education evaluation.

Special Education: From Referral to Eligibility

The special education referral process is a gateway to ensuring students' equal opportunity and access to a free appropriate public education. Referral to special education is nuanced, and although it is guided by federal legislation, the process is influenced by state and district policies and procedures. Guided by Child Find mandates within the Individuals With Disabilities Act (IDEA), early identification and school-based identification may vary. However, teachers can work together to ensure that children who may have a disability are identified and evaluated promptly and accurately.

Identifying Students Who Require Special Education and Related Services

Identification for special education typically occurs in one of two ways. First, all states are required by federal law to have a system to actively identify, locate, and evaluate children who are suspected of having a disability for special education and related services. This system is known as Child Find. The second way students can be identified for special education and related services is by parent or school personnel (e.g., teacher) referral. Students with disabilities can be identified at any age beginning at birth until age 21 (or high school graduation).

Child Find Mandate

Child Find is a legal mandate that applies to all children ages birth to 21. To serve the education needs of a child, the Child Find section of IDEA requires that public schools identify, locate, and evaluate infants, toddlers, and school-age children who are known to or suspected to have a disability and may need special education and related services. Child Find is required regardless of the severity of the disability and applies even if they are advancing from grade to grade. All states are required to have policies and procedures for the identification, location, and evaluation of students, and Child Find requires that evaluation services are provided at no cost to the family. This mandate applies to all children, including children who are unhoused, are legal wards of the state, attend private schools, or are homeschooled. In addition, Child Find must also include "highly mobile children, including migrant children" (IDEA, Section 300.111[c][2]). Table 6.1 outlines Child Find.

To locate children who may need special education and related services, public schools are required to do outreach. Outreach includes local media campaigns, posting notices in public spaces, and coordination with healthcare providers.

TABLE 6.1. *Child Find*

Child Find applies to all children ages birth to 21 and requires public schools to do the following at no cost to the student or parent/caregiver:
Identify
Locate
Evaluate
Provide special education and related services
Child Find applies to all children ages birth to 21 when
The child is known to have a disability
The child is suspected to have a disability
Child find applies to all children ages birth to 21, including children who are
Unhoused
Wards of the state
Enrolled in private school
Homeschooled
Highly mobile, including migrants
Advancing from grade to grade

Parent/Caregiver-Initiated Referral

Some parents/caregivers may notice that their child is having a difficult time with academic tasks or functional skills. As a result of these difficulties, the parent/caregiver might suspect their child has a disability. If a parent suspects that their child has a disability, parents/caregivers have the right to request an evaluation in writing from the public school or district regardless of whether the child attends public school. If the child is involved in the response to intervention (RtI)/MTSS process, the public school must still complete the evaluation and must collect all data from the RtI process before the end of the time frame set in place by parent consent (Learning Disabilities Association of America, 2023). IDEA requires public schools to complete an evaluation within 60 days of parent consent.

A parent/caregiver's request for evaluation is protected by IDEA through the Child Find mandate. As such, the public school has the responsibility to fulfill the request and must do so at no cost to the parent. If a child is found eligible for special education and related services, the public school is also required to provide special education and related services unless the family does not want them. If a public school refuses to evaluate a child, parents/caregivers can request a written explanation and have the right to dispute the decision as part of IDEA procedural safeguards (IDEA, Section 300.504[a][1]). Procedural safeguards also protect parents/caregivers' right to obtain independent educational evaluation.

Public School-Initiated Referral

Prior to IDEA (1997), PL 94-142 required a discrepancy between intellectual ability and academic performance to determine a student's eligibility for special education services for several disability categories, including a specific learning disability (Fuchs et al., 2008). This discrepancy became known as the discrepancy model. Adherence to the discrepancy model left students who were not yet identified for special education services without much-needed interventions until they were in upper elementary grade levels. To be eligible for special education and to receive much-needed support, the discrepancy between their performance and their peers had to grow significantly, and in some cases the discrepancy grew beyond repair (Siegel & Hurford, 2019). In addition, the federal legislation at that time required the documentation of a discrepancy between intellectual ability and academic performance but did not define eligibility criteria (Bradley et al., 2005), leaving its interpretation to the states and school districts. The lack of accepted definitions and eligibility criteria resulted in students being unidentified or misidentified (Vaughn & Fuchs, 2003).

During the 1990s and early 2000s, there was a growing concern that the discrepancy model was "neither necessary nor sufficient" in identifying students with specific learning disabilities (Bradley et al., 2005). These concerns prompted the National Joint Committee on Learning Disabilities (NJCLD) to write a letter to the Office of Special Education Programs (OSEP), which later became known as the Learning Disabilities (LD) Initiative (Bradley et al., 2007). The discrepancy model, now referred to as the "wait-to-fail" approach (Fuchs & Fuchs, 2007), was the catalyst for reauthorization of IDEA legislation in 2004.

When IDEA was reauthorized in 2004, the reauthorization emphasized early and accurate identification of students with disabilities. This emphasis replaced the wait-to-fail model with an RtI model, a problem-solving approach for identification of learning disabilities (Bradley et al., 2007). RtI had the potential "to reduce the prevalence of academic difficulty while enhancing the validity with which learning disabilities (LD) are identified" (Fuchs & Vaughn, 2012, p. 195). The RtI framework focused on early screening and prevention, progress monitoring for learning gains, and the positive effects of small-group interventions and tutoring (Fuchs & Vaughn, 2012). RtI was later integrated into an MTSS framework to address academic concerns. Also integrated within an MTSS framework are positive behavior intervention and supports (PBIS) and methods for addressing social-emotional learning (SEL) (see chapter 4 for more details on MTSS, RtI, PBIS, and SEL development). Table 6.2 highlights key differences between the discrepancy model and RtI.

The Path to Special Education

IDEA provides guidelines to states that create a blueprint for the special education referral and eligibility process. The blueprint includes the minimum standards that all states must meet, providing flexibility for states to establish their own eligibility criteria and identification policies and procedures that are responsive to their local context (U.S. Government Accountability Office, 2019). After conducting an audit of state approaches to referral and eligibility, the U.S. Government Accountability Office (2019) developed a flowchart to illustrate the *typical* process for school-aged children (ages three to 21). Figure 6.1 illustrates this typical process.

Stage One: Prereferral

For school-aged children (ages three to 21), the referral process typically begins when a teacher recognizes that a student would benefit from intervention to further develop their academic, behavioral, or social-

TABLE 6.2. *From Failing to Responsiveness*

Discrepancy (Wait-to-Fail) (Berkeley et al., 2009; Bradley et al., 2007)	Response to Intervention (MTSS) (Clark, 2021)
• Failed to deliver support or intervention	• Provides immediate evidence-based support and intervention
• Delayed identification and support until upper elementary grades	• Requires prevention, early intervention, and early identification
• Widened the achievement gap since students were left to struggle until the discrepancy was significant	• Aims to reduce the achievement gap by reducing barriers and providing access and opportunity
• Provided limited information about a student's academic need	• Utilizes multiple sources of data to identify, understand, target, and respond to student strengths and needs
• Lacked plan for addressing academic discrepancies	• Provides a blueprint for addressing academic discrepancies
• Increased opportunity for misdiagnosis due to lack of procedures and definitions	• Reduces opportunity for misdiagnosis due to clarified procedures and definitions
• Failed to acknowledge students' cultural capital	• Acknowledges and leverages students' cultural capital
Persistent overrepresentation of marginalized and minoritized students. including multilingual students	

emotional abilities (U.S. Government Accountability Office, 2019; Maryville, 2023). The prereferral stage is a preventative measure designed to reduce or eliminate inappropriate referrals to special education and provide students with beneficial support and targeted intervention (IRIS Center, 2022). Even though data collection is important during this stage, the emphasis should be on student support and intervention. During this stage, the teacher uses a problem-solving approach to evaluate if changes to instruction or the learning environment can address the student's difficulties (IRIS Center, 2019). Classroom teachers can collaborate with other school personnel or parents/caregivers to identify strategies that meet student needs. During this stage, the classroom teacher is able to adjust instruction, collect information, consult with other professionals, implement interventions, and monitor student response to intervention. This stage also allows the classroom teacher to identify specific skills students need support in mastering.

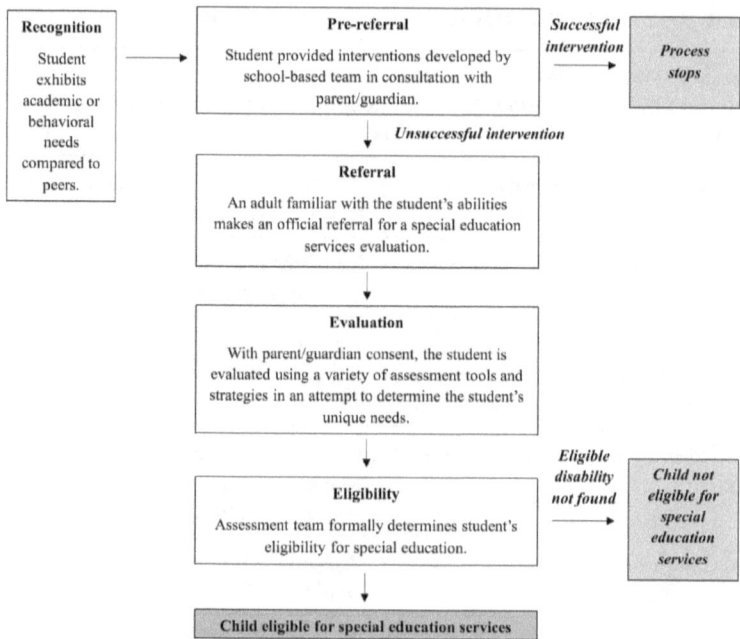

FIGURE 6.1. *Typical Process for Referral and Eligibility for School-Aged Children. Adapted from US Government Accountability Office, 2019.*

If adjustments to the instruction or environment or the targeted or individualized interventions at Tier 2 or Tier 3 are successful, the referral process will stop. However, the interventions may continue in response to student need in a fluid and flexible way (e.g., students move up and down the tiers in response to their needs).

Stage Two: Formal Referral

If the interventions during the prereferral stage are not successful, and the difficulties persist, then the referral process is formalized. At this stage, the teacher or other educators who are familiar with the student's strengths and needs will make an official referral for special education evaluation. With the parent's consent, the student is evaluated by a school psychologist using a variety of assessments designed to determine a student's unique educational needs (academic, behavioral, or social-emotional).

Stage Three: Evaluation

IDEA requires an evaluation to be administered by a qualified and trained professional to (1) determine if a student has a disability consistent with the federal disability categories and (2) identify an appropriate educational program for the student (e.g., content of the IEP). Prior to administering the evaluation, the public agency (i.e., school) must obtain informed consent from the student's parent/caregiver(s). The initial evaluation may be requested by either the parent/caregiver(s) or the public agency (i.e., school). Once requested, the evaluation must be conducted within 60 days of receiving parental consent (or the time frame established by the state).

According to IDEA (Section 300.304), the public agency *must*

- Use a variety of assessment tools and strategies to gather relevant functional, developmental, and academic information
- Use technically sound instruments that may assess the relative contribution of cognitive and behavioral factors in addition to physical or developmental factors
- Ensure prompt completion of full evaluations
- Ensure assessments or other evaluation measures are not discriminatory on a racial or cultural basis
- Administer the evaluation in the student's native language or other mode of communication and in the form most likely to yield accurate information
- Ensure assessments are used for the purposes for which they are valid and reliable (e.g., they assess what they are meant to assess)
- Ensure assessments are not designed to provide a single general intelligence quotient (IQ)
- Administer the evaluation in a way that accurately reflects the student's aptitude or achievement rather than reflecting their impaired sensory, manual, or speaking skills
- Assess students in all areas of suspected disability, including, if appropriate, health, vision, hearing, and social-emotional status
- Ensure assessments are completed expeditiously if the student is transferring from one public agency to another
- Ensure the assessment is sufficiently comprehensive to identify all of the student's special education and related services needs, whether or not it is commonly linked to the disability category in which this student has been classified

In addition to reviewing the evaluation assessment results, an interdisciplinary team must review parent/caregiver information and responses to evaluations, classroom performance data including local or state assessments, and classroom observations from teachers and related service providers.

Stage Four: Eligibility

Once the evaluation is complete, a team of specialists (e.g., classroom teachers, interventionists, special educators, related service personnel, school psychologist, parents/caregivers) will determine eligibility for special education and related services.

To determine if a student is eligible for special education and related services, the interdisciplinary team must establish that *both* of the following criteria have been met:

1. The student meets the definition of one or more of the disability categories recognized by IDEA.
2. The disability affects the student's academic or functional performance to the extent they require special education services.

Given that both of the criteria must be met, it is important to recognize that it is not enough for a student to meet the definition of a disability category. The disability must also impact their academic or functional performance to the extent that they would benefit from special education services. IDEA recognizes thirteen disability categories for students ages three to 21. In addition, IDEA recognizes developmentally delayed (DD) as a disability category for students ages three to nine.

Table 6.3 describes the federal disability categories as outlined in IDEA, Part B, Subpart A, Section 300.8, "Child With a Disability." Note the following two considerations. First, some of the words used to identify the federal disability categories (e.g., emotional disturbance) or to describe defining characteristics (e.g., subaverage, unusual) may no longer reflect contemporary descriptions since their adoption in 2006. Second, although the federal regulations provide defining characteristics for each disability category, it is important to note that every child is unique and the way they experience their disability is equally unique.

If the interdisciplinary team determines the student is not eligible using these established criteria, the process ends and the student will not receive special education or related services. In this situation, the team may consider if (1) the student would benefit from continued targeted or individualized interventions or (2) the student is eligible for accommodations and protections under Section 504 (see chapter 7 for more details on Section 504). If a student is determined to be eligible for special education, the team will draft the IEP using data from the evaluation to identify services and supports. Chapter 7 introduces the IEP and details all required components.

TABLE 6.3. *IDEA Disability Categories*

Federal Disability Category	Federal Description
Developmentally Delayed (DD) (ages three to nine, or any subset of this age group [e.g., three to five])	• Students with DD may be experiencing delays in one or more of the following areas: • Physical development • Cognitive development • Communication development • Social or emotional development • Adaptive development • And, by reason thereof, needs special education and related services.

Autism	• A developmental disability that significantly affects verbal and nonverbal communication
	• Generally evident before age three
	• Characteristics associated with autism include
	  • Engagement in repetitive activities and stereotyped movements
	  • Resistance to environmental change or change in daily routines
	  • Unusual responses to sensory experiences
	
	Note: A child who manifests the characteristics after the age of three could be identified as having autism if the preceding criteria are satisfied. Autism does *not* apply if a child's educational performance is affected primarily because of an emotional disturbance (see definition).

Deaf-Blindness (DB)	• Defined as having a concomitant hearing and visual impairment, the combination of which causes severe communication and other developmental and educational needs that cannot be accommodated in special education programs solely for children with deafness or children with blindness
Deafness	• A hearing impairment so severe that the child is impaired in processing linguistic information through hearing, with or without amplification, that adversely affects a child's educational performance

Emotional Disturbance (ED)	• Condition where a child exhibits one or more of the following:
	• Inability to learn that cannot be explained by intellectual, sensory, or health factors
	  • Inability to build or maintain satisfactory interpersonal relationships with peers and teachers
	  • Inappropriate types of behavior feelings under normal circumstances
	  • General pervasive mood of unhappiness or depression
	  • Tendency to develop physical symptoms or fears associated with personal or school problems
	• Includes schizophrenia
	• Does not apply to children who are socially maladjusted, unless determined that they have an emotional disturbance as defined in the preceding description

(Continued)

TABLE 6.3. *(Continued)*

Federal Disability Category	Federal Description
Hearing Impairment	• An impairment in hearing, permanent or fluctuating, that adversely affects educational performance but that is not included under the definition of deafness
Intellectual Disability (ID)	• Significantly subaverage general functioning • Exists concurrently with deficits in adaptive behavior manifested during the developmental period • Adversely affects a child's educational performance
Multiple Disabilities (MD)	• Concomitant impairments (such as ID and blindness, or ID and OI) • The combination of which causes such severe educational needs that they cannot be accommodate in special education programs solely for one of the impairments • Does not include deaf-blindness

Orthopedic Impairment (OI)	• A severe orthopedic impairment that adversely affects a child's educational performance
	• Includes impairments caused by
	  • Congenital anomaly
	  • Disease (e.g., poliomyelitis, bone tuberculosis)
	  • Other causes (e.g., cerebral palsy, amputations, fractures or burns that cause contractures)

Other Health Impaired (OHI)	• Limited strength, vitality, or alertness, including a heightened alertness to environmental stimuli, that results in limited alertness with respect to the educational environment, that
	  • Is due to chronic or acute health problems such as
	    • Asthma
	    • Attention deficit disorder or attention deficit hyperactivity disorder
	    • Diabetes
	    • Epilepsy
	    • A heart condition
	    • Hemophilia
	    • Lead poisoning
	    • Leukemia
	    • Nephritis
	    • Rheumatic fever
	    • Sickle cell anemia
	    • Tourette syndrome
	• Adversely affects a child's educational performance

Visual Impairment (VI)	• Impairment in vision that, even with correction, adversely affects a child's educational performance • Includes both partial sight and blindness

(Continued)

TABLE 6.3. *(Continued)*

Federal Disability Category	Federal Description

Speech or Language Impairment (SLI)	• Communication disorder such as
	  • Stuttering
	  • Impaired articulation
	  • Language impairment
	  • Voice impairment
	• Adversely affects a child's educational performance

Traumatic Brain Injury (TBI)	• Acquired injury to the brain caused by an external physical force, resulting in total or partial functional disability or psychosocial impairment, or both
	• Applies to open or closed head injuries resulting in impairments in one or more areas, such as
	  • Cognition
	  • Language
	  • Memory
	  • Attention
	  • Reasoning
	  • Abstract thinking
	  • Judgment
	  • Problem solving
	  • Sensory, perceptual, and motor abilities
	  • Psychosocial behavior
	  • Physical functions
	  • Information processing
	  • Speech
	• *Does not* apply to brain injuries that are congenital or degenerative, or brain injuries induced by birth trauma

Specific Learning Disability (SLD)	• Disorder in one or more of the basic psychological processes involved in understanding or in using language, spoken or written
	• May manifest itself in the imperfect ability to
	  • Listen
	  • Think
	  • Speak
	  • Read
	  • Write
	  • Spell
	  • Do mathematical calculations
	• Includes conditions such as
	  • Perceptual disabilities
	  • Brain injury
	  • Minimal brain dysfunction
	  • Dyslexia
	  • Developmental aphasia
	• *Does not* include learning problems that are primarily the result of
	  • Visual disabilities
	  • Hearing disabilities
	  • Motor disabilities
	  • Intellectual disability
	  • Emotional disturbance
	  • Environmental, cultural, or economic disadvantage

> Pause and Reflect:
>
> Consider the vignette at the beginning of this chapter. What stage is Mr. Emmett in with Elijah? How do you know? What steps are next in the process? Who should Mr. Emmett involve in the current and remaining stages? What happens if Elijah is not eligible for special education and related services?

Eligibility for Specific Learning Disability

Nearly 35% of students who qualify for special education and related services fall under the category of SLD, making it the most prevalent disability category (U.S. Department of Education, 2023). In light of the widespread occurrence of SLD, there are additional regulations that govern eligibility. Additionally, IDEA provides states with the flexibility to add (not remove) procedures for identification and eligibility under SLD. IDEA stipulates that criteria adopted by the state (1) *must* permit the use of a process that evaluates a student's response to research-based interventions, (2) *must* be applied consistently, and (3) *may* permit the use of alternative, research-based methods for determination. However, states *cannot* establish criteria that require the use of a severe discrepancy between intellectual ability and achievement.

IDEA allows the determination of the existence of SLD if the assessment team determines (IDEA, Sec. 300.309)

(1) The student does not achieve adequately for their age to meet State-approved grade-level standards in one or more of the following areas: oral expression, listening comprehension, written expression, basic reading skill, reading fluency skills, reading comprehension, mathematics calculation, or mathematics problem solving;
AND

(2) The student does not make sufficient progress to meet State-approved grade-level standards when using appropriate assessments;
AND

(3) The findings are not the result of a visual, hearing, or motor disability, intellectual disability, emotional disturbance, cultural factors, environmental or economic disadvantage, or limited English proficiency.

As part of the evaluation for SLD, the public agency must ensure that the student is observed in their learning environment by at least one member of the team who is not the student's classroom teacher. For students eligible for special education under the category of SLD, IDEA requires a report to document the determination of eligibility that must be certified in writing by all team members. The report must include a statement about (IDEA Sec. 300.311)

- Whether the student has SLD
- The basis for making the determination
- Any relevant behavior noted during the observation
- The relationship of that behavior to their academic functioning
- The educationally relevant medical findings, if any
- The determination of the group concerning the effects of visual, hearing, motor disability, intellectual disability, or emotional disturbance
- The determination of the group concerning cultural factors, environmental or economic disadvantage, or the influence of limited English proficiency on their achievement level
- Whether the student is achieving adequately for their age or to meet grade level standards
- If the student participated in a process to assess their response to research-based intervention and the instructional strategies used and student-centered data collected

> Pause and Reflect:
> What must the interdisciplinary team do if Elijah is being considered for eligibility within the disability category of SLD?

Challenges and Best Practices

Variation in State Referral and Eligibility Criteria

Challenge: Federal guidelines include minimum standards but provide states with limited flexibility to establish their own eligibility criteria and identification processes by adding (not removing) requirements (U.S. Government Accountability Office, 2019). This flexibility can lead to variation in the referral and eligibility process, resulting in eligibility for services in one state but not another. Experts, advocates, and the media raised concerns about the variation in state referral and eligibility criteria, which in many states has led to the systematic delay or denial of special education services and the over- and underidentification of marginalized and minoritized students, including multilingual students.

These concerns led the U.S. Congress to request an audit of state systems for special education referral and eligibility by the U.S. Government Accountability Office in 2019. The audit found that the variation in referral and eligibility criteria existed across states and across districts within the same state. Significantly contributing to differences in the percentage of students receiving special education services were variations in procedural implementation, definitions of disability categories, identification and referral procedures, quality of RtI implementation, and guidance for eligibility decisions (U.S. Government Accountability Office, 2019).

Best practices: Even though educators may not be able to influence the variation across state or district lines, they can commit to ensuring consistency in their own adherence to referral and eligibility processes. To reduce or limit variation in implementation, educators can increase their knowledge of state or district referral and eligibility policies and procedures, advocate for students and their families, and center students in their practice.

School System Barriers

Challenge: The U.S. Government Accountability Office (2019) indicated that staffing limitations may impact the referral and eligibility process. When schools are facing shortages, especially in critical need areas, existing staff are burdened with additional workloads. The increased responsibility with limited resources may influence a classroom teacher's decision to refer a student for special education due to the increased paperwork, lengthy timelines (especially for the prereferral stage), limited access to resources, and budget constraints.

Best practices: To mitigate these barriers, classroom teachers can establish strong relationships for collaboration for a shared responsibility, participate in training and professional learning to improve systems and efficiency of the process, and advocate for access to resources and adequate budgets.

Parental/Caregiver Resistance

Challenge: When initiating the referral process, classroom teachers may be met with parental/caregiver resistance. Parents/caregivers' resistance can be rooted in culture, be emotionally driven, or stem from practical concerns. Cultural norms shape perspectives of disability and special education and may result in an unwillingness to provide consent for evaluation or for receiving special education services. Understandably, some parents/caregivers may be resistant due to an emotionally driven response that manifests as guilt, anger, or sadness and stems from a fear of labeling their child due to the associated stigma, a denial of disability, or previous negative experiences with special education. Practical concerns can also influence a parent/caregiver's decision to provide consent. Parents/caregivers may believe that additional or alternative interventions are needed or might be more effective than special education services. Concerns about the quality of special education services may arise, especially if parents/caregivers believe their child will be placed in a more restrictive setting and be held to lowered expectations.

Best practices: Addressing parent/caregiver concerns begins with building a relationship, establishing a welcoming environment, fostering open and respectful communication, and honoring cultural assets. By engaging in these practices, classroom teachers communicate that they value parent/caregiver agency and their participation in the decision-making.

Bias in Referral and Evaluation

Challenge: The referral and evaluation process is vulnerable to the influence of implicit bias. The subjectivity in the process can arise from educator perception, assessment interpretation, or ambiguity in federal or state guidance. Referrals originate at educator discretion, underscoring the significance of using culturally responsive instruction and assessment practices, evaluating the influence of the classroom environment on student learning, and ensuring the use of evidence-based instructional practices aligned with student need. Approximately 73% to 90% of students referred for special education are determined to be eligible (Fish, 2016; Harry & Klingner, 2006). Interpretation of evaluation results can lead to inequitable outcomes when influenced by implicit bias (unconscious judgment) or confirmation bias (asking questions that support existing diagnosis) (National Association of School Psychologists, 2017).

Best practices: To eliminate bias in the referral and evaluation process, educators can participate in targeted professional learning for cultural competence or bias workshops. Collaboration is also an effective approach for addressing bias. A team-based approach ensures multiple perspectives are considered and included in the decision-making process. Additionally, a data-driven approach is critical for reducing bias. When using multiple sources of objective and culturally responsive assessment results to drive decision-making, subjective judgment can be reduced.

> Pause and Reflect:
>
> What types of challenges could Mr. Emmett potentially encounter during the referral and eligibility process? What can Mr. Emmett do to mitigate the challenges? What types of challenges do you think Mr. Emmett will not encounter? Why?

HIGH-IMPACT: THE CONNECTION WITH HIGH-LEVERAGE PRACTICES

HLP 1: Collaborate with professionals to increase student success

HLP 2: Organize and facilitate effective meetings with professionals and families

HLP 3: Collaborate with families to support student learning and secure services

HLP 4: Use multiple sources of information to develop a comprehensive understanding of a student's strengths and needs

HLP 5: Interpret and communicate assessment information to collaboratively design and implement educational programs

HLP 6: Use student assessment data, analyze instructional practices, and make necessary adjustments that improve student outcomes

HLP 10: Conduct functional behavior assessments to develop individual student behavior support plans

HLP 11: Identify and prioritize long- and short-term learning goals

HLP 12: Systematically design instruction toward a specific goal

HLP 13: Adapt curriculum tasks and materials for specific learning goals

Review and Reflect

The referral and eligibility process paves the path for providing equitable access to special education and related services. Grounded in federal legislation and guided by state policy and procedures, the referral and eligibility process centers the student at each stage. By having a clear understanding of the requirements and criteria for eligibility, classroom teachers can make informed decisions that improve student outcomes.

Equally as important is understanding the potential challenges that can arise through the process and the best practices that can mitigate their impact. Classroom teachers are an integral part of the process and are often the originating source of the referral, underscoring the significance of building their skills for meaningful participation.

Guiding Questions

1. Who can initiate a referral for special education and related services?
2. Describe the stages of the referral and eligibility process and who is involved.
3. Why is the prereferral process a significant part of the eligibility process?
4. Explain IDEA's requirements for assessments used in the evaluation process.
5. What criteria has IDEA established for eligibility? What supplemental criteria are included for SLD eligibility?
6. Explain challenges to the referral and eligibility process.

Extend Your Learning

TABLE 6.4. *Resources*

Resource	Description	Link
Project IDEAL (Informing and Designing Education for All Learners)	Modules and videos for disability categories, attitudes, special education law, RtI	https://www.projectidealonline.org/
IRIS Center	Modules, tools, skill sheets, and information briefs for the prereferral process and perceptions of disability	https://iris.peabody.vanderbilt.edu/
National Center for Learning Disabilities	Briefs, reports, and fact sheets for SLD eligibility, learning disabilities, disproportionality, assessment, and federal data	https://ncld.org/

References

Berkeley, S., Bender, W.N., Gregg, L., & Saunders, L. (2009). Implementation of response to intervention: A snapshot of progress. *Journal of Learning Disabilities, 42,* 85–95.

Bradley, R., Danielson, L., & Doolittle, J. (2005). Response to intervention. *Journal of Learning Disabilities, 38,* 485–86. https://doi.org/10.1177/00222194050 380060201

Bradley, R., Danielson, L., & Doolittle, J. (2007). Responsiveness to Intervention: 1997 to 2007. *Teaching Exceptional Children, 39*(5), 8–12. https://doi.org/10 .1177/004005990703900502

Clark, A. (2021, June 9). 10 benefits of MTSS. *Shaped.* https://www.hmhco.com/blog/benefits-of-mtss

Fish, R. E. (2016). The racialized construction of exceptionality: Experimental evidence of race/ethnicity effects on teachers' interventions. *Social Science Research, 62,* 317–34. https://doi.org/10.1016/j.ssresearch.2016.08.007

Fuchs, L. S., & Fuchs, D. (2007). A model for implementing responsiveness to intervention. *Teaching Exceptional Children, 39*(5), 14–20.

Fuchs, L. S., Fuchs, D., & Zumeta, R. O. (2008). Response to intervention. In E. L. Grigorenko (Ed.), *Educating individuals with disabilities: IDEIA 2004 and beyond* (pp. 225–33). Springer.

Fuchs, L. S., & Vaughn, S. (2012). Responsiveness-to-intervention: A decade later. *Journal of Learning Disabilities, 45*(3), 195–203.

Harry, B., & Klingner, J. K. (2006). *Why are so many minority students in special education? Understanding race and disability in schools.* Teachers College Press.

Individuals With Disabilities Education Improvement Act. (2004). 20 U.S.C. § 1400 et seq.

IRIS Center. (2019). *IEPs: Developing high-quality individualized education programs.* https://iris.peabody.vanderbilt.edu/module/iep01/

IRIS Center. (2022). *The pre-referral process: Procedures for supporting students with academic and behavioral concerns.* https://iris.peabody.vanderbilt.edu/module/preref/#content

Learning Disabilities Association of America. (2013). *Right to an evaluation of a child for special education services.* https://ldaamerica.org/advocacy/lda-position -papers/right-to-an-evaluation-of-a-child-for-special-education-services/

Maryville, M. (2023, April 6). *Special education referrals.* National Education Association. https://www.nea.org/professional-excellence/student-engagement/tools-tips/special-education-referrals

National Association of School Psychologists. (2017). *Implicit bias: A foundation for school psychologists.* https://www.nasponline.org/resources-and-publications /resources-and-podcasts/diversity-and-social-justice/social-justice/implicit-bias-a -foundation-for-school-psychologists

Siegel, L., & Hurford, D. (2019). The case against discrepancy models in the evaluation of dyslexia. *Perspectives on Language and Literacy, 45*(1), 23–28.

Slanda, D. D., Pike, L. M., Herbert, L., Wells, E. B., & Pelt, C. (2022). Dismantling disproportionality in special education through antiracist practices. In T. M.

Mealy & H. Bennet (Eds.), *Equity in the classroom: Essays on curricular and pedagogical approaches to empowering all students* (pp. 218–64). McFarland.

U.S. Department of Education. (2023). *45th annual report to Congress on the implementation of the Individuals With Disabilities Education Act, 2023.* https://sites.ed.gov/idea/files/45th-arc-for-idea.pdf

U.S. Government Accountability Office. (2019). *Report to congressional requesters: Special education varied state criteria may contribute to differences in percentages of children served* (GAO-19-348). https://www.gao.gov/assets/gao-19-348.pdf

Vaughn, S., & Fuchs, L. S. (2003). Redefining learning disabilities as inadequate response to instruction: The promise and potential problems. *Learning Disabilities Research & Practice, 18*(3), 137–46.

7

The IEP

A Blueprint for Individualizing Instruction

The classroom teacher is an essential member of the team involved in developing and implementing an individualized education program (IEP) for a student with a disability. Nearly 70% of students with disabilities spend 80% of their day in the general education classroom (U.S. Department of Education, 2024). These data emphasize the pivotal role classroom teachers assume in the execution of the IEP, not only by providing accommodations and support but also by gathering performance data to monitor the student's progress toward annual goals. Therefore, it is important for classroom teachers to understand the specific tasks and responsibilities they hold as a member of the IEP team to ensure students with disabilities receive inclusive and equitable education to meet rigorous state standards. This chapter provides an overview of the classroom teacher's role in co-developing an IEP, implementing accommodations and evidence-based teaching practices, and collecting data related to student progress.

Chapter Objectives

After reading this chapter, students will be able to

- Explain the purpose of an IEP
- Describe the essential and required components of an IEP
- Describe the role of the classroom teacher in ensuring access to the general education curriculum for students with disabilities

- Describe the classroom teacher's responsibilities related to co-developing and implementing an IEP for a student with a disability
- Determine the classroom data and observational information needed to support the construction of data-driven goals for the IEP related to a student's academic or behavioral progress
- Select evidence-based instructional practices to deliver instruction and provide accommodations to students with disabilities

Key Terms

accommodation: An alteration made to the environment, curriculum format, or equipment that allows a student with a disability to access educational content or complete a task.

appropriate and measurable annual goal: An academic, behavioral, or social goal developed for a student based on their disability and designed to support their involvement and progress within the general education environment. The goal indicates what the student is reasonably expected to achieve within a 12-month period when provided appropriate special education services.

assistive technology (AT): Assistive technology is (1) a tool that addresses barriers to developing academic or functional skills and (2) an accommodation that helps students with disabilities access the general education curriculum (IRIS Center, 2010, 2020).

free appropriate public education (FAPE): All students, regardless of the severity of their disability, are entitled to a free appropriate public education under federal and state law. Schools and districts have the responsibility to provide an appropriate education, which includes special education and related services, and this must be provided without any financial burden to the parent or caregiver. This education must meet the unique needs of a student with a disability to support their preparation for further education, employment, and independent living.

IEP team: A team of individuals involved in co-constructing and implementing an IEP for a student with a disability. The IEP team must include parents/caregivers of the student, a classroom teacher, a special education teacher, a representative of the local education agency (LEA) who is qualified to supervise the provision of the IEP, an individual who can interpret the evaluation results and their implications for instruction, where appropriate the student with a disability, and other individuals invited by the parent/caregiver or agency with knowledge or expertise regarding the student.

- **inclusive education/inclusion:** Schools and classrooms where all children, including those with disabilities and diverse learning needs, learn together within the same space with equitable access to a continuum of support and services matched to their needs (UNESCO, 1994, 2015), providing individual learning goals, modifications, accommodations, and high expectations for students with disabilities to ensure access to the general education curriculum in the least restrictive environment.
- **individualized education program (IEP):** A formal, legally binding document that delineates the specially designed instruction, supports, and services required by a child with a disability to ensure their academic growth and success within a school setting. IDEA further defines an IEP as a "written statement for each child with a disability that is developed, reviewed, and revised in accordance with section 614(d)" (Section 602, 20 U.S.C. 1401[14]).
- **least restrictive environment (LRE):** A principle within IDEA (2004) intended to ensure students with disabilities are served in an environment with peers who are not disabled to the maximum extent appropriate. LRE is most commonly interpreted as the general education classroom.
- **modification:** A change made to the curriculum, content, or what a student is taught or expected to learn.
- **paraprofessional:** An educational support staff member who assists teachers by providing instructional, behavioral, and administrative support to meet the needs of all students.
- **present levels of academic achievement and functional performance (PLAAFP):** A comprehensive summary of the student's current levels of functioning. The statement describes the impact of the student's disability on their involvement in the general education curriculum, documents data related to the student's current levels of performance, describes the student's needs in all appropriate academic or functional skill areas, and is the basis for the development of annual goals and selection of special education services and supports required to meet the goals (IRIS Center, 2019).
- **progress monitoring:** The process of collecting and interpreting data to assess a student's performance and the effectiveness of instruction in relation to the student's progress toward an annual goal.
- **related services:** A service provided to a child with a disability to support their access to or benefit from special education (e.g., transportation, occupational therapy, interpreting services).
- **special education services:** Specially designed instruction and related services necessary to ensure a student with a disability receives an FAPE aligned with their IEP.

specially designed instruction (SDI): Instruction designed for a student with a disability that addresses their IEP, accounts for their disability, provides modifications or adaptations to content, and supports access to the general education curriculum (PROGRESS Center, 2024a).

transition plan: A plan comprised of (1) the student's postsecondary goals around education and training, employment, and independent living; (2) the student's current performance in these areas; and (3) the instruction and services in place to assist the student in taking steps to reach these goals. This must be included in a student's IEP starting at age 16 (age 14 in some states).

Vignette

As you read this chapter, consider what you have learned about the student, Travis, in the vignette provided below. Connect the information you learn about the IEP to Travis and his education. There will be prompts and examples related to Travis throughout the chapter.

Mr. Martinez is preparing for an IEP meeting to be held in two weeks. The meeting is for a student in his sixth grade math class, Travis. Travis is an energetic student who enjoys video games, computers, cooking, and science. He especially likes collaborating with peers or small groups to complete classroom assignments and activities. Travis has an IEP for a specific learning disability (SLD) called dyscalculia, which impacts his mathematical reasoning and computation skills. His most recent diagnostic evaluation shows Travis would benefit from interventions to build foundational skills he is missing to meet proficiency in mathematics. He has difficulty following a sequence of steps to solve multiple-step problems and often makes mistakes with basic multiplication and division facts (numbers under 10) and regrouping and borrowing in addition and subtraction. Travis does not like to be called on in class to give an answer, and during independent work time he requires additional prompting to stay on task and complete assignments. Some of Travis's IEP accommodations include the use of visuals and manipulatives, graph paper for writing and organizing math problems, additional time on assessments, previewed content, and guiding notes. He is also able to use a calculator for activities that do not assess his computation skills.

Mr. Martinez is collecting and analyzing data to provide input on Travis's progress to share during the upcoming IEP annual review meeting. Using this data, the special education teacher will revise Travis's annual goals. Mr. Martinez looks over his documentation notes for implementing Travis's accommodations and begins reviewing Travis's classroom data. These data include curriculum-based assessment scores, data from the computer-based mathematics assessment program the school uses (MathPrep) three times a year, and scores from his most recent state-required mathematics assessment.

What Is an IEP?

The Individuals With Disabilities Education Act (2004) federal law requires the development and implementation of an IEP for eligible students ages three to 21. An IEP is a written document that outlines specific details about the special education instruction, supports, and services an eligible student with a qualifying disability requires to make progress. An IEP is designed to meet the unique needs of each eligible student with a qualifying disability. The IEP serves as a roadmap ensuring eligible students have equitable access to the curriculum. Essentially, the IEP is a promise to the student for their education detailing how specialized instructional support personnel (SISP) leverage their strengths to meet academic, behavioral, and functional needs. To access the general education curriculum, students with disabilities may require additional support, related services, and specially designed instruction (SDI). Specific expectations and procedures for tracking the implementation of the program and student progress are also included.

The Classroom Teacher's Role in Developing IEPs

As an important member of the IEP team, the classroom teacher is legally responsible for the development and implementation of IEPs for their students with disabilities. The IEP team is a group of individuals involved in co-constructing and implementing an IEP for a student with a disability. Figure 7.1 displays the members of an IEP team required by IDEA (2004).

Each member of the IEP team is involved in collaborating to develop an IEP for a student with a disability. Each section below describes how the classroom teacher is involved in developing the listed section of the IEP.

FAPE and LRE

Components of the IEP are developed to ensure students make ambitious academic progress through a free appropriate public education (FAPE) regardless of their disability within the least restrictive environment (LRE). Because all students are guaranteed FAPE, IDEA ensures special education and related services are provided at no charge. Special education is tailored to address the individual needs of a student with a disability, preparing them for college, career, and community living.

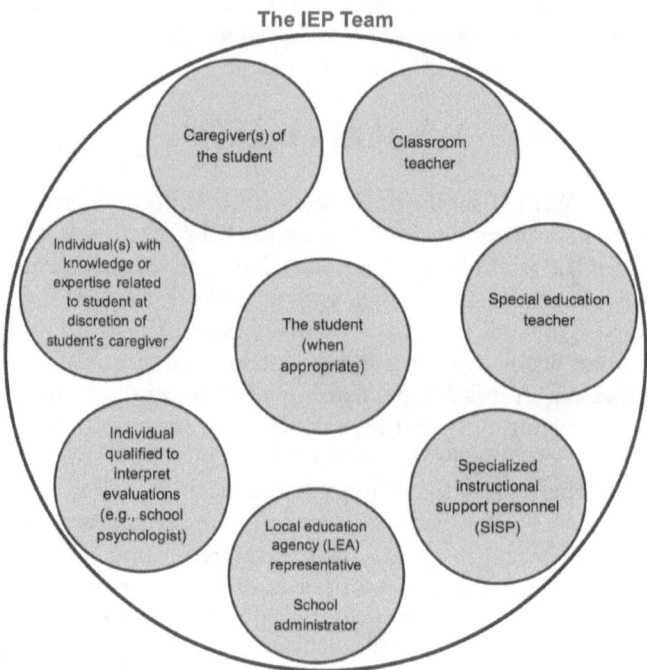

FIGURE 7.1. *IEP Team Members.*

Within IDEA, the LRE is a principle intended to ensure students with disabilities are educated with their peers who are not disabled to the maximum extent appropriate. IEPs must include a description of where services will be provided and if a student will receive any part of their education outside of the general education environment or separate from their nondisabled peers. The description must also include a rationale for why the student's educational needs cannot be met in the general education classroom through accommodations, SDI, or related services.

The classroom teacher is involved in the development, implementation, and monitoring of an IEP, making them essential to protecting a student's civil and educational rights. The classroom teacher's knowledge of students' academic and behavioral/social strengths and needs creates an important foundation for providing FAPE within the LRE. In collecting and sharing this information, the classroom teacher has detailed knowledge to support the development and implementation of a strong IEP and continuously monitor and adjust as needed to enhance and affirm access and progress.

The Endrew F. Supreme Court Ruling and IEP Standards

Although the IEP is guided by legislation (e.g., IDEA), the guidelines can sometimes be ambiguous due to the use of subjective terminology, leaving room for interpretation. To clarify terms, families, schools, or districts often turn to the judicial system, asking the courts to provide additional guidance. Sometimes litigation results in landmark court cases decided by the U.S. Supreme Court, which clarifies the rights of students with disabilities and further defines the responsibilities of educators and schools. One such court case was the *Endrew F. v. Douglas County School District*. In the Endrew F. case, the U.S. Supreme Court was asked the following question: to what extent must schools provide a free appropriate public education?

Endrew F. was a child with autism and attention deficit disorder who attended public school in Douglas County from kindergarten through fourth grade. During that time, Endrew failed to make academic and functional progress. In response, his parents withdrew him from public school and enrolled him in a private school, where he flourished academically and behaviorally. When Endrew's parents attempted to receive reimbursement for his private school expenses, the district refused, forcing the parents to file a lawsuit. Initially, the lower courts ruled in favor of the district, citing that Endrew's IEPs were created to provide an educational benefit that was *de minimis* (minor standard). The parents appealed the ruling to the U.S. Supreme Court, which would later rule that "to meet its substantive obligation under the IDEA, a school must offer an IEP reasonably calculated to enable a child to make progress appropriate in light of the child's circumstances" (*Endrew F. v. Douglas County School District*, 2017, p. 15). This ruling established a higher standard by clarifying what substantiates a free appropriate public education. To meet the FAPE requirement within IDEA, educators must furnish students with disabilities with an education designed to provide more than a minimum educational benefit (Yell & Bateman, 2017).

The Endrew F. case had profound implications for the development and implementation of IEPs. According to the U.S. Supreme Court, the IEP must be developed based on the unique needs of the student and must be *reasonably calculated* to enable the student to make meaningful progress. According to the IRIS Center (2024), for an IEP to be considered *reasonably calculated*, it must be developed by a team and take the following in to account: (1) the student's previous rate of academic growth, (2) the likelihood the student will achieve or exceed proficiency, (3) any behaviors impeding their progress, and (4) insights and contributions from the student's parents/caregivers. The U.S. Supreme Court underscored that although annual goals may vary, students must receive the necessary services and supports to achieve ambitious goals. As such, the IEP outlines a substantive education for students with disabilities, and classroom teachers play a crucial role in maintaining a high standard for that education.

Key Components of an IEP

The IDEA outlines eight requirements that must be included in an IEP and establishes an additional (eighth) requirement once the student reaches the age of transition. These components include

- Present levels of academic achievement and functional performance (PLAAFP) statement
- Appropriate (ambitious) and measurable annual goals
- Statement of special education services and supplementary aids and services
- Progress monitoring methods and reporting
- Explanation of educational setting
- Participation in statewide/district assessment
- Date of initiation, duration, frequency, and location of services
- Transition plan and age of majority

Figure 7.2 provides more information about each IEP component required by IDEA (2004). Each component will be discussed in detail below.

Connecting IEP Components for Consistency

Each element of the IEP serves an important purpose in forming an individualized, appropriate, and effective education plan for a student with a disability. The key components do not stand on their own but rather interconnect and inform each other in their development and implementation. Figure 7.3, from the PROGRESS Center (2024b), illustrates the connection between each key component of the IEP and the internal consistency they form. The student data and information presented in the PLAAFP directly inform the student's annual goals and the subsequent special education and related aids and services required for the student to make progress toward those goals. Similarly, data collected from monitoring student progress toward their goals is used to adjust goals or set new goals when they are met. When adjustments are made or new goals are set, the student's special education and aids and services may also change to align and provide support for the student in pursuing those goals. The student's special education and aids and services also determine their participation outside the general education curriculum

THE IEP

Present Levels of Academic and Functional Performance (PLAAFP) Statement	Appropriate (Ambitious) and Measurable Annual Goals	Statement of Special Education Services and Supplementary Aids and Services	Progress Monitoring Methods and Reporting	Explanation of Educational Setting	Participation in Statewide/District Assessment	Date of Initiation, Duration, Frequency, and Location of Services	Transition Plan and Age of Majority
summary of the student's present levels of academic achievement and functional progress	statement or multiple annual goals developed by the IEP team	description of special education services the student will receive, including specially designed instruction and accommodations/modifications	description or methods for monitoring and reporting the student's progress toward their annual goals	description and justification of any time the student will spend outside of the general education setting (the typical interpretation of the least restrictive environment [LRE])	information about student participation in district and statewide assessments	date when all special education services and supplementary aids and services will begin and end	required in a student's IEP starting at age 16 (14 in some states)
addresses all academic, behavioral, and functional areas	based on student data to support progress	description of related services that support access to and benefit from special education also listed in the IEP (e.g., occupational therapy, special transportation, or interpretation)	information about what types of assessments or documentation will be used and how and when this data will be reported to the IEP team, including a parent/guardian	statement of total time the student will be outside the general education environment	indication if the student will participate in alternative assessments	statement of how often the student will receive each service or aid	statement of the student's postsecondary goals for education and training, employment, and independent living
based on student data submitted by teachers and specialized instructional service personnel	goals must be measurable and ambitious			reasoning why providing accommodations and services within the general education classroom will not allow the student to progress toward their goals	list of any accommodations the student may need for participating in assessments	description of the location where each service or aid will be provided	description of the student's current performance in these areas
	supports the IEP team in determining if the IEP is providing meaningful educational benefit						description of instruction and services needed to assist the student in progressing toward goals, including needed linkages to community-based organizations
	benchmarks may be used as shorter-term indicators of progress toward the larger goal						

FIGURE 7.2. *Key Components of an IEP.*

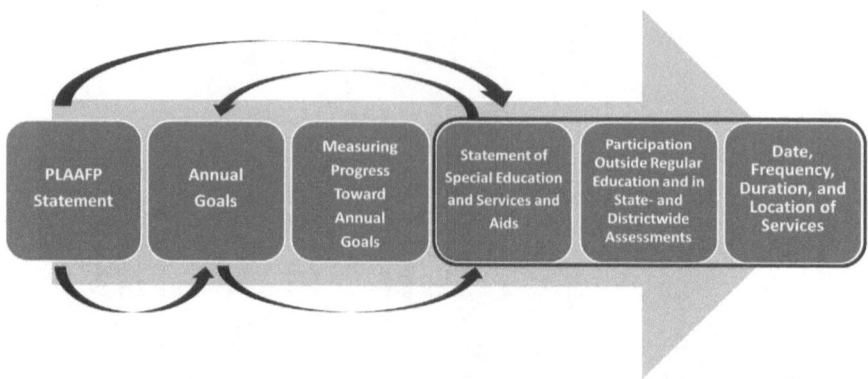

FIGURE 7.3. *Internal Consistency: Connecting the Parts of the IEP* (PROGRESS Center, 2024b). Public domain.

and classroom and in statewide and district assessments. Subsequently, the date, frequency, duration, and location of services are determined based on the types of services the student receives and where they can best be provided in their educational setting. The classroom teacher and all members of the IEP team are responsible for realizing this connection and consistency through their development of the program and their implementation of the IEP to serve and support the student.

Present Levels of Academic Achievement and Functional Performance (PLAAFP) Statement

The PLAAFP statement serves as the foundation for the rest of the IEP. The PLAAFP statement includes a summary of specific information and data related to all aspects of the student's education—academic areas, behavior, and functional skills (daily living, persona, social, and work skills), as appropriate. The classroom teacher supports the development of the PLAAF statement by providing data that can include results from diagnostic assessments and evaluations, formal and informal assessments, observations, student work samples, and other sources.

Prior to the IEP meeting, an elementary classroom teacher will share core content area data, including mathematics, reading, science, and social studies, as well as data for behavior and functional skills. At the secondary level, a classroom teacher will provide data related to their content area (e.g., science, social studies, language arts, mathematics) and related behavior and functional skills. During the IEP meeting, the data is used to collaboratively develop ambitious annual goals, identify accommodations and related services, and inform best approaches for monitoring progress and implementation of the IEP. Table 7.1 lists questions the IEP team can use to reflect on student performance.

TABLE 7.1. *Guiding Questions for IEP Development*

Questions to Consider and Respond To	Monitoring Progress
1. What are the student's strengths and abilities (academic, behavioral, functional)?	1. How will the student's progress be measured?
2. What are the student's difficulties and areas of need (academic, behavioral, functional)?	2. How often will the student's progress be measured?
3. What activities can the student complete without extra support?	3. Who is responsible for collecting the data?
4. In what activities does the student require additional support/services?	4. Where will the data collection occur?
5. What supports/services would be required?	5. When will the data collection occur?
6. How often should these supports/services be provided?	6. How will you know if the student achieved their goal?
7. How much time each day/week should the supports/services be provided?	
8. Who will provide the supports/services?	
9. Where will the supports/services be provided?	
10. When will the supports begin and end?	

Pause and Reflect:

Based on the information in the vignette about Travis at the start of the chapter, how do you think Travis's disability is impacting him in the classroom? What are Travis's strengths and areas of need in math class that Mr. Martinez should include as part of his input for the IEP meeting?

TABLE 7.2. *Key Components of an Annual IEP Goal*

Condition	The context or environment in which the target behavior(s) is to be exhibited; this may also include the measurement tool
Target Behavior	The academic, behavioral, or functional skills to be addressed
Performance Criterion	The level of performance that indicates that the goal was achieved
Time Frame	The length of time within which the student is expected to meet the performance criteria

Appropriate (Ambitious) and Measurable Annual Goals

IDEA (2004) requires IEPs to include a statement of measurable annual goals, including academic and functional goals, that will (1) meet the student's needs resulting from their disability and (2) enable the student to participate and make progress in the general education curriculum. When designed in this way, annual goals allow the IEP team to evaluate a student's educational progress and ensure the special education program provides a meaningful educational benefit. To develop annual goals, the IEP team analyzes, interprets, and synthesizes student data.

According to the IRIS Center (2024), annual goals must (1) address academic, behavioral, and functional needs set forth the PLAAF; (2) be aligned with grade level benchmarks and standards (or short-term assessment objectives for students taking alternative assessment); (3) describe what the student should be able to achieve in the next 12 months; and (4) be connected to supplemental aids and services. Aligning annual IEP goals with grade level benchmarks and standards ensures the participation of students with disabilities in the general education curriculum. Key components of an annual IEP goal are shared in table 7.2.

Writing an annual goal can prove to be difficult. Formulas can be used to assist with the process. To build capacity to write annual goals, review and reflect on the information on Javion.

TABLE 7.3. *Sample Annual Goals*

Javion is a third grade student at Casa Vista Elementary School. He is shy and enjoys learning about all kinds of animals. Javion has an IEP for a specific learning disability (SLD) that impacts his reading comprehension skills. Although data indicates Javion is reading on level, he struggles to comprehend the text. Specifically, data indicate that Javion struggles to correctly sequence story events and identify the main idea.

Javion's Annual IEP Goal for Reading: When given a grade-level nonfiction text, Javion will identify the main idea and provide at least three supporting details with 95% accuracy in three out of four trials.

Condition	Given a grade-level nonfiction text
Target Behavior/Skill	Javion will identify the main idea and provide at least three supporting details
Performance Criterion	95% accuracy in three out of four trials
Time Frame	Annual (by the end of the IEP duration)

> Pause and Reflect:
>
> Revisit the information and data provided for Travis in the vignette at the beginning of the chapter. What might be a measurable mathematics goal for Travis based on this information? What accommodations and instructional supports might Mr. Martinez provide to assist Travis in making progress toward this goal?

Statement of Special Education Services and Supplementary Aids and Services

An IEP details the special education services and supplementary aids and services (SAS) a student will receive. According to IDEA (2004), SAS are aids, services, and supports provided in the general education classroom that enable students with disabilities to be educated with their nondisabled peers to the greatest extent possible. All services included in the IEP are aligned with the PLAAFP statement, connected to the student's strengths and needs, and promote progress toward their academic and functional goals. There are three main types of SAS: instructional accommodations, instructional modifications, and other aids and services.

TABLE 7.4. *Types of Accommodations*

Accommodation Type	Purpose	Examples
Presentation	Provides access to curriculum through alternative means	• Read aloud or screen reader • Enlarged text • Multimedia
Response	Allows student to produce information and demonstrate knowledge/skills by alternative means	• Oral response instead of written • Voice-to-text or text-to-voice technology
Setting	Changes the setting/location where a student completes a task	• Quiet room/space • Flexible seating (standing desk, group table, area rug, etc.)
Timing and Scheduling	Adjusts when/how long a student has to complete a task	• Additional time • Frequent breaks

Note: Adapted from the IRIS Center (2024).

Instructional Accommodations

An instructional accommodation is an alteration made to the environment, format, or equipment that allows a student with a disability to access educational content or complete a task. Accommodations do not alter what a student learns but alter how a student accesses or demonstrates their learning. The four types of accommodations include presentation, response, setting, and timing and scheduling and are presented in table 7.4.

Instructional Modifications

Instructional modifications change what a student learns or is expected to learn. Modifications can influence the access a student has to the general education curriculum. Although some modifications may be appropriate for students with high-incidence disabilities such as SLD, they are often reserved for students with low-incidence disabilities such as an intellectual disability. Students with more severe and persistent cognitive disabilities often work toward a modified curriculum aligned with alternative standards, measured by alternative assessments, and result in an alternative diploma. Table 7.5 presents different types of modifications to content, instruction/production, and expectations and assessment (adapted from IRIS Center 2024).

TABLE 7.5. *Types of Modifications*

Modification Type	Examples
Content	• Alternative text • Alternative standards
Instruction/Production	• Student receives one-on-one or individualized instruction and support throughout the day from an educator or paraprofessional • Student asked to write two sentences instead of a whole paragraph to respond to a question. • Tasks mirror the general education curriculum but vary in difficulty. For example, a student practices addition and subtraction with single-digit problems instead of two-digit computations.
Expectations and Assessment	• Alternative assessments including projects • Reduced number of responses • Assessed for completeness rather than accuracy

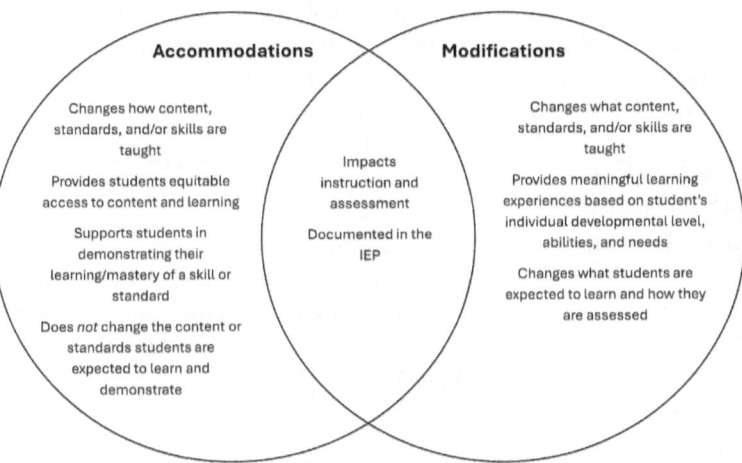

FIGURE 7.4. *Similarities and Differences between Accommodations and Modifications.*

Although the terms *accommodations* and *modifications* are often used interchangeably, they have vastly different definitions. Most predominantly, accommodations adjust *how* a student learns, while modifications change *what* a student learns. Figure 7.4 illustrates the similarities and differences between accommodations and modifications.

Assistive Technology

Assistive technology can be used to provide accommodations and supports to students with varying needs, allowing them to engage with the curriculum more effectively. Assistive technology (AT) is any device, equipment, or software designed to enhance the functional capabilities of individuals with disabilities or special needs, enabling them to perform tasks and activities they might otherwise struggle with, and aims to improve accessibility, communication, and independence. AT addresses the unique needs of students with and without disabilities, providing them with the necessary accommodations to access the curriculum and participate fully in the classroom (IRIS Center, 2010, 2020). Types of AT are typically categorized into high, medium, and low tech based on the complexity and sophistication of the devices and tools. Low-tech AT are simple, often nonelectronic devices that are easy to use and require minimal training. Medium-tech AT includes devices that involve some electronic components and require a certain level of training, but are less complex than high-tech options. High-tech assistive technologies are advanced devices that often incorporate complex electronics and software and usually require specialized training for effective use. Each level of assistive technology plays a crucial role in enhancing the independence and capabilities of individuals with disabilities, enabling them to access and participate more fully in the general education environment. Table 7.6 includes commonly used examples of low-, medium-, and high-tech AT and how they support learners.

> Pause and Reflect:
>
> Think about Mr. Martinez and his student Travis from the vignette at the start of the chapter. How might Mr. Martinez and the IEP team consider integrating assistive technology as a support for Travis? What are some specific examples of AT that might benefit Travis in accessing the curriculum and progressing toward his goals?

TABLE 7.6. *Examples of Assistive Technology*

Low-Tech AT	Medium-Tech AT	High-Tech AT
pencil grips: help individuals with fine motor difficulties to hold a pencil correctly, which improves their writing ability **math manipulatives:** physical objects such as base-ten blocks, number lines, or fraction bars that help students visualize and understand mathematical concepts **emotion cards:** cards with pictures or illustrations representing different emotions, which help students identify and discuss their feelings; these can be used in activities or therapy sessions to facilitate conversation about emotions	**digital hearing aids:** amplify sound for individuals with hearing impairments and can be programmed to suit the specific hearing loss profile of the user **calculators:** help users perform arithmetic calculations quickly and accurately, reducing cognitive load, and enhancing student ability to engage with mathematical concepts **social skills training apps:** software that offers interactive scenarios and exercises for students to practice social skills, conflict resolution, and empathy	**speech-to-text:** converts spoken words into written text using advanced algorithms and natural language processing, enabling students with physical disabilities or motor impairments to interact with computers and create documents efficiently **screen reader:** software that converts digital text displayed on a screen into synthesized speech or braille, enabling students with reading difficulties or visual impairments to access and interact with digital content **wearable biometric devices:** wearables, like watches, that monitor student's physiological signals such as heart rate and stress levels, offering real-time feedback for managing emotions

Other Aides and Services

Other aides and services refer to direct services and supports that are provided to a student based on their unique needs. Related services are provided to a student with a disability to support their access to or benefit from special education. Related services are provided by specialized instructional support personnel (SISP) and can include (but are not limited to) special transportation, speech/language therapy, occupational therapy, interpreting services, care provided by a school nurse, physical therapy, and counseling services. The classroom teacher collaborates with the SISP to ensure the student receives the appropriate services consistently and with fidelity. For example, the classroom teacher would need to coordinate with an occupational therapist who provides biweekly therapy sessions to a student in their class with motor skill challenges. A student with a

TABLE 7.7. Special Education, Supplementary Aids and Services, and Related Services in the IEP

Special Education Services

Specially Designed Instruction (SDI)	Frequency	Duration	Location
Support from a special education teacher in reading	3 times per week	30 minutes	General education classroom

Supplementary Aids and Services

Modification/Accommodation/Support for Student or Personnel	Frequency	Location
Directions provided orally	Daily	General education classroom and resource room
Directions repeated and clarified	Daily	General education classroom and resource room
Items and answer choices presented orally	Daily	General education classroom and resource room
Chunked instruction	Daily	General education classroom and resource room
100% extra time on assessments	Daily	General education classroom and resource room

Related Services

Service Type/ Description	Frequency	Duration	Location
Speech-language therapy	60 mins/week	09/01/2023–09/01/2024	Resource room

medical condition like multiple sclerosis might require the administration of medication throughout the day and support with toileting. The classroom teacher would need to coordinate with the school nurse to ensure the child receives their medication when needed and work with the nurse, paraprofessionals, or other support personnel to assist the student in the bathroom.

In addition to scheduling related services, the classroom teacher collaborates with SISP to inform instruction, assessment, and classroom practices. This collaboration enhances their understanding of the student and the progress they are making toward their annual goals. The classroom teacher can use this understanding to support the student, better understand their strengths and needs, and align expectations and strategies across classroom settings and activities. For example, if a student receives social skills instruction, the classroom teacher could collaborate with the behavior specialist to review student progress data, discuss student behaviors, and align classroom expectations with behavior supports. For a student receiving speech therapy, a classroom teacher could collaborate with the SLP to track student progress on speech goals, provide language and literacy supports, and connect skills acquired in speech therapy to classroom activities.

Although IEP formats may vary across states and districts, table 7.7 provides an example of SAS. Note that they are each listed with a location where they will be provided and their duration or frequency. Listing these details fulfills the seventh key component of an IEP.

Specially Designed Instruction

Specially designed instruction (SDI) is instruction designed for a student with a disability that addresses their IEP and accounts for their disability (PROGRESS Center, 2024a). SDI supports access to the general education curriculum, and accommodations, adaptations, or modifications may be included. Instructional practices, interventions, and supports provided through SDI are designed to address a student's academic, behavioral, and functional needs. The classroom teacher provides data to support the development and identification of appropriate SDI. The classroom teacher is also responsible for providing accommodations and modifications outlined in the IEP. Through SDI, the classroom teacher provides small group or individual instruction, opportunities for additional practice or enrichment, targeted skill instruction, and other supports to meet student needs. Examples of SDI include

- Teaching a student with a disability how to use a graphic organizer to support reading comprehension

- Providing a student with instruction and practice opportunities in self-management strategies and organizational skills
- The classroom teacher and special education teacher engaging in co-teaching models during instruction and learning activities to provide students with IEPs individualized support

> Pause and Reflect:
>
> Go back and review the information in the chapter vignette about Travis. As Mr. Martinez considers Travis's performance in his class so far this year, what additional accommodations or instructional practices might he recommend to support Travis's progress toward his goals?

Progress Monitoring Methods and Reporting

While a student receives special education or related services, the classroom teacher collects data to monitor the student's progress. Progress monitoring is the process of collecting and interpreting data to assess a student's performance and the effectiveness of instruction in relation to the student's progress toward annual goals. According to IDEA, IEP team members are required to collect progress monitoring data and report it to the team members, including the student's parents/caregivers, on a regular basis throughout the school year.

Progress monitoring data can include classroom-based assessments, work samples, district/statewide assessments, and intervention assessment probes. Progress monitoring data collected by the classroom teacher is directly related to the annual IEP goals. Classroom teachers may share the responsibility for delivering interventions in collaboration with the special education teacher. Evidence-based intervention curriculum includes progress monitoring assessment probes to frequently track student performance throughout the provision of intervention. Each assessment probe serves as a data point when graphing a student's progress related to their peers or in comparison to the benchmark or grade level performance criterion. Figure 7.5 illustrates how a progress monitoring data tracker might look. This Excel-based tool was created by the National Center on Intensive Intervention and is available for free to download on their website with instructions (https://intensiveintervention.org/resource/student-progress-monitoring-tool-data-collection-and-graphing-excel).

Data must be graphed to provide a visual representation of a student's progress and performance compared to their peers. Similar to the example in chapter 5, figure 7.6 provides an example of a progress monitoring graph. By collecting and graphing data on student progress, the classroom teacher supports the development, refinement, or changing of goals, accommodations, modifications, or services in a student's IEP.

Graph #	Last Name	First Name	Grade	Tested Measure	Tested Grade	Tested Benchmark	Tested ROI	Start Date	Weeks Left	Week 1	Week 2	Week 3	W
1	Ramirez	Marcus	2	Computation	2	19	0.7	9/10/15	30	8	4	5	
				Maze	2	25	0.8	2/19/16	15	7	9	6	
				WIF	2	32	1.4	3/2/16	12	15	17	16	

Graph #	Last Name	First Name	Grade	Tested Measure	Tested Grade	Tested Benchmark	Tested ROI	Start Date	Weeks Left	Week 1	Week 2	Week 3	W
2	Doe	Jane	3	Maze	3	22	0.9	5/11/15	16	5	5	5	
				Computation	2	30	1.0	6/13/15	13	8	8	8	
				WIF	3	33	1.3	4/2/15	9	20	20	21	

Graph #	Last Name	First Name	Grade	Tested Measure	Tested Grade	Tested Benchmark	Tested ROI	Start Date	Weeks Left	Week 1	Week 2	Week 3	W
3	Camper	Happy	3	Maze	3								
				Computation	3								
				WIF	2								

Graph #	Last Name	First Name	Grade	Tested Measure	Tested Grade	Tested Benchmark	Tested ROI	Start Date	Weeks Left	Week 1	Week 2	Week 3	W
4													

Graph #	Last Name	First Name	Grade	Tested Measure	Tested Grade	Tested Benchmark	Tested ROI	Start Date	Weeks Left	Week 1	Week 2	Week 3	W
5													

FIGURE 7.5. *NCII Progress Monitoring Data-Collection Excel.*

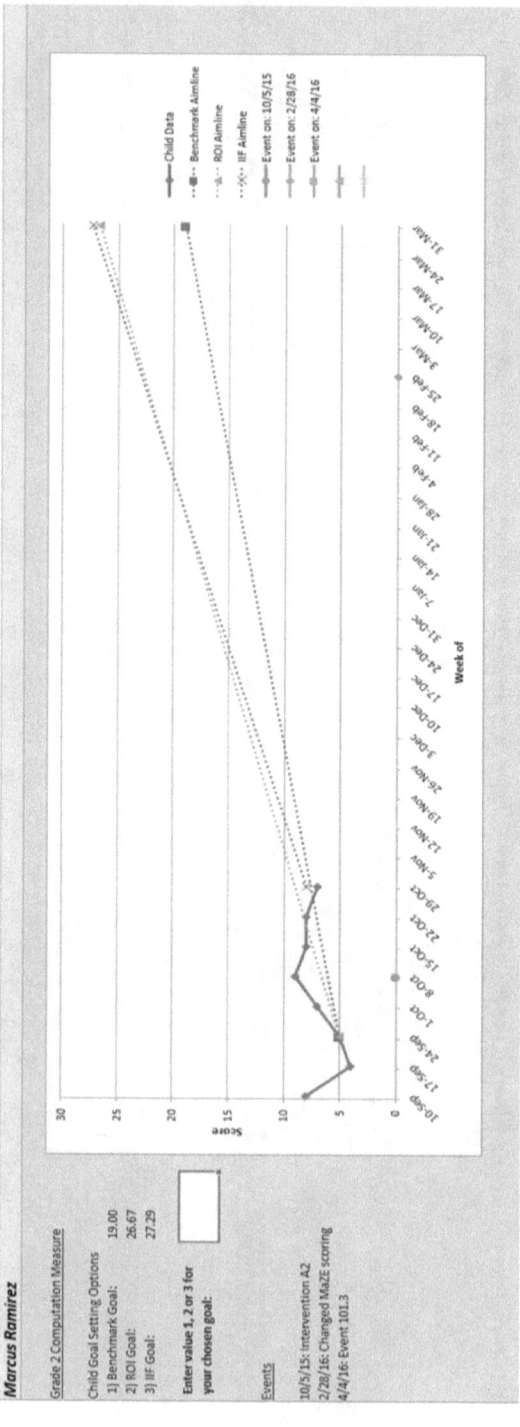

FIGURE 7.6. *Example Progress Monitoring Graph.*

> Pause and Reflect:
> Review the vignette about Travis and the chapter section on writing annual measurable goals. Once Mr. Martinez has an annual measurable goal in mathematics for Travis, what kinds of data should he collect to monitor Travis's progress?

LRE Statement

An IEP must include a statement about the extent to which a student with a disability will *not* be educated with nondisabled students in the general education setting. The LRE statement is intentionally phrased in a negative way to elicit a rationale for the time a student spends in a more restrictive setting. In other words, educators are forced to explain why they are choosing to remove a student from the general education classroom. The LRE statement must include the percentage of total instructional time expressed in minutes and the frequency at which the student will be educated outside the general education classroom.

The classroom teacher plays an integral role in the provision of education in the LRE for students with disabilities. Their commitment to inclusion, advocacy for students, implementation of evidence-based practices and supports, and effective collaboration is a cornerstone in advancing fully inclusive education in the LRE.

Participation in State and District Assessments

Both ESSA (2015) and IDEA (2004) require students with disabilities to be included in state and district assessments. Participation in accountability measures ensures students with disabilities receive access to high-quality instruction. An IEP includes a statement about the student's participation in the state and district assessments. Students who will earn a standard diploma must participate in the same standards-based assessments completed by their peers. Students working toward an alternative diploma may participate in an alternative assessment. However, no more than 1% of students will utilize alternative assessments (ESSA, 2015).

Because a majority of the students with disabilities take the same standards-based assessments as their peers, they must have equitable access. Classroom teachers share in the responsibility for preparing students with disabilities to show proficiency on these assessments by making the curriculum and assessments accessible. For access to the assessment, students may receive additional time, preferential setting (separate and less distracting environment), assessment directions, items, and answer choices read aloud, and other accommodations listed in their IEP.

Transition Plan

According to the National Technical Assistance Center on Transition (n.d.), transition planning is the "intentional, organized and coordinated process of guiding young people with disabilities with education, experiences, supports and services to help them have successful and meaningful lives beyond high school." Successful transition planning is dependent on the collective commitment of IEP team members to help a student achieve their postsecondary goals. Even though postsecondary outcomes should be considered throughout the life of an IEP, federal guidance requires a transition plan to begin with the first IEP in effect when a student turns 16 and continues until the student exits high school. However, transition plans can be included in an IEP prior to age 16 if the IEP team member deems it appropriate or necessary. Given the significance of reduced postsecondary outcomes for students with disabilities, some states have policies that require transition planning to begin at age 14.

Transition plans are not separate plans but are a significant part of the IEP when a student is of age. To assist students achieve their postsecondary goals, a transition plan outlines how a student will transition from K–12 education to postsecondary life. Plans must include measurable goals in three areas: (1) education and training, (2) employment, and (3) independent living. In addition, a transition plan must state the student's current level of performance in each of these areas (education/training, employment, independent living) and describe the instruction and services that will be delivered to help the student reach these goals. The IEP team works with the student to identify postsecondary education, employment, and living goals and then designs a cumulative plan across their secondary education (middle/high school) to ensure they receive the education, training, and experiences necessary to reach them after high school. Postsecondary goals might include college and a career requiring a four-year or advanced degree, vocational or technical training, employment skills, and independent living and life skills. Annual goals for transition should support meeting objectives related to the student's postsecondary goal.

As with all elements in an IEP, the transition plan should be based on data from a variety of evidence-based, developmentally appropriate transition assessments designed to determine the student's interests, goals, current strengths, and areas of need. Transition plans can vary in complexity. Goals and supports for functional and independent living skills will vary depending on the profoundness of the student's disability. Table 7.8 provides an example of a student's postsecondary goals for education/training,

TABLE 7.8. *Sample Transition Plan With Example Goals and Activities*

Serena (16 years old): Using data from the Transition Planning Inventory administered by the special education teacher, Serena wants to pursue a career working with animals, work in a pet store, and live independently in an apartment with a roommate.

Transition Plan Area	Sample Postsecondary Goal	Sample Activity for Annual Goal
Postsecondary education and training	Within one year of graduating high school, Serena will successfully enroll in a postsecondary program at a local college to pursue a certification as a veterinary technician.	Serena will meet with the guidance counselor to identify two postsecondary programs at local colleges that offer veterinary technician certification. Serena will meet with the guidance counselor to discuss academic requirements of pursuing postsecondary certification at a local college. Serena will enroll in academic classes that will prepare her for postsecondary education.
Employment	Within one year of graduating high school, Serena will be employed part-time at a local pet store.	Serena will develop a career portfolio to compile all vocational-related materials. Serena will participate in three career trips to area pet stores. Serena will develop a resume.
Independent living	Within two years of graduating high school, Serena will live in an apartment with a roommate.	Serena will identify personal medical management needs. Serena will demonstrate appropriate use of household appliances. Serena will demonstrate her ability to locate and purchase items in a store for meal preparation.

employment, and independent living. The table also shares examples of activities the school and community can provide to prepare the student for postsecondary life.

The requirement to include a transition plan as part of an IEP was developed partially in response to the persistent barriers faced by individuals with disabilities that resulted in low employment rates and prevented access to postsecondary education and training. Although the employment rate for individuals with disabilities has increased since 2008 (when these data first began being collected), individuals without disabilities were still three times more likely to be employed than individuals with disabilities (U.S. Bureau of Labor Statistics, 2023). Similarly, in 2023 only about half the number of individuals with disabilities held a bachelor's degree when compared to individuals without disabilities (20% vs. 41%, respectively) (Welding, 2023). Barriers to postsecondary employment and education often translate to reduced access to health care and earning potential as well as contribute to other diminished postsecondary outcomes.

Section 504: Protecting Students With Disabilities

Section 504 is part of the Rehabilitation Act of 1973, one of the first U.S. civil rights laws to protect individuals with disabilities. Governed by the Office of Civil Liberties, Section 504 prohibits discrimination against an individual with a disability and prohibits schools from discriminating against students on the basis of their disability. Similar to IDEA, Section 504 upholds a student's right to a free appropriate education (FAPE). Specifically, Section 504 prevents schools from excluding students from programs, experiences, facilities, benefits, activities, or services that are provided to students without disabilities.

Students who are eligible for special education services as defined by IDEA (2004) are also protected under Section 504. However, not all students with disabilities who are protected under Section 504 are eligible for special education services under IDEA. Although IDEA and Section 504 protect the rights of students with disabilities, there are some notable differences. First, IDEA is an education law and falls within the scope of the U.S. Department of Education. In contrast, Section 504 is governed by the Office of Civil Rights. In addition, IDEA and Section 504 differ in how they define disability. IDEA defines a child with a disability as a child who has been evaluated in accordance with Sections 300.304 through 300.311, has one of the recognized 13 disability categories (i.e., intellectual

TABLE 7.9. *Comparing IEPs and 504s*

IEP	Both	504
• Governed by IDEA • Applies to students in K–12 • Must have one or more of the 13 disabilities recognized by IDEA • Provides specially designed instruction and related services • Requires parent/caregiver participation • Includes measurable annual goals and requires progress monitoring	• Prohibits discrimination on the basis of disability • Protects students' right to FAPE • Provides accommodations with documented need	• Governed by Section 504 of the Rehabilitation Act • Applies to students in K–12 and postsecondary settings • No formal list of disabilities • Does not provide special education or related services • Does not require parent/caregiver participation • Does not include annual goals or require progress monitoring

disability, hearing impairment/deafness, speech language impairment, visual impairment/blindness, emotional disturbance, orthopedic impairment, autism, traumatic brain injury, other health impairment, specific learning disability, deaf-blindness, multiple disabilities, and developmental delay), and requires special education and related services. On the other hand, Section 504 defines disability as a physical or mental impairment that substantially limits one or more major life activities. According to the Office of Civil Rights, a physical or mental impairment is defined as

> any physiological disorder or condition, cosmetic disfigurement, or anatomical loss affecting one or more of the following body systems: neurological; musculoskeletal; special sense organs; respiratory, including speech organs; cardiovascular; reproductive; digestive; genitourinary; hemic and lymphatic; skin; and endocrine; or any mental or psychological disorder, such as intellectual disabilities, organic brain syndrome, emotional or mental illness, and specific learning disabilities. (34 C.F.R. 104[j][2][i])

To be protected under Section 504, the student must have a record of the impairment or be regarded as having such an impairment. Table 7.9 summarizes the similarities and differences between an IEP and a 504.

> **HIGH-IMPACT: THE CONNECTION WITH HIGH-LEVERAGE PRACTICES**
>
> **HLP 1:** Collaborate with professionals to increase student success
>
> **HLP 2:** Organize and facilitate effective meetings with professionals and families
>
> **HLP 3:** Collaborate with families to support student learning and secure services
>
> **HLP 4:** Use multiple sources of information to develop a comprehensive understanding of a student's strengths and needs
>
> **HLP 5:** Interpret and communicate assessment information to collaboratively design and implement educational programs
>
> **HLP 6:** Use student assessment data, analyze instructional practices, and make necessary adjustments that improve student outcomes
>
> **HLP 10:** Conduct functional behavior assessments to develop individual student behavior support plans
>
> **HLP 11:** Identify and prioritize long- and short-term learning goals
>
> **HLP 12:** Systematically design instruction toward a specific goal

Review and Reflect

The IEP serves as both a roadmap and a source of accountability to support the academic, behavioral, functional, and postsecondary outcomes of students with disabilities. The classroom teacher plays an integral role on the IEP team, including in development, implementation, and monitoring. Given their critical role throughout the IEP process, classroom teachers *are* special educators, making them important contributors to the inclusive and equitable education of students with disabilities. Having a strong understanding of the legal foundation of the IEP, the required components, and how it is implemented ensures classroom teachers can provide the best instruction, support, and learning opportunities to all students.

Guiding Questions

1. In your own words, list and describe the required components of an IEP. Who is involved in developing it?
2. What is the purpose of an IEP?
3. Identify which HLPs are connected with the development and implementation of an IEP. Describe how these HLPs align.

4. Think about the role of the classroom teacher in the development and implementation of an IEP. In your opinion, what are the three most important roles or responsibilities of a classroom teacher? Describe why you think they are the most important.
5. What is something you learned about the classroom teacher's role and responsibilities for a student's IEP that you did not know before? Did you learn anything surprising or unexpected?

Extend Your Learning

TABLE 7.10. *Resources*

Resource	Description	Link
IRIS Center	"IEPs: Developing High-Quality Individualized Education Programs"	https://iris.peabody.vanderbilt.edu/module/iep01/
PROGRESS Center	"IEP Tip Sheet Series"	https://promotingprogress.org/resources/iep-tip-sheet-series
National Center on Intensive Intervention (NCII)	Progress monitoring	Academic: https://charts.intensiveintervention.org/aprogressmonitoring?_ga=2.168976930.2089777127.1675199164-1286360179.1522772112#content Behavioral: https://charts.intensiveintervention.org/bprogressmonitoring

References

Bateman, D. F., & Cline, J. L. (2016). *A teachers' guide to special education.* Association for Curriculum Development.
Endrew F. v. Douglas County School District. (2017). 798 F. 3d 1329 (10th Cir.).
Every Student Succeeds Act. (2015). Public Law 114-95, 114th Cong., 1st sess.
Individuals With Disabilities Education Improvement Act. (2004). 20 U.S.C. § 1400 et seq.
IRIS Center. (2010, 2020). *Assistive technology: An overview.* https://iris.peabody.vanderbilt.edu/module/at/
IRIS Center. (2019). *IEPs: Developing high-quality individualized education programs.* https://iris.peabody.vanderbilt.edu/module/iep01/

IRIS Center. (2024). *Accessing the general education curriculum: Inclusion considerations for students with disabilities.* https://iris.peabody.vanderbilt.edu/agc

National Technical Assistance Center on Transition. (n.d.). *Transition planning.* https://transitionta.org/topics/secondary-education/transition-planning/

PROGRESS Center. (2024a). *IEP tip sheet: What is special education? A focus on specially designed instruction.* American Institutes for Research. https://promotingprogress.org/sites/default/files/2021-05/SDI_IEP_Tips.pdf

PROGRESS Center. (2024b). *Back to basics how the IEP helps to promote progress for students with disabilities.* American Institutes for Research. https://promotingprogress.org/news-events/prepping-progress-event-2024.

Section 504 of the Rehabilitation Act. (1973). 29 U.S.C. 28 CFR 35.104.

UNESCO. (1994). *The Salamanca statement and framework for action on special needs education.* World Conference on Special Needs Education. https://unesdoc.unesco.org/ark:/48223/pf0000098427

UNESCO. (2015). *Incheon declaration: Education 2030; Towards inclusive and equitable quality education and lifelong learning for all.* https://uis.unesco.org/en/document/education-2030-incheon-declaration-towards-inclusive-equitable-quality-education-and

U.S. Bureau of Labor Statistics. (2023). *Persons with a disability: Labor force characteristics summary* (Economic News Release USDL-23-0351). https://www.bls.gov/news.release/disabl.nr0.htm

U.S. Department of Education. (2024). *45th annual report to Congress on the implementation of the Individuals with Disabilities Education Act.* https://sites.ed.gov/idea/2023-individuals-with-disabilities-education-act-annual-report-to-congress/

Welding, L. (2023, March 29). *Students with disabilities in higher education: Facts and statistics.* Best Colleges. https://www.bestcolleges.com/research/students-with-disabilities-higher-education-statistics/

Yell, M. L., & Bateman, D. F. (2017). *Endrew F. v. Douglas County School District* (2017) FAPE and the US Supreme Court. *Teaching Exceptional Children, 50*(1), 7–15.

Yell, M. L., Bateman, D. F., & Shriner, J. G. (2021). *Developing educationally meaningful and legally sound IEPs.* Rowman & Littlefield.

8

Access and Equity by Design

Students with disabilities exhibit a wide range of academic, behavioral, and social skills. Further contributing to diversity in a learner's profile is their background, cultural values, personal interests, previous skill acquisition, and learning preferences. Although these factors are unique to each individual learner, evidence- and research-based practices such as differentiated instruction, universal design for learning, high-leverage practices, and culturally inclusive pedagogies and practices can promote equitable access to the general education curriculum. Understanding a learner's profile allows the classroom teacher to match a student's strengths and needs with impactful instructional practices.

Chapter Objectives

After reading this chapter, readers will be able to

- Explain differentiated instruction and identify the instructional elements for differentiation, including environment, content, process, and product
- Distinguish between differentiated instruction and specially designed instruction
- Define universal design for learning and explain each of the guiding principles (engagement, representation, and action and expression)
- Analyze culturally inclusive pedagogies and practices and explain differences across culturally relevant pedagogy, culturally responsive teaching, and culturally sustaining pedagogy

Key Terms

culturally inclusive pedagogy and practice (CIPP): Practices that consider cultural context, content, and constructs and how they interact to influence education and life-centered outcomes (Aceves & Kennedy, 2024).

culturally relevant pedagogy (CRP): Culturally relevant pedagogy is a theoretical framework that affirms students' cultural identity by fostering academic success, promoting cultural competence, and encouraging critical consciousness (Ladson-Billings, 1995).

culturally responsive teaching (CRT): Culturally responsive teaching is a research-based teaching approach that actively connects and integrates students' cultural backgrounds, cultures, languages, and experiences with their learning and the curriculum (Gay, 2002).

culturally sustaining pedagogy (CSP): Culturally sustaining pedagogy is a strengths-based approach that moves beyond integrating diverse identities in the classroom by centering and sustaining the cultural and linguistic identities, experiences, ways of knowing, and expertise of diverse students, parents/caregivers, and communities (Paris & Alim, 2017).

differentiated instruction: Differentiated instruction is a proactive approach to improving student outcomes and meeting learner diversity by adjusting content, process, or product.

flexible grouping: Flexible grouping is an asset-based, culturally responsive, and data-driven strategy that uses both heterogenous groups (students with varied strengths, interests, preferences, and needs) and homogenous groups (students with similar strengths, interests, preferences, and needs) (IRIS Center, 2010).

universal design for learning (UDL): A scientifically valid framework for guiding educational practice that provides flexibility in the ways students are engaged, the ways information is presented, and the ways students respond or demonstrate knowledge and skills. UDL reduces barriers in instruction; provides appropriate accommodations, supports, and challenges; and maintains high achievement expectations for all students, including students with disabilities and multilingual learners (CAST, 2024; IRIS Center, 2023).

Vignette

As you read this chapter, connect the information you learn about access and equity in the general education curriculum to Mr. Hill, his class, and his upcoming lesson described in the vignette below. There will be prompts and examples related to Mr. Hill and his class throughout the chapter.

Mr. Hill is a fifth grade teacher at Booker T. Washington Elementary School, a Title 1 urban public school with a diverse population of students. The school serves a multicultural student population, including families with heritage from Cuba, the Dominican Republic, Haiti, and other Caribbean nationalities, and the overwhelming majority of students are multilingual.

Mr. Hill plans to deliver a lesson to his fifth grade students on the impact adjectives can have on a reader. Aligned with grade level standards, the learning objective requires students to demonstrate their ability to write a short paragraph that correctly includes multiple adjectives to create imagery that appeals to the senses. During the lesson, Mr. Hill will ask students to compare text with sensory descriptors against text without sensory descriptors. Once students demonstrate understanding of adjectives and how they contribute to producing imagery for the reader, Mr. Hill will share a basic paragraph void of descriptive language. Students will work collaboratively to add descriptive language to the paragraph.

Mr. Hill recently took an online professional learning module where he learned strategies to provide access to the general education curriculum to his students with disabilities. When planning lessons, Mr. Hill wonders how he can implement his recent learning about access and select aligned evidence-based practices to support his students to meet the learning objective.

Promoting Access to the General Education Curriculum

At the foundation of IDEA is the promise of a free appropriate public education. Realizing this promise begins with high expectations. By having high expectations, students with disabilities can work toward ambitious and meaningful goals that are standards based and data driven. These goals can only be achieved when provided with equal opportunity and access to the general education curriculum. All teachers are responsible for providing access, which includes eliminating barriers and delivering specially designed instruction, related services, and supports (including accommodations) detailed in a student's individualized education program (IEP). In addition, teachers can eliminate barriers and provide access by engaging in various evidence-based instructional practices that underpin an inclusive and equitable education, including differentiated instruction, universal design for learning, high-leverage practices, and culturally inclusive pedagogies and practices. When implemented consistently and with fidelity, these practices promote meaningful participation in the general education curriculum within the least restrictive environment (LRE).

Universal Design for Learning

Universal design for learning (UDL) is a framework for guiding educational practice based on the science of learning. According to CAST, the goal of UDL is to proactively remove and reduce barriers to learning. This framework emphasizes flexibility and providing multiple methods for student *engagement*, *representation* of information, and student *action and expression* of learning (CAST, 2024). The UDL principles create inclusive and meaningful ways for students to access their learning in a flexible environment.

Through this flexibility, UDL reduces barriers in instruction; increases student engagement; provides appropriate accommodations, supports, and challenges; and maintains high expectations for all students, including students with disabilities and students who are multilingual learners (Higher Education Opportunity Act, 2008). Classroom teachers can utilize UDL principles to develop instructional methods, resources, activities, and assessment materials to support a broad spectrum of learner variability in their classroom. This includes differences in how students see, hear, communicate, move, read, write, attend to tasks, organize, engage, and recall. Content, materials, and instructional activities developed using UDL offer multiple options for teachers to engage students, provide instruction, and support student action and expression of their knowledge and skills toward curriculum- and standards-aligned learning opportunities. Using UDL as a framework for providing access to the general education curriculum ensures all learners work toward high expectations aligned with established learning standards. Table 8.1 describes the UDL principles and provides examples of each.

By integrating UDL principles into teaching practices, classroom teachers can proactively address barriers to learning, foster a culture of equity, and empower all students to achieve academic success (Fritzgerald, 2020). UDL promotes multiple means of engagement, encouraging teachers to provide options that motivate and sustain student interest and ensuring that all learners feel valued and connected. It also advocates for the provision of multiple means of representation, allowing educators to present content in various formats to accommodate diverse learning profiles and preferences. Additionally, UDL supports multiple means of action and expression, enabling students to demonstrate their understanding and knowledge in ways that best suit their abilities and strengths.

> Pause and Reflect:
>
> Based on the information in the vignette about Mr. Hill and his class, how could he apply the principles of UDL as he develops his lesson plan? What are some examples of multiple methods of engagement, representation, and action and expression he could provide to meet the strengths and needs of all of his students?

TABLE 8.1. *UDL Principles*

Principle	Description/Examples
Engagement: Why of learning	• Adapt how students engage with their learning environment and the content • Increase student motivation to learn • Customize the learning environment • Incorporate real-world examples • Vary resources • Tier activities
Representation: What of learning	• Connect learning to students' backgrounds and experiences • Display or deliver content in multiple ways • Solicit varied ways for students to interact with content • Present content in various formats (e.g., digital media) • Use explicit instruction • Provide graphic organizers or semantic maps • Clarify vocabulary or symbols • Use technology for vocabulary development • Use analogies to connect with learning and prior knowledge
Action and Expression: How of learning	• Build fluency with fading supports • Vary methods of response during and after instruction • Provide alternatives in assessment (e.g., projects, portfolios) • Integrate digital media in assessment • Provide manipulatives or other task-specific tools

Note: Adapted from CAST (2024).

Differentiated Instruction

Differentiated instruction is the systematic planning and implementation of educational experiences tailored to meet each student's unique needs by recognizing and leveraging their strengths while supporting their challenges (Tomlinson, 2003). It is a student-centered approach using intentional design to help every student achieve their highest potential (O'Meara, 2010). This proactive and equity-driven approach is not a straightforward process but a dynamic one with key decisions and adjustments made along the way. Differentiated instruction is used both in planning and delivery, focusing on students' relationship to the content. It requires teachers to know their students well and use knowledge of student strengths, interests, backgrounds, and needs in their planning. The goal of differentiated instruction is to promote access to learning by providing effective support to meet curriculum standards and learning goals. The process includes specific steps to create an inclusive learning environment that respects learner variability and promotes equity (Herner-Patnode & Lee, 2021; Tomlinson, 2003). To differentiate instruction, teachers

1. Examine learning standards and identify the facts, skills, and concepts students need to learn (IRIS Center, 2010).
2. Determine what knowledge and skills students must show to demonstrate progress and mastery.
3. Design activities for students to engage with the content and create assessments to measure their learning and mastery.

In addition to supporting academic progress, differentiated instruction also supports students' social development and learning (CASEL, 2018) by creating a responsive and inclusive classroom environment that fosters emotional well-being, resilience, and positive relationships (Duquette, 2022). For example, differentiated instruction builds a positive classroom atmosphere through offering flexible seating arrangements and creating quiet spaces for independent work, making students feel safe and valued. Differentiated instruction supports students in self-awareness, self-management, and responsible decision-making through personalized learning goals, flexible pacing, and student choice. Group projects, peer discussions, and other collaborative learning activities promote social awareness and relationship skills. Culturally relevant materials and resources based on student interests foster respect for diversity and learner variability. Tailored support, like scaffolding challenging tasks, helps students manage their emotions and develop resilience, while positive feedback builds a growth mindset. In these ways, differentiation supports both the academic and social-emotional development of all students.

Differentiation of Instructional Elements

Classroom teachers can differentiate across four instructional elements: environment, content, process, and product. Table 8.2 describes each element and provides examples and guiding questions that can be used to inform their implementation.

TABLE 8.2. *Domains of Differentiated Instruction*

Instructional Element	Examples
Environment *Where a student learns* The physical and psychological aspects of the classroom that influence learning	Teachers adjust the learning environment by • arranging flexible seating • providing quiet spaces/headphones for independent work • connecting to students' cultural capital • including student voice and choice • communicating high expectations • developing structures, routines, and procedures
Content *What is taught* The standards-based knowledge and skills a student is expected to master	Teachers adjust content by • scaffolding of prerequisite skills • building background knowledge • scaffolding and modeling • providing enrichment or extension activities • using varied instructional and curricular materials • incorporating multicultural materials • including images, videos, podcasts, and other multimedia
Process *How learning is structured* The activities and methods that lead to student learning and mastery of content	Teachers adjust content delivery by • delivering explicit instruction • providing tiered learning activities • using varied instructional strategies • offering choices in how students engage with the material (e.g., through discussions, role-playing, or experiments) • pairing or grouping students using flexible grouping arrangements
Product *How learning is assessed* What students do or create to demonstrate content understanding and mastery.	Teachers assess mastery by • providing assessment options aligned with students' strengths and preferences • offering multiple versions of the same assessment (larger font, blank spaces, digital, etc.) • providing opportunities for take-home assessments • incorporating the use of digital tools

(Continued)

TABLE 8.2. *(Continued)*

Instructional Element	Examples
Guiding Questions:	

- What knowledge and skills do students need to meet the standard or objective?
- What resources can I use to deliver content?
- What evidence-based practices can I use to teach this standard and meet learner variability?
- What data can inform differentiation?
- How can I integrate formative and summative assessments (formal or informal) throughout the lesson to track student progress?
- How can I evaluate student progress toward the standard? What assessment tool(s) can I use to accurately measure progress?

Note: Adapted from Bondie et al., 2019; Grimes & Stevens, 2009; Jenkins et al., 2013; Tomlinson, 2001.

Essential Practices in Differentiated Instruction

Teachers can elect to differentiate across instructional elements, which benefits students academically, socially, emotionally, and behaviorally. When classroom teachers differentiate instruction, they honor students' preferences, affirm they have multiple ways of taking in information, and recognize the many ways students can demonstrate their learning. Spanning the four instructional elements of differentiation are the essential practices of differentiated instruction: (1) discover student interests, strengths, and needs; (2) use ongoing assessment and progress monitoring; and (3) integrate flexible grouping. To inform differentiation during instruction and in planning for future lessons, classroom teachers should utilize both informal and formal assessments throughout current lessons.

Discover student's interests, strengths, and needs: To provide high-quality learning, teachers can learn about their students in meaningful ways to identify their interests, strengths, and needs. Building relationships with students and including their interests in lesson planning and delivery increases engagement and positively influences learner outcomes. Discovering student interests can be initiated by asking them directly, observing them, or by providing choices in their learning.

Use ongoing assessment and progress monitoring: Before a lesson, employ diagnostic assessments to identify a student's current knowledge and skill levels. This will inform where to start and what to include in the lesson. During the lesson, track student progress using formative assessments. By continually assessing student's progress toward a learning objective, teachers can adapt instructional strategies, adjust pacing, or increase support. At the end of the lesson, administer summative assessments to evaluate student learning and standard mastery.

Integrate flexible grouping: Flexible grouping is an asset-based, culturally responsive, and data-driven strategy that uses both heterogenous groups (students with varied strengths, interests, preferences, and needs) and homogenous groups (students with similar strengths, interests, preferences, and needs) (IRIS Center, 2010). When selecting groups, teachers should vary how they group students, not relying on a single grouping strategy. Grouping should honor student strengths and needs and not be based on ability. Placing students in groups based on their perceived ability, or ability grouping, is a controversial practice that is not equitable or beneficial (Park & Datnow, 2017; Hattie, 2009). Ability grouping can look like placing students in high-, middle-, or low-achievement groups. In the differentiated classroom, groups are not static and change depending on the lesson and activity. Flexible grouping promotes students' learning from and with students who are very similar to or different from them.

Teachers integrate each of the essential practices of differentiation described previously (student interests/strengths/needs, assessment, flexible grouping) to inform decisions for differentiated instruction. To further facilitate this process, classroom teachers use a student's current level of performance, interests, and learning profile. The IRIS Center (2010) describes each of these components as

- **current level of performance:** a student's current knowledge and skill level in the given content
- **interests:** a student's passions, curiosities, and inspirations
- **learning profile:** a student's preferred method of learning new information or skills (e.g., visually, hands-on) and environmental factors that influence their learning (e.g., small group, bright lights, no distractions); student profiles can also be influenced by gender, culture, and other social identities

Teachers should use data and information collected from assessments, observations, the parent/caregiver, other education professionals, and the student themselves to develop a comprehensive understanding of the student. Truly knowing each student enables the classroom teacher to make intentional decisions when differentiating to ensure all students are engaged and supported to meet learning goals and objectives.

Distinguishing Between Differentiated Instruction and Specially Designed Instruction

Specially designed instruction (SDI) is not differentiated instruction. While a teacher differentiates instruction to meet the learning needs of all students, SDI is unique to students with disabilities and is guaranteed by IDEA. All students with an IEP *must* receive SDI. SDI is described in a student's IEP and is designed to help students with disabilities access the general education curriculum, meet ambitious IEP goals, and make meaningful progress in their learning. In this way, SDI ensures "access of the child to the general curriculum, so that the child can meet the educational standards" in the least restrictive environment (IDEA, 2004, Section 300.39).

For SDI, the content (what a student will learn), methodology (how a student will learn), and delivery (when/where a student will learn) of instruction is individually adapted to address a student's disability-related needs. Although these three areas may mirror the essential elements of differentiation of instruction, SDI is linked to a student's IEP goals and is provided to address academic or functional skill development. SDI may include related services such as speech-language therapy or instructional services such as vocational training. The IEP details SDI, including a clear description of

- the type of service
- amount
- frequency
- duration
- location

SDI is more than an accommodation, it *is* special education. Students with disabilities receive explicit, focused, and systematic instruction aligned with their disability-related need in

- reading, math, and other academic content areas
- language and communication
- functional skills
- social skills
- behavior skills
- independent living and self-determination
- use of accommodations and supplementary aids and services

The effectiveness of SDI is evaluated by monitoring student progress toward annual goals.

Pause and Reflect:

Consider Mr. Hill and his class at Booker T. Washington Elementary from the vignette at the start of the chapter. What kinds of differentiated instruction might he anticipate needing to provide for his students during the ELA lesson he is planning? How can he use differentiation to ensure all of his students make progress toward the learning objective?

High-Leverage Practices and Evidence-Based Practices

Teachers can use high-leverage practices to deliver evidence-based instruction. As emphasized throughout this textbook, leveraging evidence- and research-based resources and practices in every aspect of teaching is critical to providing effective, inclusive, equitable, and meaningful education.

High-Leverage Practices

High-leverage practices (HLPs) are instructional strategies built on a foundation of research and exemplify core teaching behaviors. HLPs transcend content, settings, and grade bands and span instructional domains including planning, delivery, and assessment. HLPs include setting clear learning goals, using explicit instruction, providing scaffolding, using assessments to guide teaching, establishing positive classroom environments, and more. HLPs are not linear, meaning they do not occur in a predictable and sequenced order. Rather, they are practices that teachers engage in simultaneously to ensure a high-quality learning environment.

As described in chapter 1, when teachers engage in HLPs, they can improve outcomes across academic, behavior, and social/functional skills. HLPs are organized to emphasize culturally inclusive pedagogies and practices (CIPP) and are designed to fit within an MTSS framework. The 22 HLPs are arranged in four domains: (1) collaboration, (2) data-driven planning, (3) instruction in behavior and academics, and (4) intensify and intervene as needed. Seven of the HLPs are designated as pillar practices: (1) collaboration among professionals; (2) collaboration with families; (3) using data, analyzing instruction, and adjusting as necessary; (4) establishing a consistent, organized, and responsive learning environment; (5) using explicit instruction; (6) providing intensive instruction for academics and behavior; and (7) creating individualized function-based support plans.

Evidence-based practices (EBP) are educational practices or strategies that have empirical evidence to support their efficacy, meaning they have been proven to produce positive student learning outcomes in real school settings (Council for Exceptional Children, 2014). Many states and school districts review and adopt textbooks and programs to meet the established curriculum standards. Curriculum experts review content resources within textbooks and programs to ensure that the resources have a published list of EBPs. The What Works Clearinghouse (https://ies.ed.gov/ncee/wwc/) was established by the federal government to review and identify programs and practices to evaluate their influence on student outcomes. Numerous educational organizations review research-validating instructional practices, programs, and interventions. As technology and society evolve, it is important that the field continues to build the knowledge base for evidence-based and standards-aligned curricular resources and materials.

EBPs can be content specific, tied a grade level, and more effective for one student group than another. Examples of EBPs include explicit instruction, collaborative grouping, previewing vocabulary, and scaffolding, to name a few. EBPs can also include various commercially packaged programs that have been evaluated to demonstrate their influence on student learning. In addition to the What Works Clearinghouse, several federally funded national centers provide examples and descriptions of EBPs, including the National Center on Intensive Intervention, PROGRESS Center, CEEDAR Center, Lead IDEA Center, and MTSS Center.

Although HLPs and EBPs differ, they complement each other, creating a powerful combination for providing access to the general education curriculum. By leveraging HLPs to deliver and implement EBPs, educators can ensure that instructional and intervention practices are not only grounded in research but are also strategic and practical. This synergy helps create environments where all students not only engage in the general education curriculum but are included and have the opportunity to grow and progress academically, socially, and emotionally.

> Pause and Reflect:
>
> Think back to the vignette at the beginning of the chapter. Where might Mr. Hill go to find EBPs and HLPs to integrate into his lesson planning and delivery of instruction? Why is it important for Mr. Hill to ensure he utilizes EBPs and HLPs in this lesson and all lessons, activities, and practices in his classroom? How do they support access to the general education curriculum for all students, including those with disabilities?

Foundational Framework: Culturally Inclusive Pedagogy and Practice (CIPP)

As emphasized in UDL, differentiated instruction, HLPs, and EBPs, understanding and integrating student's identities, experiences, and cultures into teaching and learning are critical to creating accessible, inclusive, and equitable classrooms. Three prominent and essential culturally inclusive pedagogies and practices (CIPP) (Aceves & Kennedy, 2024) in the classroom are culturally relevant pedagogy, culturally responsive teaching, and culturally sustaining pedagogy. CIPP represent "theories and practices that have centered multiple layers of sociocultural diversity and understanding in the educational sphere" (Aceves & Kennedy, 2024). Classroom teachers can integrate these theories and pedagogical approaches to create learning environments and experiences to recognize and incorporate students' cultural identities. CIPP are essential to building learning environments, opportunities, and experiences that reflect an understanding of intersectionality and how it applies to schools and education (Boveda, 2016). By employing these practices, teachers communicate that they recognize students' culture as an intersectional part of their personal and educational identity and experience.

Culturally relevant pedagogy (CRP) is an educational approach introduced by Gloria Ladson-Billings (1995) that aims to empower students by incorporating their cultural backgrounds and experiences into the teaching and learning process. This pedagogical framework focuses on three main goals:

- Fostering academic success
- Promoting cultural competence
- Encouraging critical consciousness

It involves creating a learning environment where students' cultural identities are respected and valued, integrating diverse cultural perspectives into the curriculum, and using teaching strategies that are responsive to the cultural needs of students. By doing so, culturally relevant pedagogy seeks to enhance student engagement, improve educational outcomes, and support students' development as critical thinkers and active participants in a diverse society.

Culturally responsive teaching (CRT) as a concept was developed by Geneva Gay (2002) and includes teaching practices that actively connect with students' cultural backgrounds, affirm their identities, and integrate diverse perspectives into the curriculum. In this way, CRT is the practical application of the principles of CRP in the classroom. Some of the key CRT practices for classroom teachers include

- Setting high academic expectations for all students
- Ensuring all students see themselves represented in what they are learning by intentionally connecting classroom content to students' personal experiences and cultural backgrounds
- Helping students develop a critical awareness of societal issues, including racism, inequality, and injustice by empowering students to question and challenge the status quo and become active participants in their communities
- Fostering a collaborative learning environment where students work together, learn from each other, and develop mutual respect

Culturally sustaining pedagogy (CSP), developed by Django Paris and H. Samy Alim (2017), goes beyond recognizing and valuing students' cultural backgrounds to promote, sustain, and nurture students' cultural and linguistic practices. This approach advocates for the continuation and revitalization of students' cultural traditions and languages within the educational system. CSP aims to prepare students to thrive in a multicultural society by fostering an environment where diverse cultural expressions are celebrated and preserved instead of assimilated. Some core practices within CSP include

- Promoting multiple cultures and languages as equally valuable and crucial to students' academic success and personal development
- Emphasizing the importance of engaging with students' families and communities as integral partners in the educational process and incorporating community knowledge and cultural resources into the curriculum
- Fostering critical consciousness by encouraging students to critically examine issues of social justice and equity and empowering students to become agents of change

Each of these theories and practices is connected to and advances the others. CRP serves as a foundation and aims to ensure students from diverse cultural backgrounds achieve academic success while maintaining their cultural integrity and to create a learning environment where students' cultural identities are not only acknowledged but also leveraged as assets in the educational process. Building on CRP, CRT focuses on the practical application of these ideas in the classroom. Classroom teachers using CRT methods include culturally relevant examples, texts, and materials and employ teaching strategies that reflect students' cultural norms and values. CRT aims to make learning more accessible and meaningful by connecting academic content to students' lived experiences. CSP takes CRP further by focusing on nurturing and sustaining students' cultural identities over time. It emphasizes the importance of linguistic diversity, challenges inequities in educational settings, and aims to promote long-term cultural resilience and empowerment. Figure 8.1 illustrates the connection between CRP, CRT, and CSP.

Culturally Relevant Pedagogy CRP	Culturally Responsive Teaching CRT	Culturally Sustaining Pedagogy CSP
An approach to education that emphasizes fostering academic success, promoting cultural competence, and encouraging critical consciousness for all students.	The practical application of the principles of CRP within the classroom. Teachers using CRT methods integrate students' cultural references into all aspects of learning.	Pedagogy and practice that actively sustains, nurtures, and promotes students' linguistic and cultural pluralism. CSP advocates for the continuation and revitalization of students' cultural traditions and languages within the educational system and prepares students for a multicultural society.

FIGURE 8.1. *Connecting CRP, CRT, and CSP.*

> Pause and Reflect:
>
> Revisit the vignette at the beginning of the chapter and consider the learner variability and diversity within Mr. Hill's classroom and school. What approaches and practices from CRP, CRT, and CSP can Mr. Hill use to ensure student's cultures, languages, and experiences are represented, integrated, celebrated, and sustained in his classroom? How will this promote access and inclusion?

HIGH-IMPACT: THE CONNECTION WITH HIGH-LEVERAGE PRACTICES

HLP 4: Use multiple sources of information to develop a comprehensive understanding of a student's strengths and needs

HLP 6: Use student assessment data, analyze instructional practices, and make necessary adjustments that improve student outcomes

HLP 7: Establish consistent, organized, and responsive learning environments

HLP 11: Identify and prioritize long- and short-term learning goals

HLP 12: Systematically design instruction toward a specific goal

HLP 13: Adapt curriculum tasks and materials for specific learning goals

HLP 14: Teach cognitive and metacognitive strategies to support learning and independence

HLP 15: Provide scaffolded supports

HLP 16: Use explicit instruction

HLP 17: Use flexible grouping

HLP 19: Use assistive and instructional technologies

HLP 8/22: Provide positive and constructive feedback to guide students' learning (HLP 22) and behavior (HLP 8)

Review and Reflect

To promote access to and equity in the general education classroom, a comprehensive approach integrates differentiated instruction, UDL, EBPs, HLPs, and CIPP (including CRP, CRT, and CSP). Classroom teachers can use these foundational practices simultaneously to ensure all students, including students with disabilities, are engaged, included, supported, and valued within an accessible and inclusive learning environment.

Classroom teachers can utilize these practices to consistently and intentionally promote equity and access. When integrated across an MTSS framework, such practices promote a deeper understanding and appreciation of diverse perspectives and abilities. Table 8.3 below provides a checklist for classroom teachers to use as they reflect on and enhance their implementation of these integrated foundational frameworks.

TABLE 8.3. *Checklist for Access and Inclusion in the General Education Curriculum*

Reflect on the following characteristics to self-assess your relative strengths and set professional development goals.	**Strength**	**Area for Development Goal**
Classroom Environment		
Environment provides all students (including those with mobility devices or needs) clear access to any part of the room.		
Desks, tables, and seating options are arranged in a way that promotes and supports cooperative and collaborative learning.		
Resources and materials are organized, easily accessible, and inclusive.		
Visual supports for academic, social, behavioral, and functional learning are clearly communicated and displayed.		
Expectations and procedures are clear, positive, and explicitly taught.		
Expectations and procedures promote respect and value learner diversity.		
Visuals and displays are representative of learner variability and diversity.		
Planning for Instruction		
Lessons include principles of UDL.		
Resources and activities align with curriculum and learning standards.		
Resources and activities reflect learner profiles.		
Resources and activities are data driven and promote access.		
Lesson integrate formative and summative assessments.		

(Continued)

TABLE 8.3. *(Continued)*

Reflect on the following characteristics to self-assess your relative strengths and set professional development goals.	Strength	Area for Development Goal
Implementing Instruction		
Educators differentiate instruction.		
Specially designed instruction is provided to students with disabilities in accordance with their IEP.		
Multiple opportunities are provided for collaboration.		
Progress is monitored throughout instruction.		
Reflective Practice and Continued Professional Growth		
Teacher regularly engages reflective practice.		
Teacher reflects on their own identities, the identities of their students, and how they interact in the classroom.		
Teacher analyzes student data and uses it to inform instruction.		
Teacher engages in regular professional learning and professional growth.		
Teacher regularly connects and collaborates with families and colleagues to inform practice.		

Guiding Questions

1. Describe differentiated instruction and explain how it promotes access to learning.
2. How does differentiated instruction differ from specially designed instruction?
3. Describe the principles of universal design for learning and explain how you can incorporate UDL in your current or future classroom.
4. Define HLPs and EBPs. How do HLPs promote the use of EBPs?
5. Explain CIPP and the significance of CIPP for student learning. Provide concrete examples of how you can integrate students' culture in the learning environment and curriculum.
6. Distinguish culturally responsive practices, culturally relevant teaching, and culturally sustaining practices.

Extend Your Learning

TABLE 8.4. *Resources*

Resource	Description	Link
IRIS Center Module on Differentiated Instruction	An online professional learning module focused on the core components of differentiated instruction, considerations for decision-making for differentiation, and essential differentiation practices and strategies	https://iris.peabody.vanderbilt.edu/module/di/
UDL Tips from CAST	Multiple quick guides and tip sheets covering a broad range of topics focused on the implementation of UDL in the classroom	https://www.cast.org/resources/udl-tips-from-cast
High-Leverage Practices for Students with Disabilities	Resources designed to support and strengthen educators' understanding of the high-leverage practices for students with disabilities	https://exceptionalchildren.org/topics/high-leverage-practices
Evidence-Based Practices: What Works Clearinghouse	Searchable database of empirical reports on instructional materials, curriculums, intervention programs, and other educational tools and resources; includes information about validity and effectiveness of use	https://ies.ed.gov/ncee/wwc
Collaboration for Effective Educator Development, Accountability, and Reform (CEEDAR) Center	"High-Leverage Practices and Evidence-Based Practices: A Promising Pair" defines the terms with examples and describes how they can be seamlessly integrated into instruction as part of an MTSS	https://ceedar.education.ufl.edu/wp-content/uploads/2017/11/HLPs-and-EBPs-A-Promising-Pair-FINAL.pdf
Culturally Responsive-Sustaining Education Framework: Learning Modules	Learning modules designed to provide an initial exploration of the importance of culturally responsive teaching, specifically related to why culturally responsive-sustaining education (CRSE) is important and necessary	https://www.weteachnyc.org/resources/collection/culturally-responsive-sustaining-education-crse-professional-learning-modules/

References

Aceves, T. C., & Kennedy, M. J. (Eds.). (2024). *High-leverage practices for students with disabilities* (2nd ed.). Council for Exceptional Children and CEEDAR Center.

Bondie, R. S., Dahnke, C., & Zusho, A. (2019). How does changing "one-size-fits-all" to differentiated instruction affect teaching? *Review of Research in Education, 43*(1), 336–62.

Boveda, M. (2016). *Beyond special and general education as identity markers: The development and validation of an instrument to measure preservice teachers' understanding of the effects of intersecting sociocultural identities* [Doctoral dissertation]. FIU Electronic Theses and Dissertations, 2998. https://digitalcommons.fiu.edu/etd/2998

CASEL. (2018). *What is the CASEL framework?* https://CASEL.org/core-competencies/

CAST. (2024). *The UDL guidelines.* https://udlguidelines.cast.org/

Council for Exceptional Children. (2014). *Standard for evidence-based practices in special education.* https://exceptionalchildren.org/sites/default/files/2021-04/EBP_FINAL.pdf

Council for Exceptional Children and CEEDAR Center. (2024). *High-leverage practices for students with disabilities* (2nd ed.). https://ceedar.education.ufl.edu/wp-content/uploads/2024/03/High-Leverage-Practices-for-Students-with-Disabilties-updated.pdf

Duquette, C. (2022). *Finding a place for every student: Inclusive practices, social belonging, and differentiated instruction in elementary classrooms.* Pembroke.

Fritzgerald, A. (2020). *Antiracism and universal design for learning: Building expressways to success.* CAST.

Gay, G. (2002). Preparing for culturally responsive teaching. *Journal of Teacher Education, 53*(2), 106–16. https://doi.org/10.1177/0022487102053002003

Grimes, K. J., & Stevens, D. D. (2009). Glass, bug, mud. *Phi Delta Kappan, 90*(9), 677–80.

Hattie, J. (2009). *Visible learning: A synthesis of over 800 meta-analyses relating to achievement.* Routledge.

Howard, M. (2009). *RtI from all sides: What every teacher needs to know.* Heinemann.

Herner-Patnode, L., & Lee, H. J. (2021). Differentiated Instruction to teach mathematics: Through the lens of responsive teaching. *Mathematics Teacher Education and Development, 23*(3), 6–25.

Higher Education Opportunity Act. (2008). Public Law 110-315.

IDEA Regulations. (2012). 34 C.F.R.300.

Individual With Disabilities Act. (2004). 20 U.S.C. 1400 et seq. and Supp.V.

IRIS Center (2010). *Differentiated instruction: Maximizing the learning of all students.* https://iris.peabody.vanderbilt.edu/module/di/

IRIS Center (2015). *Intensive intervention (Part 1): Using data-based individualization to intensify instruction.* https://iris.peabody.vanderbilt.edu/module/dbi1/

IRIS Center. (2023). *Universal design for learning: Designing learning experiences that engage and challenge all students.* https://iris.peabody.vanderbilt.edu/udl/

Jenkins, J. R., Schiller, E., Blackorby, J., Thayer, S. K., & Tilly, W. D. (2013). Responsiveness to intervention in reading: Architecture and practices. *Learning Disability Quarterly, 36*(1), 36–46.

Ladson-Billings, G. (1995). Toward a theory of culturally relevant pedagogy. *American Educational Research Journal, 32*(3), 465–91. https://doi.org/10.3102/00028312032003465

O'Meara, J. (2010). *Beyond differentiated instruction.* Corwin.

Paris, D., & Alim, H. S. (Eds.). (2017). *Culturally sustaining pedagogies: Teaching and learning for justice in a changing world.* Teachers College Press.

Park, V., & Datnow, A. (2017). Ability grouping and differentiated instruction in an era of data-driven decision making. *American Journal of Education, 123*(2), 281–306. https://doi.org/10.1086/689930

Tomlinson, C. A. (2001). *How to differentiate instruction in mixed-ability classrooms.* ASCD.

Tomlinson, C. A. (2003). *Fulfilling the promise of the differentiated classroom: Strategies and tools for responsive teaching.* ASCD.

Tomlinson, C. A., & Imbeau, M. B. (2023). *Leading and managing a differentiated classroom.* ASCD.

9

A Shared Responsibility

Collaborating for Access, Inclusion, and Equity

It takes an effective team of educators, professionals, and parents/caregivers to provide accessible, inclusive, and equitable education to students with disabilities. Implementing the various frameworks, services, and supports discussed throughout this book requires the classroom teacher to collaborate effectively with all members of the IEP team and school-based teams. This chapter describes the key elements of collaboration and the necessary practices and strategies for effectively collaborating with educators, administrators, specialized instructional service personnel, and parents/caregivers. Best practices in collaboration, effective communication methods, and other team-based tasks related to inclusive education are discussed. This chapter also provides essential, research-based practices for culturally responsive and equitable collaboration with parents and caregivers.

Chapter Objectives

After reading this chapter, readers will be able to

- Identify and define the key components of effective collaboration
- List and describe effective communication practices
- Describe several culturally responsive and equitable practices for collaborating with parents/caregivers

- Evaluate the role classroom teachers play in collaborating with other educators, administrators, specialized instructional service personnel, and parents/caregivers
- Analyze how effective collaboration supports accessible, inclusive, and equitable education for students with disabilities

Key Terms

active listening: The process of fully focusing, understanding, responding, and remembering what is being said and demonstrating this engagement through verbal and nonverbal cues.

collaboration: Style for direct interaction between at least two coequal parties voluntarily engaged in shared decision-making as they work toward a common goal.

consultation: The provision of professional input or services in a field of special knowledge or training, or consulting with another for a specific purpose.

co-teaching: A partnering of two teachers with different expertise (typically a classroom teacher and a special education teacher) to provide more comprehensive and effective instruction for students with disabilities within the general education classroom. Co-teaching involves collaborative planning, teaching, and assessing within the least restrictive environment.

family engagement: An active practice in which families and school personnel collaborate to support and improve the learning and development of children; educators are committed to listening and collaborating with families and actively encourage families to participate in meaningful ways, and families are committed to prioritizing their children's education at home and at school (IRIS Center, 2020).

interdisciplinary team: A group of professionals from different disciplines or fields who work together to address common educational goals or problems by combining their expertise and perspectives.

nonverbal communication: The transmittal of information, feelings, or ideas using body language, facial expressions, gestures, posture, eye contact, and tone of voice instead of spoken or written words to convey meaning.

problem-solving process: A set of skills formulated to collaboratively address issues, progressing from data gathering to problem identification, to development of a plan, to evaluation of progress, to the follow-up of results.

verbal communication: The exchange of information or ideas using spoken words, involving both the content of the message and the way it is delivered, such as tone, pitch, and pace.

written communication: The process of conveying information, ideas, or messages through written symbols, such as text, letters, or emails.

Vignette

Consider the following vignette about Ms. Jones as you read this chapter. Connect the information you learn about the importance of effective collaboration and key collaborative strategies to Ms. Jones and the practices she will need to engage in to support all students. There will be prompts and examples related to this vignette throughout the chapter.

Ms. Kingston is starting her very first year as a ninth grade world history teacher at Springfield High School. She is feeling excited, motivated, and a little nervous to welcome her students for the start of the year in just a few weeks. Recently, Ms. Kingston received her class rosters and student data for the freshman who will be taking her class. After reviewing this information, she recognizes that her students represent a wide range of learner variability and student diversity, including students of multiple races and cultures, students who are multilingual, and students with IEPs and 504 plans. Ms. Kingston is looking forward to having such a diverse group of students with exciting strengths, interests, and perspectives to contribute to the class. However, she also feels a bit nervous about how she will manage to provide great instruction and support that best serves each student as an individual.

Ms. Kingston remembers the emphasis placed on collaboration during her courses and experiences within her university teacher education program. She learned about and experienced collaboration with other educators, specialized instructional service professionals, and parents/caregivers. However, this was all under the supervision and support of faculty and the supporting teacher within her internships and student teaching. Ms. Kingston knows that she will need to collaborate effectively to provide accessible, inclusive, and equitable education to all of her students. However, as a new teacher, she is not sure how to begin these collaborative processes, the skills and practices she should focus on, or her specific roles in collaboration with other teachers, professionals, and families. Ms. Kingston feels like she is prepared to do her part and deliver great educational experiences and supports to her students, but she needs more clarity on exactly how she will work with her school-based colleagues and the parents/caregivers of her students.

Collaboration: Types, Purposes, and Collaborators

Collaboration is essential for providing access and equity in education for students with disabilities regardless of the environment where they are served (Aceves & Kennedy, 2024). Collaboration improves programming by leveraging the content knowledge of a classroom teacher and the knowledge of high-leverage and evidence-based strategies to support students with disabilities. However, collaboration can be challenging for a number of reasons. Classroom teachers will collaborate with parents/caregivers and a number of professionals to support students with disabilities; therefore, developing collaboration skills can bolster effectiveness and increase student success.

Collaboration Along a Continuum of Placement

Currently, classroom teachers participate in a spectrum of collaborative opportunities with a wide range of professionals as they serve students with disabilities. The frequency and duration of the collaboration is dependent on the student's least restrictive environment (LRE). Within the general education classroom, the classroom teacher is fully involved in collaborating around all aspects of the student's education. As a student's placement becomes more restrictive, the classroom teacher's involvement is typically more limited.

Because each student's individual supports and services can vary, the LRE exists across a continuum of placement options ranging from least restrictive to most restrictive. Just like any other essential component of an IEP (e.g., specially designed instruction), the LRE is not standardized across disability categories but rather is determined by an IEP team and is responsive to each individual student. The continuum of LRE placement options moving from least to most restrictive is (1) general education classroom, (2) general education classroom with consultation, (3) resource program, (4) separate classroom, (5) separate school, (6) residential school, and (7) hospital homebound.

Although a growing number of students with disabilities are served in the general education classroom, receiving services in the general education classroom may not meet every student's individual needs. As discussed in chapter 2 and emphasized in the Individuals With Disabilities Education Act (IDEA), *special education is a set of services, not a place.* Therefore, the IEP team must identify the supports and services a student needs in advance of determining the LRE.

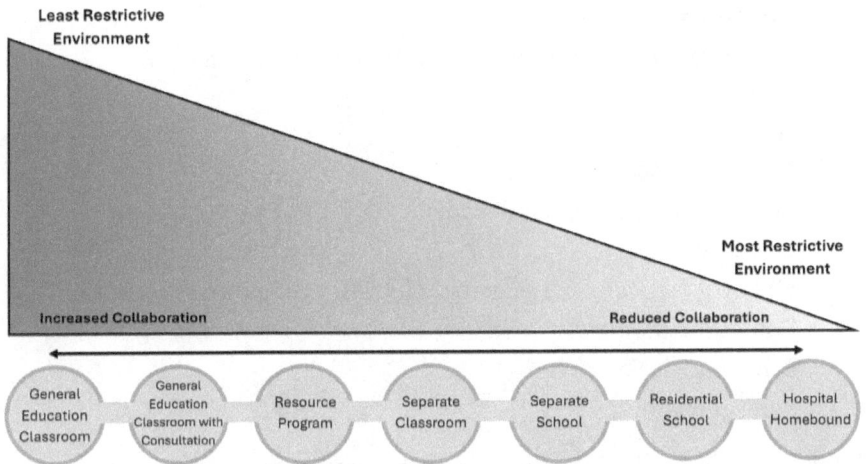

FIGURE 9.1. *Collaboration Continuum to Support Students with Disabilities.*

Regardless of LRE placement, the classroom teacher remains an essential member of the IEP team. However, the frequency and duration of their involvement increases or decreases along the continuum, with the greatest involvement for students who receive services in the general education environment and least involvement for students who receive services in a hospital or homebound environment.

As educators provide appropriate education in the LRE for students with disabilities, the classroom teacher's involvement in collaboration continues to grow. Effective collaboration among educators, specialized instructional support personnel (SISP), and parents/caregivers is essential to expanding inclusive education for all students. Figure 9.1 illustrates the continuum of placement options, defining each and articulating the involvement of the classroom teacher.

Collaboration With Teams

Classroom teachers are key collaborators and are essential to the success of students with disabilities. When students receive special education services in the general education classroom, classroom teachers assume increased responsibilities to ensure students receive accommodations, specially designed instruction, and related services and supports. Educators can collaborate in a variety of ways. Collaboration can occur across a variety of meeting types (e.g., student study, MTSS, IEP) across a variety of tasks (instructional planning), and in instructional delivery (co-teaching). Collaboration also occurs with a variety of individuals who are responsible for educating students with disabilities including the following:

- Parents/caregivers
- Classroom teachers in the same/different grade bands or content areas
- Special education teachers
- Interventionists
- Instructional coaches and leaders
- Administrators
- SISP (e.g., speech-language pathologists, occupational therapists)
- School psychologists
- Behavior specialists
- Paraprofessionals

Table 9.1 includes the key areas, common types, and function and purpose of the types of collaboration.

TABLE 9.1. *Collaboration for Classroom Teachers*

Key Area	Common Approach	Purpose
Team Meetings	Participate in Student Study Meeting	• analyze multiple sources of data to identify student academic, behavioral, social, or emotional needs • develop strategies and interventions • establish a plan for monitoring student progress • determine if further assessment or referral for other resources or special education services is necessary based on student response to initial interventions
	Participate in MTSS Team Meetings	• provide and analyze student data across all three tiers of MTSS • discuss and develop instructional and intervention practices (Tier 1—universal, Tier 2—targeted small group, Tier 3—intensive individual) • evaluate MTSS practices
	Participate in IEP Team Meetings	• determine eligibility • develop IEP • implement IEP • share progress monitoring data for IEP goals • evaluate and revise the IEP

(*Continued*)

TABLE 9.1. *(Continued)*

Key Area	Common Approach	Purpose
Instructional Planning	Engage in Collaborative Planning	• ensure instructional methods and strategies are aligned with IEP goals • deliver specialized instruction, including accommodations • utilize UDL, EBPs, HLPs, and CIPP to frame instructional and intervention planning • analyze, interpret, and utilize data to drive instruction and intervention
	Receive Consultation	• acquire information, strategies, resources, or tools to facilitate the learning of students with disabilities • discuss the provision of specially designed instruction in the general education setting
Instructional Delivery	Co-teach	• co-plan for instruction • co-instruct • co-assess student progress and teacher practices • co-deliver specially designed instruction • provide intervention • support classroom management • provide appropriate accommodations

---

Pause and Reflect:

Consider Ms. Kingston from the vignette at the beginning of the chapter. Whom can she expect to collaborate with to provide accessible, inclusive, and equitable education to students with disabilities in her classes? What structures and teams will she be a part of? Which colleagues and coworkers might she connect with to learn more about her collaborative roles as a classroom teacher?

Classroom teachers are essential members of MTSS teams and IEP teams. MTSS and IEP teams are types of interdisciplinary teams. Interdisciplinary teams represent a group of professionals from different disciplines or fields who work together to address common educational goals or challenges. The advantage of an interdisciplinary team is its ability to combine their diverse expertise to develop a holistic understanding of a student and design instruction or intervention to meet their needs. Each interdisciplinary team can collaboratively develop appropriate, evidence-based, and effective instruction, support, and intervention. As a member of this team, the classroom teacher is able to couple their knowledge of content and related standards with the delivery expertise of special educators (including SISP). Although both interdisciplinary teams may overlap in some of their functions, they have different foci and serve different purposes. Figure 9.2 illustrates the similarities and differences between the MTSS team and IEP team. As a member of each team, the classroom teacher is the strong link between delivering intervention to support students with high-intensity needs and delivering specialized instruction as part of an IEP within an MTSS framework to maximizes the benefits for students with disabilities (Choi et al., 2020).

MTSS Team Collaboration

A multitiered system of support (MTSS) provides a framework to provide students with responsive, evidence-based instruction and intervention. As an essential member of the MTSS team, the classroom teacher is the primary source of instruction and intervention across all the tiers (Scanlon et al., 2021). As they support their students across the tiers, the classroom teacher may choose to consult with special education teachers or related services personnel (e.g., speech-language pathologists, behavior specialists) to identify strategies and approaches for intervention aligned with the

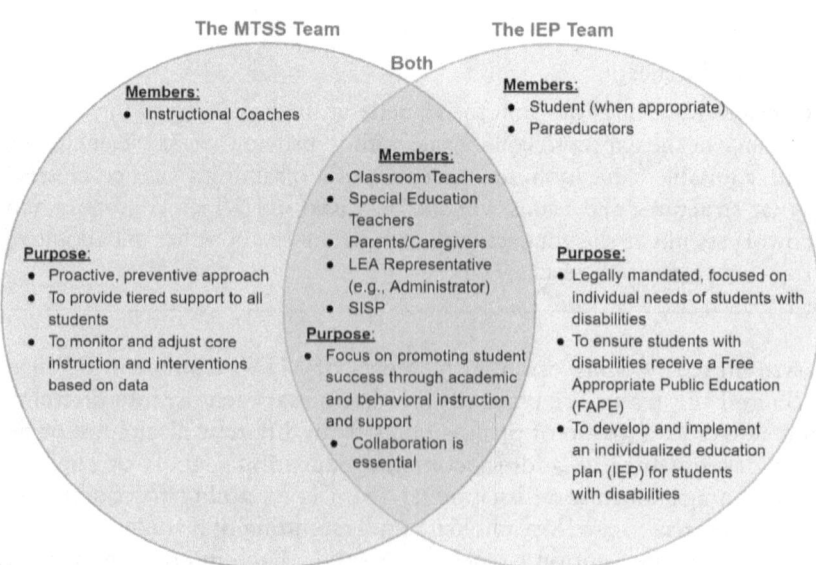

FIGURE 9.2. *The MTSS Team and the IEP Team.*

student's individual needs (Eisenman et al., 2011; Todd, 2012). In response to this consultation, special educators, school psychologists, instructional coaches, or other types of educators provide indirect services to support students. Providing indirect services allows educators to support students indirectly by directly supporting the classroom teacher. Indirect services can include observation, data collection, or recommending resources, materials, strategies, or intervention approaches. In addition, indirect services delivered by the MTSS team may include meeting regularly to collaboratively review data and monitor progress for students receiving Tier 2 or Tier 3 intervention. During these recurring meetings, the MTSS team reviews data and assesses the effectiveness of interventions, provides recommendations for adjustment, and determines levels of effective support.

If needed, a classroom teacher may request direct services from an MTSS team member (e.g., interventionist, special educator, speech-language pathologist). When providing direct services, an educator supports the classroom teacher by modeling, scaffolding, or delivering instruction or intervention directly to the student. If the student is not responsive to Tier 3 intervention, all members of the MTSS team may convene to determine the need for special education evaluation. This meeting is typically referred to as the "student study meeting."

IEP Team Collaboration

Once a student is determined eligible for special education services, the IEP team will convene to develop the IEP. Or, if the student is already receiving services, the IEP team will meet to revise a student's IEP. Similar to the MTSS team, the IEP team is interdisciplinary. And, although there may be similarity in the members of the team, the teams differ in their roles and responsibilities. To develop an IEP, the team will use assessment and evaluation data to collaboratively identify a student's strengths and needs, determine long- and short-term goals, and develop specially designed instruction and related services to support the student's academic, behavioral, and functional development (IDEA, 2004). Once the IEP is developed, the classroom teacher will share the responsibility for delivering specially designed instruction (including accommodations), monitoring progress toward annual goals, and evaluating the effectiveness of an IEP.

Collaboration in the Classroom

Collaboration can take a variety of forms, including the implementation of collaborative teaching models. Collaborative teaching, or co-teaching, is the partnering of two teachers with different expertise (typically a classroom teacher and a special education teacher) to provide comprehensive and effective instruction for students with disabilities within the general education classroom (Friend, 2016; Murawski & Ricci, 2019). Co-teaching can be configured in a variety of ways to deliver accessible and inclusive learning experiences. The six most common configurations of co-teaching are one-teach-one-observe, one-teach-one-assist, parallel teaching, team teaching, station teaching, and alternative teaching. Each configuration provides a different level of support. Therefore, the co-teaching configuration should be aligned with instructional objectives as well as learner strengths and needs. Co-teaching configurations do not need to be static and can change in response to objectives, lesson plans, or other needs. Additionally, being flexible and fluid in the selection of co-teaching models can result in multiple models being used within the same lesson or unit. Table 9.2 describes the six co-teaching models, provides an illustration of the model, and lists the potential benefits and challenges for each configuration.

The following characteristics contribute to the effectiveness of co-teaching (Jortveit & Kovač, 2022; Scruggs & Mastropieri, 2017):

- a common vision and goal for collaborative teaching
- a shared understanding of learning standards and curriculum/lesson objectives
- a common understanding of student strengths and needs
- an intentional plan for assessment opportunities
- a clear, detailed plan for each teacher's roles throughout the lesson

After a co-taught lesson, both teachers can (1) engage in reflection to identify strengths and areas for adjustment to their instructional approaches, (2) review and reflect on student data, and (3) identify areas for focus for the next lesson. Figure 9.3 provides an instructional planning template that co-teachers can use to develop and deliver a lesson.

> Pause and Reflect:
>
> Think back to Ms. Kingston in the vignette at the start of the chapter. As she plans and prepares for her new students, how can she work with the special education teachers, paraeducators, and SISP within her school to deliver appropriate and effective instruction, support, and intervention for students with disabilities? What will she need to consider in planning for and implementing each of these elements? Who else might she connect with to inform her preparation and practice?

Date:	Grade Level:	Content Area:
Teacher 1:		Aligned Standards:
Teacher 2:		
Learning Objectives:		Materials/Resources:
Whole-Group Instruction: Room arrangement Grouping Teacher locations		**Small-Group Instruction:** Room arrangement Grouping Teacher locations
Supports, aids, and/or services for specific students:		
Accommodations/Modifications for specific students:		

Teacher Tasks	Co-Teacher #1:	Co-Teacher #2:
***Before* instruction** *What specific tasks am I responsible for to prepare the lesson?*		
***During* instruction** *What specific tasks and responsibilities do I have during instruction?*	**Introduction** **Main Activity** **Closure** **Formative Assessment:** **Summative Assessment:**	**Introduction** **Main Activity** **Closure** **Formative Assessment:** **Summative Assessment:**
***After* instruction** *What specific tasks am I responsible for after instruction?*		

FIGURE 9.3. Co-Taught Lesson-Planning Template.

TABLE 9.2. *Co-teaching Models*

Configuration	Illustration	Potential Benefits and Challenges
One-Teach-One-Observe: One teacher provides instruction to the whole class while the second teacher observes and collects data on one or more students.		*Benefits:* Informs instructional decisions and provides insight to student needs through observation and data collection. *Challenges:* Observing teacher may be underutilized for their expertise. Students may view the observing teacher as having less authority.
One-Teach-One-Assist: One teacher provides instruction to the whole class while the second teacher provides individual assistance to students.		*Benefits:* Provides immediate assistance to students who require additional support. *Challenges:* Reinforces hierarchies of one teacher leading rather than promoting parity in collaboration. Students may perceive one teacher as an assistant rather than as an expert.
Parallel Teaching: Students are split into two equal groups. Both teachers each deliver the same lesson/instruction to one of the groups simultaneously.		*Benefits:* Supports individualized attention and engagement by reducing student-teacher ratio. *Challenges:* Both teachers need to be equally skilled in the content area. Instructional consistency across groups may be difficult.

(Continued)

TABLE 9.2. (*Continued*)

Configuration	Illustration	Potential Benefits and Challenges
Team Teaching: The classroom teacher and the special education teacher provide instruction to the whole class together. They trade off leading throughout the lesson.		*Benefits:* Promotes teachers' equal contributions to learning and enhances instructional quality. Models effective collaboration and communication skills. *Challenges:* Requires strong rapport and careful planning between teachers. May cause conflict or inconsistencies if teaching philosophies or styles do not align.
Station Teaching: Students are placed in groups and rotate through three stations with related learning activities. Both teachers provide instruction at one of the stations. The third station is typically an independent activity for students.		*Benefits:* Stations can be designed to meet diverse learning needs, making this configuration ideal for providing differentiated instruction. This model increases student engagement through varied activities. *Challenges:* Requires increased planning time and careful coordination and management of station transitions.
Alternative Teaching: One teacher provides instruction to the majority of the students while a second teacher provides instruction to a small group of students. Small-group instruction is typically specialized instruction for remediation or enrichment.		*Benefits:* Students who need additional support or enrichment receive targeted instruction. *Challenges:* Students in the smaller group may be stigmatized. Students in the larger group may not receive the benefit of additional support and small-group instruction.

Essential Practices for Effective Collaboration

Essential collaborative practices can improve the effectiveness and efficiency of collaboration. Strong communication skills, consistency in collaboration, and a focus on organization create a robust foundation for effective collaboration (Aceves & Kennedy, 2024; Da Fonte & Barton-Atwood, 2017; Vangrieken et al., 2015). As both a leader and a supporting team member, classroom teachers can add to the success of any collaborative structure or practice with these essential skills.

Communication Skills

Strong communication requires attention to relaying and receiving information, which includes verbal, written, and nonverbal forms of communication as well as active listening (Da Fonte & Barton-Atwood, 2017; Khan et al., 2017; Vangrieken et al., 2015).

Verbal communication is the exchange of information or ideas using spoken words, involving both the content of the message and the way it is delivered, such as tone, pitch, and pace. Written communication is the process of conveying information, ideas, or messages through written symbols, such as text, letters, or emails. In addition to what and how we say or write information, it is also important to be aware of what our body language conveys. Nonverbal communication involves the transmittal of information, feelings, or ideas using body language, facial expressions, gestures, posture, eye contact, and tone of voice instead of spoken or written words to convey meaning. Through all three of these forms of communication, collaborative team members can ensure information and their ideas and feelings are communicated clearly and effectively.

Active listening is the process of fully focusing, understanding, responding, and remembering what is being said and demonstrating this engagement through verbal and nonverbal cues. As such, verbal, written, and nonverbal communication can all be leveraged as part of active listening.

Strong communication involves transmitting and receiving information. Listening is just as important as speaking or writing. By engaging in active listening, collaborators ensure they are listening to truly hear and understand others in a way that is productive and moves toward the purpose and goals of their collaboration. Developing strong communication skills supports collaboration with colleagues and parents/caregivers and can improve the quality and consistency of programming, services, and supports. In this way, effective communication is a cornerstone of effective collaboration. Table 9.3 provides examples of effective communication skills and practices that increase engagement, understanding, and empathy.

TABLE 9.3. *Essential Communication Skills for Effective Collaboration*

Type of Communication	Skills and Practices	Examples
Verbal	Active Listening	• Use phrases like "I see" or "I understand" to show engagement and attention • Paraphrase what someone else said to communicate engagement and attention ("What I heard you say is . . ." or "What I understood is . . .")
	Empathetic Language	• State "I see what you mean," "I understand how that might make you feel ___," "I appreciate your perspective," or other similar phrases
	Clarity and Conciseness	• Articulate thoughts clearly and in an organized way • Avoid the overuse of jargon or technical terms or providing definitions and explanations • Utilize professional translators and interpreters when necessary
	Tone and Pacing	• Speak with a warm, welcoming, and respectful tone to communicate empathy and genuineness • Avoid speaking too fast and include time and space for processing, input, and questions
Written	Active Listening	• Paraphrase key information from the other person's previous communication, using phrases like "From your last email, I understood . . ." or "When we spoke, you stated . . ."
	Empathetic Language	• Include phrases like "I appreciate you sharing your feelings and ideas" or "I understand this is challenging"
	Clarity and Precision	• Write clear and concise messages that utilize greetings (e.g., Dear ___, To the Parents/Caregivers of ___) and complimentary closes (e.g., Sincerely, Thank you, Best) • Employ proper grammar and structure to reduce possible misunderstandings

(Continued)

TABLE 9.3. *(Continued)*

Type of Communication	Skills and Practices	Examples
	Timely Responses	• Respond to collaborators' messages and communications promptly to show engagement, commitment, and respect
Nonverbal*	Body Language	• Maintain eye contact • Face the speaker • Nod to demonstrate engagement/understanding • Lean toward the speaker to show engagement
	Facial Expressions	• Smile when greeting and engaging with others • Show facial expressions appropriate to the topic or context to convey understanding and empathy
	Gestures	• Use open hand gestures • Keep arms uncrossed to indicate openness

* Be aware that cultures differ in their use and interpretation of body language.

Consistency in Collaboration

Consistency is key for maximizing the effectiveness of collaboration (Leko et al., 2015; Vangrieken et al., 2015). When educators collaborate with consistency, they contribute to the successful development, implementation, and evaluation of instruction, intervention, and support for students with disabilities (Francisco et al., 2020; Hargreaves, 2021). Regular formal and informal collaboration based on consistent and reliable practices supports and facilitates significant student progress toward their IEP goals. Collaboration can be optimized through consistent contact, collaborative structures, and procedures that create and prioritize the time needed to engage and work together in meaningful ways with follow-through and accountability. Centering the strengths, perspectives, and needs of students and their caregivers/families within a consistent collaborative system promotes access, inclusion, and equity.

Classroom teachers can lead and support the development of consistent collaboration structures, including the following:

1. Establishing and maintaining regular meeting times and shared meeting protocols
2. Setting clear team member roles and expectations for documentation
3. Monitoring, reviewing, and discussing progress regularly

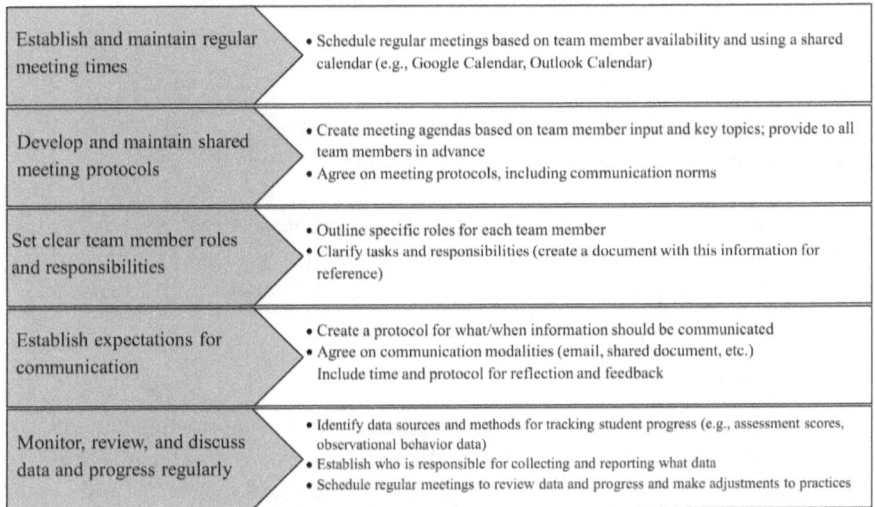

FIGURE 9.4. *Strategies for Consistency in Collaboration.*

Prioritizing these three practices to establish consistency will leverage the strengths of each collaborator and allow teams to work together in effective and productive ways. Figure 9.4 provides suggested strategies to support the three key practices for consistent collaboration.

Organization

To communicate effectively and maintain consistency, educators must prioritize organization. Whether it is scheduling regular and consistent meetings, establishing agendas and protocols, or sharing documents and data, organizing collaboration improves the efficiency of school-based teams. Efficient and effective collaborative teams in turn improve the education and outcomes for students with disabilities (Da Fonte & Barton-Arwood, 2017; Hargreaves, 2021; Zagona et al., 2017).

Technology to Support Collaboration

Technology can be leveraged to support collaborative organization. Many platforms and applications include features for organizing and scheduling meetings, setting agendas, communicating with team members, developing and storing documents, sharing and reviewing data, and providing feedback. Some platforms and applications are specifically designed to support collaboration in education and can be used to store the tools, resources, and products for collaborative planning, implementation, and evaluation all in one place. Examples of these platforms and applications include

- Google Drive
- Ed Plan (https://www.edplan.com/)
- PowerSchool (https://www.powerschool.com)
- SameGoal (https://samegoal.com/sm/lp)

Utilizing shared technology can ensure all members of MTSS teams, IEP teams, co-teaching teams, and other collaborative groups stay organized and aligned and maintain access to all relevant information and resources.

> Pause and Reflect:
>
> As Ms. Kingston continues to learn about her roles in supporting students with disabilities, what essential practices should she focus on to ensure her collaboration is effective? How might technology support her and her fellow collaborators in providing strong and cohesive instruction, services, and supports to students with disabilities?

Effective and Culturally Informed Collaboration With Families

The importance of parents/caregivers as collaborators with educators cannot be overstated. Parents/caregivers provide essential insight and expertise on their child, including their strengths and needs. Partnering with parents/caregivers strengthens the provision of appropriate, meaningful, culturally responsive, and effective education. Through effective collaboration, families and educators "create an environment where all students feel a sense of belonging across intersectional identities to reach their full potential and support an inclusive and equitable educational system" (Aceves & Kennedy, 2024, p. 26).

Because parents/caregivers are an integral part of a students' success, especially students with disabilities, it is important for classroom teachers to engage in practices that promote family engagement (Ishimaru, 2019; Ruiz, 2024). Parents/caregivers are essential team members for providing an equitable education. Parents/caregivers assume three essential roles when collaborating: (1) offering insights about their child, (2) participating in the decision-making process for the student's IEP, and (3) providing logistical and personal support at home.

Offering Insight

Parents/caregivers offer unique insights into their student's strengths and needs as well as provide cultural context. Cultural context can inform personalized and effective educational strategies. Parents/caregivers have a deep understanding of their child's daily life, communication preferences, and how their disability impacts their learning, behavior, social skills, and personal skills. Involving parents/caregivers fosters a learning environment where the student feels valued, understood, and supported. Collaboration with parents/caregivers can ensure instructional strategies are relevant and reinforced at home.

Participating in the Decision-Making Process

Active participation from parents/caregivers in decision-making processes helps align educational programs and interventions with the student's strengths and needs as well as family values, circumstances, and expectations. Centering data from parents/caregivers in the development of the IEP enables them to advocate for their student's specific needs and preferences and ensure plans are realistic and culturally informed. This kind of ongoing collaboration fosters trust and mutual respect that leads to more effective and sustained support for the student's education (Turnbull et al., 2022).

Providing Logistical Support

Parents/caregivers provide essential emotional and logistical support at home, reinforcing learning and behavioral goals. They can create encouraging home environments where students can practice and apply skills learned in school to maintain consistency. This additional support, opportunity for practice and consistency bridges the gap between school and home and contributes to the student's emotional well-being. Building a cohesive approach between educators and families to address and support a student's academic and functional/behavioral strengths and needs increases the opportunity for student progress and development (Sheridan et al., 2019; Strickland-Cohen et al., 2021).

TABLE 9.4. *Culturally Informed Practices for Collaborating With Parents/Caregivers of Students With Disabilities*

Culturally Informed Collaboration Outcome	Practices and Strategies	Examples
Reflexivity and Cultural Competency	• Reflect on personal biases and assumptions that may influence interactions with parents/caregivers • Continuously educate oneself about the diverse cultural backgrounds of students and their families • Integrate culturally informed practices into all aspects of teaching and educational decision-making	→ Journal on interactions with families to identify potential biases → Participate in workshops on cultural diversity and inclusion; attend community cultural events; engage with media about and by people from diverse backgrounds → Use culturally relevant examples in lesson plans and classroom materials
Equitable Relationships	• Establish trust by respecting and valuing each family's cultural beliefs, traditions, and perspectives • Foster a partnership approach where parents/caregivers are seen as equal collaborators in the educational process • Recognize and address power dynamics, ensuring that all parent/caregiver voices are heard and inform decision-making. • Engage cultural brokers (a person with an understanding of multiple cultures who provides important information about cultural norms and can mediate between groups from different backgrounds) (Aceves & Kennedy, 2024, p. 39) to facilitate communication and understanding between educators and parents/caregivers	→ Ask parents/caregivers to share cultural practices that can be integrated into instruction, intervention, and supports → Involve parents/caregivers in the development of IEP goals and strategies by centering their input and suggestions → Hold meetings in neutral settings and ensure all parents/caregivers have the opportunity to speak → Collaborate with a cultural broker who understands the family's cultural context and can support and mediate during meetings
Consistent and Effective Communication	• Use clear, respectful, and culturally responsive language in all communications • Provide information in the parent/caregiver's preferred language and format, utilizing translators or interpreters when necessary • Maintain regular and proactive communication, offering updates on the student's progress and seeking parent/caregiver input regularly	→ Avoid jargon and use plain language in emails, letters, and other communications with families → Translate IEP documents and other important communications into the parent/caregiver's preferred language → Send weekly or biweekly updates via the parent/caregiver's preferred communication method (e.g., text, email, phone)

Culturally Informed Collaboration With Parents/Caregivers

It is critically important that educational plans and decisions are informed by a student's cultural background and other aspects of identity. Parents/caregivers are the key source for learning about a student's culture and life outside of school. Culturally informed practices aid in establishing relationships built on trust and respect, improve the efficiency of communication, and ensure plans and decisions made for a student's education are realistic and compatible with family values, beliefs, and lifestyles. Table 9.4 describes foundational practices for culturally informed collaboration with parents/caregivers (Aceves & Kennedy, 2024; Barrio et al., 2017; Ishimaru, 2019; Robinson, 2016; Rossetti et al., 2017).

> Pause and Reflect:
>
> Ms. Kingston knows she will be teaching students from diverse backgrounds and communities and that it is essential to develop good relationships and communication with parents and caregivers. This is especially important for students with disabilities who receive special education. As she prepares for the upcoming school year, what are some plans, strategies, and tools Ms. Kingston can develop to ensure she is engaging with parents/caregivers in culturally informed ways? Where can she get more information and resources for collaborating with CLD parents and caregivers?

Collaboration for Professional Growth

Professional growth and reflection are essential to all education practices, including for collaboration. Professional learning can be completed collaboratively to support collective professional growth. Educators can participate in workshops, synchronous and asynchronous modules, or other professional learning opportunities to expand their knowledge and skills. Learning opportunities may be developed by school, district, or state-level educators or administrators, but they can also be identified by teachers and their professional learning communities.

In addition to formalized professional learning opportunities, educators can collaborate with each to build their knowledge and skills or acquire resources. By leveraging their own expertise and experience, educators can collectively grow each other's knowledge and skills. Educators can elect to

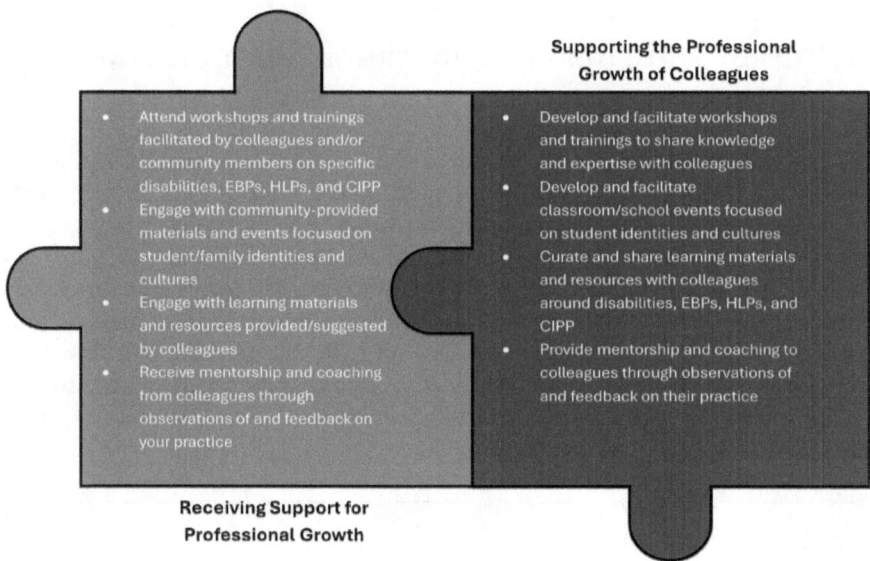

FIGURE 9.5. *Classroom Teacher Collaboration for Professional Growth.*

participate in learning opportunities or develop and facilitate the learning of others. Either way, educators can play a transformative role by growing their own capacity or the capacity of their colleagues through coaching or mentoring. Figure 9.5 displays potential opportunities and topics for classroom teachers to both receive and provide professional learning that improves education for students with disabilities.

HIGH-IMPACT: THE CONNECTION WITH HIGH-LEVERAGE PRACTICES

HLP 1: Collaborate with professionals to increase student success
HLP 2: Organize and facilitate effective meetings with professionals and families
HLP 3: Collaborate with families to support student learning and secure services
HLP 5: Interpret and communicate assessment information to collaboratively design and implement educational programs

Review and Reflect

Collaboration is an essential component of every aspect of special education and paves the way for student success. Effective collaboration among educators, SISP, and parents/caregivers is vital for ensuring access, inclusion, and equity in education for students with disabilities. Classroom teachers are core team members and engage in various forms of collaboration, from co-teaching and interdisciplinary teaming to professional learning and growth. Strong communication skills, consistency, and organization are key to fostering productive collaboration between educators and their colleagues and with parents/caregivers. Engaging in culturally informed practices ensures parents/caregivers are centered on developing plans and making educational decisions for students with disabilities. By prioritizing effective and responsive collaborative practices, classroom teachers support the creation of inclusive educational environments and opportunities that meet the diverse strengths, backgrounds, and needs of all students.

Guiding Questions

1. In your own words, describe the types of collaboration classroom teachers are involved in and their roles in each. Who can classroom teachers expect to team with? How does the classroom teacher's professional collaboration support access and equity for students with disabilities?
2. How does both verbal and nonverbal communication impact collaboration? What are some verbal and nonverbal communication practices you can implement to ensure you communicate effectively?
3. Why are both consistency and organization essential for effective collaboration? List specific practices and strategies you can use to support consistency and organization in collaboration. Include technology-based resources and tools.
4. Why is it important to center students and parents/caregivers in all forms of collaboration? What role do they play and how do they contribute?
5. How can you ensure collaboration with parents/caregivers is culturally informed, inclusive, and equitable? What practices can you use and how do these practices increase the effectiveness of collaboration?

Extend Your Learning

TABLE 9.5. *Resources*

Resource	Description	Link
Harvard University Graduate School of Education—Project Zero, "The Good Collaboration Toolkit"	Web-based resource with articles, checklists, organizers, and other tools to further learning and effective practices around professional collaboration	https://pz.harvard.edu/resources/the-good-collaboration-toolkit
CAST Resource Page	Web page on the CAST website that provides additional information and resources to support learning about and implementing co-teaching	https://publishing.cast.org/stories-resources/stories/co-teaching-introduction-inclusion-stein
IRIS Center Module: "Family Engagement: Collaborating With Families of Students With Disabilities"	A learning module that addresses the importance of engaging the families of students with disabilities in their child's education; highlights key factors that affect these families and outlines practical ways to build relationships and create opportunities for involvement	https://iris.peabody.vanderbilt.edu/module/fam/
National Center on Dispute Resolution in Special Education (CADRE)	Webinar that examines current barriers that impact overall culturally and linguistically diverse family engagement and collaboration during the IEP meeting; provides recommendations to remove these barriers and increase collaboration between CLD families and educational teams during IEP meetings	https://www.youtube.com/watch?v=jMlnhSYb2QQ

References

Aceves, T. C., & Kennedy, M. J. (Eds.). (2024). *High-leverage practices for students with disabilities* (2nd ed.). Council for Exceptional Children and CEEDAR Center.

Barrio, B. L., Peak, P. L., & Murawski, W. W. (2017). English language learners with disabilities. In W. W. Murawski & K. L. Scott (Eds.), *What really works with exceptional leaners* (pp. 262-81). Corwin & Council for Exceptional Children.

Choi, J. H., McCart, A. B., & Sailor, W. (2020). Achievement of students with IEPs and associated relationships with an inclusive MTSS framework. *Journal of Special Education, 54*(3), 157-68. https://doi.org/10.1177/00224669198974

Da Fonte, M. A., & Barton-Arwood, S. M. (2017). Collaboration of general and special education teachers: Perspectives and strategies. *Intervention in School and Clinic, 53*(2), 99-106.

Eisenman, L. T., Pleet, A. M., Wandry, D., & McGinley, V. (2011). Voices of special education teachers in an inclusive high school: Redefining responsibilities. *Remedial and Special Education, 32*(2), 91-104. doi:10.1177/0741932510361248

Francisco, M. P. B., Hartman, M., & Wang, Y. (2020). Inclusion and special education. *Education Sciences, 10*(9), 238. https://doi.org/10.3390/educsci10090238

Friend, M. (2016). Co-teaching as a special education service: Is classroom collaboration a sustainable practice? *Educational Practice and Reform, 2*.

Hargreaves, A. (2021). Teacher collaboration: 30 years of research on its nature, forms, limitations and effects. In A. Hargreaves (Ed.), *Policy, teacher education and the quality of teachers and teaching* (pp. 103-21). Routledge.

Individuals With Disabilities Education Improvement Act. (2004). 20 U.S.C. § 1400 et seq.

IRIS Center. (2020). *Family engagement: Collaborating with families of students with disabilities.* https://iris.peabody.vanderbilt.edu/module/fam/

Ishimaru, A. M. (2019). From family engagement to equitable collaboration. *Educational Policy, 33*(2), 350-85. https://doi.org/10.1177/0895904817691841

Jortveit, M., & Kovač, V. B. (2022) Co-teaching that works: Special and general educators' perspectives on collaboration. *Teaching Education, 33*(3), 286-300. https://doi.org/10.1080/10476210.2021.1895105

Khan, A., Khan, S., Zia-Ul-Islam, S., & Khan, M. (2017). Communication skills of a teacher and its role in the development of the students' academic success. *Journal of Education and Practice*, 8(1), 18-21.

Leko, M. M., Brownell, M. T., Sindelar, P. T., & Kiely, M. T. (2015). Envisioning the future of special education personnel preparation in a standards-based era. *Exceptional Children, 82*(1), 25-43.

Miller, G. E., Lines, C., Sullivan, E., & Hermanutz, K. (2018). Preparing educators to partner with families. In R. L. Quezada, V. Alexandrowicz & S. Molina (Eds.), *Family, School, Community Engagement and Partnerships* (pp. 36-49). Routledge.

Murawski, W. W., & Ricci, L. A. (2019). UDL and co-teaching. In W. W. Murawski & K. L. Scott (Eds.), *What really works with universal design for learning* (pp. 141-56). Sage.

Robinson, G. G. (2016). Culturally responsive beliefs and practices of general and special education teachers within a response to intervention framework. *Multiple Voices for Ethnically Diverse Exceptional Learners, 16*(2), 22-36.

Rossetti, Z., Sauer, J. S., Bui, O., & Ou, S. (2017). Developing collaborative partnerships with culturally and linguistically diverse families during the IEP process. *Teaching Exceptional Children, 49*, 328–38. doi:10.1177/0040059916680103

Ruiz, E. A. (2024). *Supporting pre-service teachers through intersectionally conscious collaboration: A multimethod study utilizing transformative learning theory* [Doctoral dissertation, Arizona State University]. ProQuest Dissertations and Theses Global.

Scanlon, D., Nannemann, A. C., & Baker, D. (2021). Lessons from research for implementing an instructional accommodations model in secondary inclusion. *Learning Disabilities: A Multidisciplinary Journal, 26*(1).

Scruggs, T. E., & Mastropieri, M. A. (2017). Making inclusion work with co-teaching. *Teaching Exceptional Children, 49*(4), 284–93.

Sheridan, S. M., Smith, T. E., Kim, E. M., Beretvas, S. N., & Park, S. (2019). A meta-analysis of family-school interventions and children's social-emotional functioning: Child and community influences and components of efficacy. *Review of Educational Research, 89*, 296–332.

Strickland-Cohen, M. K., Kyzar, K. B., & Garza-Fraire, F. M. (2021). School–family partnerships to support positive behavior: Assessing social validity and intervention fidelity. *Preventing School Failure, 65*(4), 362–70.

Todd, N. A. (2012). Assisting secondary support teachers to work in the recommended service delivery model: Introducing the concept of a subculture of learning support. *Support for Learning, 27*(4), 177–83.

Turnbull, A., Turnbull, R., Francis, G. L., Burke, M., Kyzar, K., Haines, S. J., Gershwin, T., Shepherd, K. G., Holdren, N., & Singer, G. (2022). *Families and professionals: Trusting partnerships in general and special education* (8th ed.). Pearson.

Vangrieken, K., Dochy, F., Raes, E., & Kyndt, E. (2015). Teacher collaboration: A systematic review. *Educational Research Review, 15*, 17–40.

Zagona, A. L., Kurth, J. A., & MacFarland, S. Z. (2017). Teachers' views of their preparation for inclusive education and collaboration. *Teacher Education and Special Education, 40*(3), 163–78.

INDEX

ableism, 40, 41, *45*
abnormalities, 23, 24
academic learning, 59
academic performance, *85*, 103
academic success, 154, 163
access, 151–52; checklist for, *166–67*; CIPP and, 162–65; differentiated instruction and, 155–60, *157–58*; differentiated instruction and SDI, 159–60; HLPs and, 161–62; promoting, 153; UDL and, 154, *155*
accommodations, 122, 126, 135, 160; IEPs and, 134, *134*; modifications compared to, *135*; types of, *134*
accountability, 7, 66, 91
Aceves, T. C., 93
achievement gaps, 92
action, 154, *155*
active listening, 172, 184, *185*
aligned alternate annual assessments, 9
Alim, H. Samy, 163
alternate academic achievement standards, 9
alternative teaching, *183*
antibias practice, 47
antidiscrimination practices and policies, 43
appropriate and measurable annual goal, 122, 132–33
ASD. *See* autism spectrum disorder
assessments, *30*; aligned alternate annual, 9; classroom, 81; criterion-referenced, 78; defined, 78; diagnostic, 78, 81, 87, *89*; district, 143–44; formative, 79, 87, *90*; high stakes, 87, 91; norm-referenced, 79, 86; ongoing, 158; state, 143–44;

summative, 79, 87–88, *90*; types of, 86–88, *89–90*. *See also* universal screening
assets, differences as, 49
assistive technology (AT), *30*, 122, 136, *137*
autism, 5
autism spectrum disorder (ASD), *109*, 127
awareness: self-awareness, 61, 156; social, 61

Balu, R., 62
baseline, 88
behavioral learning, 59
behavior performance, *85*
behavior skills, 160
best practices, for referral process, 113–16
bias, 44; antibias practice, 47; cultural, 107; examining your own, 47; racial, 107; recognizing, *93*; in referral process, 115–16; religious, 46; of social systems, 45–46. *See also* explicit bias; implicit bias
Black History Month, 49
Black women, 40
Bocala, C., *93*
body language, *186*
Booker T. Washington Elementary School, 153, 160
Brown v. Board of Education, 4, 8

CADRE. *See* National Center on Dispute Resolution in Special Education
calculators, *137*

Campbell, Ms. (teacher), 57, 59, 63, 65
Casa Vista Elementary School, 133
CASEL. *See* Collaborative for Academic, Social, and Emotional Learning
CAST Resource Page, *194*
categories of disabilities, 5, 108, *109–11*
CEC. *See* Council for Exceptional Children
CEEDAR Center, 14, *16*, 71, *168*; CIPP and, 37; Course Enhancement Module on Inclusion, 35; EBPs and, 162; HLPs and, 13; Resource Bank, 52
Center for Excellence in Teaching Learning Resource Bank, 52
Center on Multi-Tiered Systems of Support, 81
Center on Positive Behavioral Interventions and Supports, 60, 71, 95
CHAMPS, 66
change: in federal legislation, *10–11*; systemic, 50, *50*
Chastain, Ms. (teacher), 21–22, 25, 31
Child Find, 100–103, *102*
CIPP. *See* culturally inclusive pedagogies and practices
civil rights: laws, 146–47; movement, 4, 40
clarity, *185*
classism, 41, *45*
classroom: assessment, 81; collaboration in, 179–80, *181–83*; responsive classroom management, *31*
classroom teachers. *See* teachers
clear expectations, *31*
collaboration, 13, *30*, 67, 171, 173; in classroom, 179–80, *181–83*; communication skills and, 184, *185–86*; conclusion, 193; consistency in, 186–87; on continuum of placement, 174–75; culturally informed, *190*, 191; decision-making in, 189; defined, 172; essential practices for effective, 184–88; with families, 188–91, *190*; HLPs and, 192; IEP team, 179; insight and, 189; logistical support in, 189; MTSS team, 178–79; organization and, 187; for professional growth, 191–92, *192*; strategies for consistency in, *187*; with teams, *175*, 175–79, *176–77*, *178*; technology to support, 187–88. *See also* co-teaching
collaborative approach, to MTSS, 67
Collaborative for Academic, Social, and Emotional Learning (CASEL), 61, *71*
collaborative inquiry, 92
collaborative learning activities, 156
collaborative teamwork, 27
Collins, Patricia Hill, 40
communication, 160; nonverbal, 172, 184, *186*; skills, 184, *185–86*; strong, 184; verbal, 173, 184, *185*; written, 173, 184, *185–86*
conciseness, *185*
Congress, U.S., 114
conscious discipline, 66
consistency: in collaboration, 186–87; in IEPs, 128, 130, *130*; strategies in collaboration, *187*
Constitution, U.S., 14th Amendment of, 6
consultation, 172
co-teaching: collaboration in classroom and, 179–80, *181–83*; collaboration with teams and, *175*; defined, 172; lesson planning template, *181*; models, *182–83*
Council for Exceptional Children (CEC), 13, *16*, 37
counseling services, 137
Crenshaw, Kimberlé, 40
criterion-referenced assessment, 78
critical consciousness, 163, 164
CRP. *See* culturally relevant pedagogy
CRT. *See* culturally responsive teaching
CSP. *See* culturally sustaining pedagogy
cultural bias, 107
cultural competence, 163, *190*

culturally inclusive pedagogies and practices (CIPP), 37, *93*, 152, 161, 162–65
culturally informed collaboration, *190*, 191
culturally relevant pedagogy (CRP), 152, 163, *164*
culturally responsive teaching (CRT), 152, 163, 164, *164*
culturally sustaining pedagogy (CSP), 152, 163–64, *164*
cultural norms, 115
cures, 21, 22

data: demographic, 85; equity in, 91–92, *93*; power of, 84; qualitative, 79; quantitative, 79; sensemaking of, 82; student performance, 81; types of, 84–85, *85*
data-based individuation, 78
data-driven decision-making (DDDM), 66, 70, 77, 78, 92; defining, 80–81; HLPs and, 94; intervention intensity and, *83*; process, 81–83, *82*; steps of, *82*
data-driven planning, 13
DB. *See* deaf-blindness
DD. *See* developmentally delayed
DDDM. *See* data-driven decision-making
deaf-blindness (DB), *109*
deaf community, 48
deafness, *109*
decision-making: in collaboration, 189; responsible, 61, 156. *See also* data-driven decision-making
deficit perspective on disability, 23–24
de minimis (minor standard), 127
demographic data, 85
Department of Education, U.S., 42; Office of Civil Rights, 92, 146–47
developmentally delayed (DD), *109*
diagnostic assessment, 78, 81, 87, 89
differences as assets, 49
differentiated instruction, 30, 152, 155; domains of, *157–58*; essential practices in, 158–59; SDI compared to, 159–60; teachers and, 156

digital hearing aids, *137*
disability: categories of, 5, 108, *109–11*; deficit perspective on, 23–24; defined, 20; ID, *110*; MD, *110*; medical model of, 21, 22–24, *23*; SLD, 100, 103, *110*, 112–13, 124, 133; social model of, 21, 24; unclear understanding of characteristics, 3. *See also specific topics*
disability/critical race theory (DisCrit), 40
discipline, 7
discrepancy model, 7–8, 100, 103–4, *105*
discrimination, 44; antidiscrimination practices and policies, 43; defined, 38; racial segregation as, 4; workforce, 43; zero-tolerance approach to, 39
DisCrit. *See* disability/critical race theory
disproportionality, 38, 44
district assessments, 143–44
Diverse Educators Toolkit, 52
due process rights, 6

EAHCA. *See* Education for All Handicapped Children Act
early intervention, 7
EBPs. *See* evidence-based practices
ED. *See* emotional disturbance
Ed Plan, 188
Education for All Handicapped Children Act (EAHCA), 4
Elementary and Secondary Education Act (ESEA), 8, *10*, *12*
eligibility, 7, 100; criteria, 113–14; for referrals, 108; for SLD, 112–13
Elijah (student), 100–101, 112
Emmett, Mr. (teacher), 101, 112, 116
emotional disturbance (ED), *109*
emotion cards, *137*
empathetic language, *185*
Endrew F. v. Douglas County School District, 127–28
engagement, 154, *155*
equality, 38

INDEX

equitable relationships, *190*
equity, 38; in data, 91–92, *93*; systemic inequity, 39, 41–42, *42*
ESEA. *See* Elementary and Secondary Education Act
ESSA. *See* Every Student Succeeds Act
Eurocentrism, *45*
evaluation, 100; for referrals, 106–7
Every Student Succeeds Act (ESSA), 1, 8–10, 59, 70; MTSS and, 55, 58, 66; SISP and, 67; state and district assessments and, 143
evidence-based practices (EBPs), 1, 13, 62; defined, 2, 14, 78; HLPs and, 14, 161; MTSS and, 59–60
Excel, 140
explicit bias: defined, 38; student identity and, 42–43, *43*; zero-tolerance approach to, 43
explicit instruction, *31*
expression, 154, *155*

facial expressions, *186*
family: collaboration with, 188–91, *190*; engagement, 172
FAPE. *See* free appropriate public education
federal disability categories, 108, *109–11*
federal legislation: changes in major tenets of, *10–11*; MTSS and, 58–59. *See also specific laws*
feedback, *30*
feminist movement, 40
fidelity of implementation, 79
first-person language, 48
flexible grouping, 152, 159
Flores, Mrs. (teacher), 31
formal referral, 106
formative assessment, 79, 87, *90*
foundational inclusive practices, 29–32, *30*, *31*
14th Amendment, 6
free appropriate public education (FAPE), 1, 4, 6; defined, 2, 20, 122; IEPs and, 125–26; inclusive education and, 25; Section 504 and, 146

Fuchs, D., 11, 83
Fuchs, L. S., 11, 83
functional performance, *85*
functional skills, 160

Gay, Geneva, 163
genderism, *45*
gestures, *186*
Google Drive, 188
Government Accountability Office, U.S., 104, 114
Green Pines Middle School, 21–22
group projects, 156

Harvard University Graduate School of Education, *194*
hearing impairments, *110*
Heritage, M., 87
heterosexism, 41, *45*
higher power, 22
high-intensity needs (HIN), 56
high-leverage practices (HLPs), 1, 12–13, *13*, 116, 162, 165; collaboration and, 192; DDDM and, 94; defined, 2; EBPs and, 14, 161; IEPs and, 148; inclusion and, 33; MTSS and, 70; student identity and, 51
High-Leverage Practices for Students with Disabilities, *168*
highly mobile children, 102
high-quality instruction, 60
high stakes assessments, 87, 91
high-tech AT, 136, *137*
Hill, Mr. (teacher), 152–53, 154, 160, 162, 165
HIN. *See* high-intensity needs
Hispanic History Month, 49
HLPs. *See* high-leverage practices

ID. *See* intellectual disability
IDEA. *See* Individuals With Disabilities Education Act
IDEIA. *See* Individuals With Disabilities Education Improvement Act
identities: social, 39, 41, 44; understanding, *93*. *See also* student identity

IEPs. *See* individualized education programs
IEP team, 122, *126*, *178*, 179
impairment, 20, 24
implicit bias: defined, 38; in referrals and evaluation, 115; student identity and, *41*, 42–43
inclusion, 123; as best model, 27; checklist for, *166–67*; defined, 20, 38–39; HLPs and, 33; IEPs and, 7; intersectionality for, 47–50; medical model of disability and, 22–24, *23*; rates of, 19; responsible, 19; social model of disability and, 24; teachers' role in, 29–32
inclusive education, 19, 20, 25–26, 123; benefits of, *30*; key components of, *26*
inclusive language: defined, 39; RtI and, 60; student identity and, 48
inclusive learning. *See* multitiered system of supports
independent living, 160
indirect services, 179
individualized education programs (IEPs), 1, 2, 5, 6, 7, 121–24, 148, 153; AT and, 136, *137*; accommodations and, 134, *134*; annual goals, key components of, *132*; annual goals, sample of, *133*; appropriate and measurable annual goals for, 132–33; components for consistency, 128, 130, *130*; defined, 123; *Endrew F. v. Douglas County School District* and, 127–28; FAPE and, 125–26; guiding questions for development of, *131*; HLPs and, 148; inclusion and, 7; key components of, *129*; LRE and, 125–26, 143; modifications and, 134–35; other aides and services, 137–39; PLAAFP and, 130–31; progress monitoring and, 140–43, *141*, *142*; SAS and, 133–40; SDI and, 139–40; Section 504 and, 146, *147*; teachers and, 125; transition plan and, 144–46, *145*

Individuals With Disabilities Education Act (IDEA), 1, 5–8, *10*, *12*, 21, 70, 153, 174; Child Find and, 101, 102; on DD, 108; disability categories, *109*; evaluation and, 106–7; IEPs and, 2, 123, 125–26, 132; inclusion and, 25; LRE and, 126; MTSS and, 58–59; outcomes of reauthorization of, 7; parent/caregiver-initiated referral for, 103; prereferral interventions and, 58–59; provisions of, 6; reauthorization of, 104; RtI and, 56, 104; on SAS, 133; on Section 504, 146–47; SLD and, 100, 112–13; state and district assessments and, 143; teacher roles and responsibilities, 10
Individuals With Disabilities Education Improvement Act (IDEIA), 8
inequity, systemic, 39, 41–42, *42*
inquiry, collaborative, 92
insight, 189
instructional delivery, *177*
instructional planning, 175, *177*
intellectual ability, 103
intellectual disability (ID), *110*
intelligence quotient (IQ), 107
intensive intervention, 79
interdisciplinary team, 172, 177–78
interpreting services, 137
intersectionality: defined, 39; examples of, *41*; for inclusion, 47–50; student identity and, 40–41, *41*, 47–50; students with disabilities and, 44–46, *45–46*
Intervention Central, 71
intervention intensity, 83
IQ. *See* intelligence quotient
IRIS Center, 14, *16*, 71, 117, 127, 132, 149, *194*; flexible grouping and, 159; Module on Differentiated Instruction, *168*
IRIS Center Professional Development Module, 35
IRIS Modules, 95

Javion (student), 133
Jones, Ms. (teacher), 173

Judeo-Christian model, moral, 22
justice, restorative, 66

Kennedy, M. J., *93*
Kingston, Ms. (teacher), 173, 177, 180, 188, 191
Kramer, S. V., 68

Ladson-Billings, Gloria, 163
language, 160; body, *186*; empathetic, *185*; first-person, 48; inclusive, 39, 48, 60; SLI, *111*; speech/language therapy, 137; student identity and, 48
LD. *See* Learning Disabilities Initiative
LEA. *See* local education agency
Lead IDEA Center, 162
learning: academic, 59; behavioral, 59; collaborative activities, 156; PLC, 56, 68; SEL, 57, 59, 60–61, 104; SLD, 100, 103, *110*, 112–13, 124, 133; UDL, 27, *30*, 152, 154, *155*
Learning Disabilities (LD) Initiative, 104
Learning for Justice Toolkit, 52
least restrictive environment (LRE), 1–2, 5, 6, 21, 25, 123, 153, 174–75; IDEA and, 126; IEPs and, 125–26, 143; statement, 143
linguicism, *46*
listening, active, 172, 184, *185*
local education agency (LEA), 122
Locke, Ms. (teacher), 80, 86, 92
logistical support, 189
low-income students, 92
low-tech AT, 136, *137*
LRE. *See* least restrictive environment

marginalization, 39, 44
Martinez, Mr. (teacher), 124–25, 131, 133, 136, 140
Maryland Coalition for Inclusive Education (MCIE), *35*
mastery line, 88
math, 160
math manipulatives, *137*
MCIE. *See* Maryland Coalition for Inclusive Education

MD. *See* multiple disabilities
medical field, 23
medical model of disability, 21, 22–24, *23*
medium-tech AT, 136, *137*
meetings: student study, 179; team, *176*
migrant children, 102
minor standard (*de minimis*), 127
modifications, 123; accommodations compared to, *135*; IEPs and, 134–35; types of, *135*
moral failings, 22
moral Judeo-Christian model, 22
MTSS. *See* multitiered system of supports
MTSS Center, 162
MTSS team, *178*, 178–79
multilingual students, 44
multiple disabilities (MD), *110*
multitiered system of supports (MTSS), 8, 13, 57, 77, 88, 103–4, 161, 177–78; collaborative approach to, 67; defined, 56; EBPs and, 59–60; ESSA and, 56, 59, 66; essential components of, 65; features of, 61; federal legislation and, 58–59; framework, 64; HLPs and, 70; overview of, 59–64; required components of, 64–65, *65*, *66*; specialized instruction in, 67–68; teachers and, 68, *69*

Naomi (student), 39–40, 46, 49
National Center for Intensive Intervention (NCII), 14, *16*, 71, 95, 140, *149*, 162
National Center for Learning Disabilities, *117*
National Center for Special Education Research (NCSER), 6
National Center on Dispute Resolution in Special Education (CADRE), *194*
National Center on Response to Intervention, 63
National Joint Committee on Learning Disabilities (NJCLD), 104

National Technical Assistance Center on Transition, 144
NCII. *See* National Center for Intensive Intervention
NCLB. *See* No Child Left Behind
NCSER. *See* National Center for Special Education Research
NJCLD. *See* National Joint Committee on Learning Disabilities
No Child Left Behind (NCLB), 9, 91
nonverbal communication, 172, 184, *186*
normalization, 21, 22
norm-referenced assessment, 79, 86
norms: cultural, 115; social, 42; societal, 24
nutrition plan, 77

Obama, Barack, 10
occupational therapy, 4, 137
Office of Civil Rights, of Department of Education, 92, 146–47
Office of Special Education Programs (OSEP), 104
OHI. *See* other health impaired
OI. *See* orthopedic impairment
one-teach-one-assist, *182*
one-teach-one-observe, *182*
ongoing assessment, 158
opportunity gaps, 92
oppression, 39, 41–42, *42*, 44
oral reading fluency (ORF), 57, 86
organization, collaboration and, 187
orthopedic impairment (OI), *110*
OSEP. *See* Office of Special Education Programs
other aides and services, 137–39
other health impaired (OHI), *110*
outreach, 102

pacing, *185*
parallel teaching, *182*
paraprofessional, 123
parental/caregiver-initiated referral, 103
parental/caregiver participation, 6
parental/caregiver resistance, 114–15
parent consent, 103

Paris, Django, 163
Parker Boudett, K., *93*
PBIS. *See* positive behavioral intervention and supports
peer discussions, 156
pencil grips, *137*
physical therapy, 137
PLAAFP. *See* present levels of academic achievement and functional performance
planning: data-driven, 13; instructional, 175, *177*; lesson planning template, *181*; transition plan, 124, 144–46, *145*
PLC. *See* professional learning community
positive behavioral intervention and supports (PBIS), 56, 60, 66
positive relationships, *31*
postsecondary goals, 139–40, 144, 146
power: of data, 84; higher, 22
PowerSchool, 188
precision, *185*
prereferral, 7, 58, 100, 104–6
present levels of academic achievement and functional performance (PLAAFP), 5, 123, 128, 130–31, 133
privilege, 39, 41–42, *42*
problem-solving approach, 56
problem-solving model, 8
problem-solving process, 172
professional development, 66
professional growth, collaboration for, 191–92, *192*
professional learning community (PLC), 56, 68
Professional Standards and Practice Committee (PSPC), 13
PROGRESS Center, *95*, 128, *149*, 162; Handout and Resource Tool, *52*
progress monitoring, 60, *65*, *66*, 90, 158; DDDM and, 81; defined, 56, 79, 88, 123; IEPs and, 140–43, *141*, *142*; in Tier 1, 62; in Tier 2, 62; in Tier 3, 63
Project IDEAL, *117*
Project Zero, *194*

PSPC. *See* Professional Standards and Practice Committee
public education, as right, 3–4. *See also* free appropriate public education
Public Law 94-142, 1, 4–5, *10*, 100. *See also* free appropriate public education
public school-initiated referral, 103–4

qualitative data, 79
quantitative data, 79

racial bias, 107
racial segregation, 4
racism, 40, 41, *46*
rate of growth, 88, *88*
reading, 160
reasonably calculated, 127
referral process, *106*; best practices for, 113–16; bias in, 115–16; challenges for, 113–16; Child Find and, 102, *102*; eligibility for, 108; evaluation for, 106–7; formal, 106; parental/caregiver-initiated, 103; parental/caregiver resistance to, 114–15; prereferral, 7, 58, 100, 104–6; public school-initiated, 103–4; school system barriers, 114; student identification for, 101–4
reflective practices, 47
reflexivity, *190*
related services, 123, 126, *138*
relationship skills, 61
religious bias, *46*
representation, 154, *155*
response to intervention (RtI), 8, 70, 105, 114; defined, 56; IDEA and, 56, 104; inclusive language and, 60; MTSS and, 57; parent/caregiver-initiated referral and, 103
responsible decision-making, 61, 156
responsible inclusion, 19
responsive classroom management, *31*
restorative justice, 66
rights: civil, 4, 40, 146–47; due process, 6; public education as, 3–4
Rinehart, Ms. (teacher), 3, 11, 14
RtI. *See* response to intervention
Ryan (student), 3, 10, 11

SameGoal, 188
SAS. *See* supplementary aids and services
school system barriers, 114
screen readers, *137*
SDI. *See* specially designed instruction
sectarianism, *46*
Section 504, 146–47, *147*
segregation, racial, 4
SEL. *See* social-emotional learning
self-awareness, 61, 156
self-determination, 160
self-management, 61, 156
sensemaking, of data, 82
sexism, *45*
short-term interventions, 64
SISP. *See* specialized instructional support personnel
skills: behavior, 160; communication, 184, *185–86*; functional, 160; relationship, 61; social, *137*, 139, 160; of teachers, *12*
SLD. *See* specific learning disability
SLI. *See* speech or language impairment
small group instruction, 62
social awareness, 61
social development, 156
social-emotional development, 61
social-emotional learning (SEL), 57, 59, 60–61, 104
social identities, 39, 41, 44
social model of disability, 21, 24
social norms, 42
social performance, *85*
social skills, 160; instruction, 139; training apps, *137*
social systems, 42, *45–46*
societal norms, 24
sociocultural diversity, 37
special education: as not always available, 3–4; services, 123. *See also specific topics*
specialized instructional support personnel (SISP), 66, 67–68, 125, 137, 139, 175, 176
specially designed instruction (SDI), 2, 124, 126; differentiated instruction

compared to, 159–60; IEPs and, 139–40
special transportation, 137
specific learning disability (SLD), 100, 103, *110*, 112–13, 124, 133
speech/language therapy, 4, 137
speech or language impairment (SLI), *111*
speech-to-text, *137*
standardized definitions, lack of, 7–8
state assessments, 143–44
state referral, 113–14
station teaching, *183*
Stecker, P. M., 11
stereotypes, 43
strong communication, 184
student identity, 37–38; biases and, 47–48; conclusion, 51; differences as assets, 49; explicit and implicit bias and, 42–43, *43*; HLPs and, 51; intersectionality and, 40–41, *41*, 47–50; language and, 48; oppression and, 41–42, *42*; privilege and, 41–42, *42*; systemic change and, 50, *50*; systemic inequity and, 41–42, *42*
student performance data, 81
students from low-income homes, 92
students of color, 44, 92
student study meeting, 179
subjectivity, 115
summative assessment, 79, 87–88, *90*
supplementary aids and services (SAS), 133–40, *138*, 160
Supreme Court: *Brown v. Board of Education*, 4, 8; *Endrew F. v. Douglas County School District*, 127–28
systematic identification procedures, 1
systemic change, 50, *50*
systemic inequity, 39, 41–42, *42*

target line, 88
TBI. *See* traumatic brain injury
teachers: CIPP and, 163; collaboration for, 176–77; competencies for, 12–14, *13*; differentiated instruction and, 156; foundational inclusive practices and, 29–32, *30*, *31*; IEPs and, 125; inclusion and, 29–32; knowledge and skills of, *12*; LRE statement and, 143; MTSS and, 68, 69; progress monitoring and, 140; roles and responsibilities of, 10–11; SEL and, 61; UDL and, 154. *See also* co-teaching; *specific teachers*
team meetings, 176
teams: collaboration with, *175*, 175–79, *176–77*, *178*; collaborative teamwork, 27; IEP, 122, *126*, *178*, 179; interdisciplinary, 172, 177–78; MTSS, *178*, 178–79
team teaching, *183*
technology: assistive, *30*, 122, 136, *137*; collaboration supported by, 187–88
test scores, 9
therapy: occupational, 4, 137; physical, 137; speech/language, 4, 137
tiered intervention, 60
tiers of support: Tier 1, 62, 66, *69*; Tier 2, 62–63, 66–67, 68, *69*, 106; Tier 3, 63–64, 67, 68, *69*, 106
TIES Center Inclusive Practices Video Bank, 35
Tomas (student), 79–80, 86
tone, *185*
transition plan, 124, 144–46, *145*
transportation, special, 137
traumatic brain injury (TBI), *111*
Travis (student), 124–25, 131, 133, 136, 140
Tremblay, P., 11
trend line, 88
Trujillo, Mrs. (teacher), 3, 10

UDL. *See* universal design for learning
UDL Tips from CAST, *168*
unconscious attitudes, 43
uniquely designed education, 6
United Nations Partnership on the Rights of Persons with Disabilities Resource Guide, 52
United Nations Women, 52
United States (U.S.): Congress, 114; Constitution, 6; Department of

Education, 42, 92, 146; Government Accountability Office, 104, 114
universal design for learning (UDL), 27, *30*, 152; access and, 154, *155*; principles of, *155*; teachers and, 154
universal screening, *65*, *66*, *89*; DDDM and, 81; defined, 79, 86–87; RtI and, 60
U.S. *See* United States

verbal communication, 173, 184, *185*
visual impairment (VI), *111*
"wait-to-fail" approach, 104, *105*

Washington (state), 92
wearable biometric devices, *137*
What Works Clearinghouse (WWC), 14, 161, *168*
women, Black, 40
workforce discrimination, 43
written communication, 173, 184, *185–86*
WWC. *See* What Works Clearinghouse

zero-tolerance approach: to discrimination, 39; to explicit bias, 43

ABOUT THE AUTHORS

Dena D. Slanda leads large-scale projects at the American Institutes for Research, delivering professional learning and coaching to state agencies, districts, and schools. She coleads technical assistance for the Lead IDEA Center, manages special projects for the Center on Great Teachers and Leaders, and provides technical assistance for the Comprehensive State Literacy Development National Literacy Center.

Lindsey Pike is an assistant professor of special education at Roger Williams University. She is passionate about teacher preparation and supporting educators in developing inclusive and equitable practices. Her research and practice as a teacher educator emphasizes the importance of intersectionality as a framework to address educational equity.

Mary E. Little is professor and program coordinator in exceptional student education at the University of Central Florida. She serves as project director of multiple research and personnel preparation grant projects focused on school and teacher leaders' use of data-driven decision-making within university and inclusive, urban school settings.

www.ingramcontent.com/pod-product-compliance
Lightning Source LLC
Chambersburg PA
CBHW031358230426
43670CB00006B/577